Beatrix
DOWAGER MARCHIONESS OF WATERFORD
MEMOIRS 1895-1908

Beatrix

DOWAGER MARCHIONESS OF WATERFORD

MEMOIRS 1895-1908

SOMERVILLE PRESS

Somerville Press Ltd
Dromore, Bantry, Co. Cork, Ireland

©2024 Maria Ines Dawnay

First published 2024

Designed by Jane Stark
Typeset in Adobe Garamond Pro
seamistgraphcs@gmail.com

ISBN: 978 1 8382544 8 3

Printed and bound in the EU

ACKNOWLEDGEMENTS

The Somerville Press would like to thank Lord and Lady Waterford for permission to reproduce the portrait of *Beatrix Waterford* by Philip de László and other photographs. We would also like to thank Mary Ashton-Bell who typed up the three Notebooks and the photographer Pawel Lorenc.

Contents

Family Tree 6

Introduction 7

Curraghmore October 16 1912. 8

Memoirs Notebook One, begun May 1895. 9

Memoirs Notebook Two, begun April 1914 95

Memoirs Notebook Three, begun May 1914. 175

Evening Standard Article about
Beatrix's husband's death December 1911 257

Ireland at War
Beatrix and her son Tyrone get mixed up in the fighting.. 259
(*'Free Staters'* was a term used to describe those in Ireland who supported the Anglo-Irish Treaty of 1921 that led to the creation of the Irish Free State in 1922. The 'Irregulars' or Republicans were anti-Treaty.)

Derreen
Beatrix Waterford and her mother, Lady Lansdowne
visit Derreen after it was burned and looted. 267

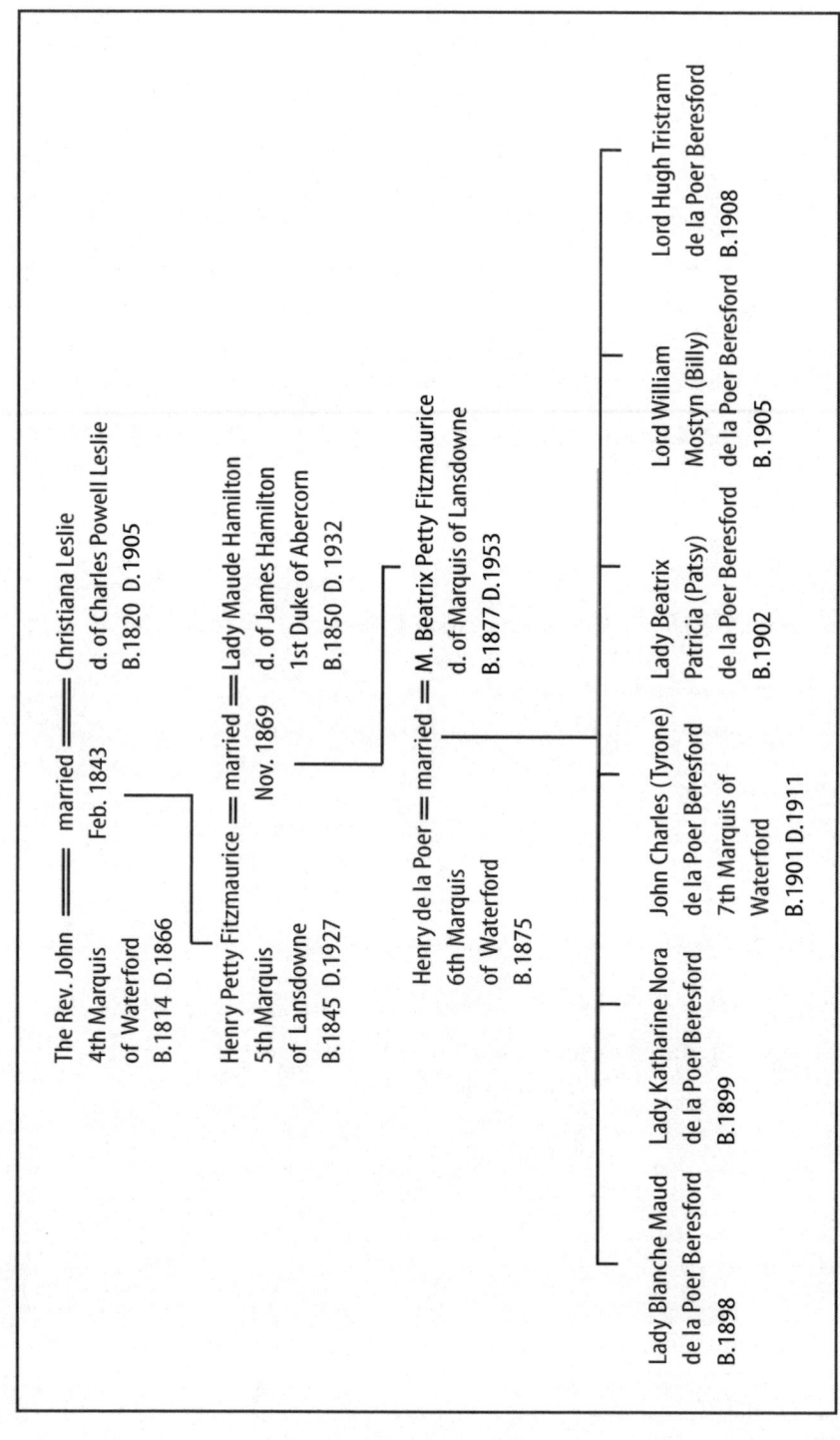

Introduction

I am the widow of Major Hugh Dawnay, legendary polo player and polo coach. His mother was Lady Katharine Dawnay, who was a daughter of Beatrix Waterford.

My mother-in law talked a lot about Beatrix Waterford and told me about these memoirs, which were in her possession. She was always keen that they should be published and passed them on to me.

My late husband's memoir, *Galloping Through Life*, was published by Somerville Press and when I thought the time was right, I approached Somerville Press and suggested that they might like to publish Beatrix Waterford's memoirs, and they happily agreed.

Maria Ines Dawnay
County Waterford May 2024

Curraghmore
October 16th 1912

This is the Anniversary of our Wedding Day, the first since my Darling was taken from me. He often talked of this day, and last year he used to say 'Just think, next year we shall have been married fifteen years!' and there would follow reminiscences of that Wedding Day, and other happy incidents in our life.

Now there is no-one with whom to talk over those bygone years, and memories stored away soon grow dim. So I am going to write down all I can remember of our life together during those 14 years, and as I have always kept a very short diary, the task should be a fairly easy one. It will be a labour of love, for every word will bring back something of him and some day it may help the children to remember him, and give them some ideas of our married life.

Beatrix Waterford

Memoirs
Notebook One
(begun May 1895)

May & June 1895

In a way I feel as if I had always known Tyrone, although I did not meet him until I was 18; but he and my brother Charlie were at private school (Chigwell's) and at Eton together, and crammed for the Army at the same time at Camberley, though at rival establishments; and they were always great friends. I had often heard Charlie talk of Tyrone and I was most anxious to meet him, but we were away from England during the best part of eleven years (while my Father was Governor General of Canada, and Viceroy of India, 1883 to 1894) and so met none of my brothers' friends. Lord William Beresford, who was Military Secretary to my Father in India, often spoke of his nephew Tyrone, and his favourite niece Susie, and Curraghmore – the most beautiful place in the World; but curiously enough, I never even saw a photograph of Tyrone, and had imagined him to be dark, with a large moustache! I must confess to a momentary disappointment when at last Charlie introduced him to me (at Lady Templemore's Ball, May 25th 1895) and I saw before me a tall, rather lanky boy, very fair, with no attempt at a moustache, and looking ridiculously young. However, as soon as I had danced with him, all disappointment vanished. He was a beautiful dancer and had besides a charm of manner which was quite irresistible. We danced together twice that night. He was then living at Camberley and used to come up on purpose for dances, and only got back in time for his work next morning. As he was not at all strong then, and had quite outgrown his strength, this kind of thing was very bad for him, and I fear he generally came up rather on the sly, as his parents strongly disapproved. We met again a week later at a dance given by the Duchess of St. Albans, and danced together and I well remember my disappointment when Mother said we must move on to another Ball at Holland House. However, he presently appeared there, so all was well, and we again danced together. After the dance he wanted me to go out in the garden with him, but I regretfully refused to go, as Mother had forbidden sitting out in the garden. We had quite a tussle over it, and he tried to drag me out, and all the time I was simply longing to go.

On the 11th June we met at a sort of children's party given by Bridie Stewart and her brother at Londonderry House, and he danced with me twice; and that evening we were both at the Ralli's dance and then went on to Mrs Charrington's, and I danced with him four times altogether. The next day, June 12th, we were at a delightful Ball at Londonderry House, and he was particularly nice to me, and twice took me down to supper after dancing. The only thing which spoilt my pleasure was a growing jealousy of Beasie Butler (Lord Ormonde's eldest daughter); she was perfectly lovely, and Tyrone was very fond of her, and one time, during nearly the whole of supper, he remained with his eyes fixed on her, and almost entirely forgot my existence, which was very trying! The only other time we met that year was when Charlie brought him to luncheon one day, and afterwards we played, and he chaffed Mother a great deal over the anxious face she put on when playing the mandoline.

On the 25th June, my Grandmother (Lady Lansdowne) died, and though we remained on some weeks in London, I saw no more of Tyrone that season, then for many months after.

In October of that year Lord Waterford died, so Tyrone was in mourning all the following season, and of course went to no dances, but we met a few times at dinner parties. He dined at Lansdowne House on May 9th 1896, but it was a big dinner party and, as he did not sit next to me, I hardly had a chance of speaking to him. After dinner I played the violin, John Baring accompanying me.

July & August 1896

On June 14th Charlie, who was then quartered in Ireland, came over for a few days, and we had a little dinner party for him, to which Tyrone came, as his friend, but this was not a very satisfactory meeting as everybody was playing the fool afterwards, and there was no chance of talking. We did not meet again until July 24th, when there was a dinner of 60 at Londonderry House, and to my delight I found he was to take me in. He was very nice to me and said he would like us to come to Curraghmore for his coming of age festivities, which, owing to mourning, were not to take place until September. After dinner, we all listened to the string band; it was a very blissful evening. We went to Derreen in the middle of August; every day I was hoping for the arrival of the invitation to Curraghmore and, as there was no sign of it, my spirits sank lower and lower, particularly as I remembered that he had said Beasie Butler would be there! At last, there came a letter from Lady Waterford, asking us to go to Curraghmore a few days later; then I was in the seventh heaven of delight! Lord William was staying with us at the time so he and Mother and I went there together, on August 31st, arriving just in time for dinner.

Beasie Butler was not there after all and I was the only girl outside the family. Sue and Clodagh of course were there, also their cousin, Kathleen Beresford, who was then 17; the rest of the party were: Lord Ormonde, Sir W. Perry, Canon McColl, Mr H. Pack-Beresford, Mademoiselle Richard (an old governess), Mr Grey (Agent at Ford), Sir Owen Slacke and the Duke & Duchess of Beaufort.

Our luggage was delayed somewhere and I remember wearing a teagown belonging to Susie, which pleased me very much as I had never been allowed to wear a teagown before!

Tyrone took me in to dinner that night. I felt rather shy, as I knew no-one there except him and Lord William, and most of the talk was somehow strange to me.

September 1896

Next day, September 1st, there was a huge garden party, to which the neighbours came from far and wide; Lady Waterford received them, sitting in her bath chair, as she was very ill at that time, and could not stand much. Later on, she made me play the violin, in the Inner Hall, and she herself accompanied me; it was very alarming, as the place was packed with people. Irene Congreve played afterwards and I think somebody sang. After dinner we all danced in the Inner Hall, the music being provided by a large Orchestrian which stood there.

On September 2nd, a great banquet was given in the Riding School for all the tenants, about 800; we went in at the end, to hear the speeches, and Tyrone made a very nice one, which was received with great enthusiasm, and of course we all drank his health. Lord William also spoke, but got so choky in the middle that he had to stop, and we all felt inclined to howl too. There was something terribly sad about this coming of age; Lord Waterford had died in a very tragic way less than a year before and Lady Waterford had a mortal illness and could not live more than a few months; in fact, it seemed as if only her indomitable pluck had kept her alive so long. But she was always cheerful and would allow no-one to be morbid.

She was most charming to me and played with me a great deal, and I afterwards heard that she told several people she would be quite happy if Tyrone married me, though she feared it was hardly likely to happen.

I have always liked to think of this. At this time I was very deeply in love with Tyrone, but I was very shy and undemonstrative and nobody guessed it, except, of course, Mother, and perhaps Lord William.

After tea on the day of the banquet, Tyrone took me out fishing all alone with him; it was delightful, though he talked very little, being very intent on his fishing. There was one very bad moment, when, in casting, his hook got entangled in my fringe; it happened to be a fake one (as I never could keep my own in curl) and I had visions of it being bodily removed and left floating at the end of the line. Luckily for me, the hook was really only caught in the fringe net and was disentangled without much difficult and, afterwards, I had the pleasure of landing a trout for Tyrone. We danced again after dinner.

On the 3rd he asked me to come out riding and I was given a mount on Belladonna, a mare we afterwards bought. We didn't go far, as he wanted to practise knocking a polo ball about, so he and two of the other men did this while I looked on. Most of the party went over to luncheon at Bessborough where there was to be a horse show; I had hoped to drive with Tyrone in the open phaeton, but at the last moment Lady Charles Beresford – who was attired in a very décolleté pink silk gown, and swathed in boas – announced her intention of going with him, much to my annoyance.

After lunching with the Duncannons we went to see the jumping at the horse show and Tyrone's hunter took a first prize. It rained most of the afternoon, so we came home fairly early. We danced again after dinner and when we went to bed Tyrone said goodbye to us, as he was going out cub hunting early next morning and would not be back before we started. However, it rained in the morning and he didn't go out, so I hoped we might see him again as we were not making a very early start. But he didn't appear and I went away feeling rather sad, as that seemed to show that he didn't care for me at all. I went to Lady Waterford's bedroom to say goodbye; she did not come down early, but did a great deal of business in her room. I never saw her again, as she died about five months later.

After this, we went back to Derreen, and back to England soon after. We went to a shooting party at Wynyard in November, and I was very much disgusted to find that Tyrone had been there just the week before.

January ~ March 1897

On January 19th 1897 we went to Badminton for a couple of Balls, Susie had been staying at Bowood, and went over with us, and Tyrone turned up soon after we arrived. We all went to the Hunt Ball at Tetbury that evening; he danced with me 3 times, and took me down to supper, where we remained a long time; it was a very happy evening. He had to go back to duty the next day, and so missed the second Ball and I was rather sad over this as I felt I looked rather nice that night!

On the 22nd February we heard of Lady Waterford's death and we felt it very much, not only because of her kindness to us, but also because of the awful loss to him and his two sisters, all so young and so alone in the world.

On March 5th, Charlie and I went to luncheon at Hampden House, and found the three of them there, but as I had to rush off to a violin lesson directly after, there was hardly time to say a word to him.

On March 7th, I again had luncheon at Hampden House. Susie and Clodagh were there, and while I was talking to them and Phyllis afterwards, Tyrone suddenly turned up. I was seized with an unwanted amount of courage and proposed that they should all come and have tea with me at Lansdowne House, which they did. Mother was away at the time, as Granny was ill. My little tea party was quite a success and I remember how Tyrone laughed at me on the way because of the stiff way I carried my umbrella and how he walked behind me imitating me. He always teased me a great deal and I seemed to amuse him enormously, because of my shyness and my rather prim ways.

We met again at dinner at Hampden House on March 14th; we had a nice quiet evening and he then suggested that we might ride together in the Park, but as he was in deep mourning he went out very early and I should have to arrange to do the same. After this, I discovered that the early morning was much the nicest time to rise! We met like this on the 15th, 19th, 20th and 24th and had some very charming rides together, but one or two other days I drew blank and returned disconsolate.

At this time, Mother had a very bad attack of influenza and on the 24th I went with her to Brighton for a change of air. We stayed at the Bedford, Lord William Beresford and 'Lily Duchess' were also there, and on the 26th the latter told us that Tyrone was coming down to see her; 'So nice of him, dear boy, particularly as Bill had just gone away'. He had told me of this little plan on our last ride, so I smiled inwardly, and felt very happy. Mother and I had a Sitting Room next to the front door and I remained with my nose flattened against the window all that afternoon; and when at last he drove up, I found I had to go and fetch something in the hall! We all went out together in the afternoon and went to the Pier and the Aquarium, and he and the Duchess dined with us that evening. The next day he came down to breakfast with us and we lunched upstairs with the Duchess.

We again walked together, both morning and afternoon, and once when we had got out of sight of our chaperones we both got into Bath Chairs and acted the invalid like two babies. It was very windy, and I remember getting thoroughly tousled and feeling rather distressed at it. He went back to London after tea, but made me promise I would go back before April 1st, as the Blues were to leave London that day, and he was anxious to have another ride with me before that. So on the 30th I basely deserted Mother and went up to London with Lord William.

April 1897

*N*ext day I was in Rotten Row at the appointed time, although it was a miserably cold and wet morning, but there was not a sign of my friend! Up and down I went, getting more and more dejected, and rode along the other ring, past the Barracks, several times, in the hopes that he might see me. He often chaffed me about this afterwards and declared that I went up and down before the window the whole time, in the most brazen way! At last, after three quarters of an hour in the wet I was thinking of going home, when he appeared smiling and not a bit penitent, and pretended to be awfully surprised to see me. The ride ended very happily, except for having to say goodbye.

The Blues moved to Windsor early next morning and the following week we went to Bowood. A few days later there came a telegram from Tyrone, to say he was coming to stay with us the following Saturday to Tuesday. He did not, however, arrive until Sunday (April 18th) in the evening, and then told us he would have to leave next day, on account of an inspection by General Luck. This was a nasty blow, but luckily he was able to stay till quite late, and we made the most of our time together, on that Easter Monday. He and I rode after breakfast; he was on Belladonna, who got rather rubbed by the saddle, so on the way home he got off and walked back by my side all the rest of the way. In the Big Wood he stopped to pick some primroses and gave me a little bunch of them, which I treasured for long afterwards; in fact, I have them still. I had a little book – the *Pocket Encyclopedia* – in which several pages were devoted to 'the language of flowers' and I was quite distressed to find in this that primroses meant 'inconstancy'. I was looking for signs in everything; but all the same, I don't think this worried me seriously.

After luncheon we went out walking, Mother was driving in the little pony-chaise, and Uncle Freddy Hamilton tactfully stayed with her, so we gradually got well ahead and had a very happy time. The walk was right round the Lake. He was always full of chaff, and loved teasing me, and taking me in; and I remember how, that day, he said he would race me and I was to run at my very fastest, though he gave me a long start. Away I went, and being a very bad mover, panted and puffed, and got extremely hot and dishevelled. I was rather surprised that he hadn't caught me up after a bit, but when I looked round, there he was, just where I had left him, roaring with laughter at having taken me in and made me run! This sort of behaviour seemed very un-loverlike, and made me fear that perhaps he meant nothing and only felt brotherly friendship for me! For all this time he had never told me that he liked me, though he looked a good deal. Before he left Bowood, he promised to come up and see us in London, whither we went the following week.

May 1897

On the 5th May he came to Lansdowne House for luncheon and stayed until after tea. It was a wet afternoon, so we wandered about in the house and I showed him the Ballroom, the New Stables etc. Twice that afternoon he called me 'Bertie', which set my heart hammering furiously, but he seemed to do it unconsciously and he was so absent minded that it might have meant nothing. Then he said he wanted to consult me about a very difficult question; he had been asked to start the 'Curraghmore Hounds' again and he was wondering whether he ought to do it and whether he should leave the Army. 'What do you think about it?', he said – and he kept on insisting on having my opinion, as if I had a real share in his life. I think I advised him to stay on in the Army and not hurry about taking the Hounds, but it was all very embarrassing and I was so diffident that I did not know what to make of it. He was really shy too, and I think he wanted to make sure that I cared for him before he committed himself. Before he left, he said he would come up again the following Sunday afternoon, when we should have to finally settle the question of the Hounds. By this, I felt sure that he meant to propose to me and I was in a wild state of excitement and anxiety the rest of the week, but by Sunday evening I was nearly in tears, for he never came! The whole afternoon I remained at the window watching the Lodge Gate, and every time they opened my heart went pip-a-pat, but I grew more and more despondent as the hours passed, and then I felt sure he must have changed his mind and that everything was over, and that perhaps it was my fault for not meeting him half-way when he made advances. It was a miserable evening. However, it turned out afterwards that he had had a bad knock at polo a day or two before and hurt his left ear: he had meant to come up all the same, but on the Sunday morning the ear got worse and he had to keep quiet and have it poulticed. He never lost the mark of this cut and often used to say that he could always be identified by it if he were lost, and this came true after his death. On Monday morning he telegraphed his excuses and ended 'have written': I waited patiently for this letter, but it never came, or rather, I think it came three days afterwards!

At this point, Lord William Beresford came to the rescue and invited us both down to Deepdene for the following Saturday to Monday.

Father and Mother and I travelled down in the afternoon, and at the station we met Tyrone, who went in the carriage. It was a fairly large party; Harbords, Mrs Colgate, Mr Burke Corkran, Col. Mackenzie, Billy Lambton, Lord Marcus Beresford etc. Tyrone took me in to dinner; he was rather 'distrait' and nervous and chopped his name card into dozens of little pieces. He told me that he particularly wanted to have a talk with me the next day about Hounds and other things, and that we must be alone. Most of us went to Church in the morning, but he didn't appear at all till we came back and then he asked me to go for a walk. As bad luck would have it, Mrs Colgate insisted on my playing the violin with her just then and I had to play piece after piece, and all the time I was longing to get off, and he stood there staring at me and frowning because I didn't come. At last, however, I got off, and we strolled up the hill, away from the house. Then he put the question; he was very very nervous as up to the last he wasn't quite sure of me, which was odd, as I simply adored him, but I was always afraid to show it.

I was so overcome when he proposed, that I could hardly answer, and he always declared afterwards that I burst into floods of tears, but this was certainly not the case, as I was able to go in to luncheon directly afterwards and, though I felt as if everybody must notice my flushed cheeks, nobody guessed that anything had happened. We had to keep the engagement private for some time, as he did not wish it known until his sisters returned from abroad, thinking that it would be kinder to tell them than to write about it. Of course, Mother, Lily Duchess, and the two Uncles were told, directly we got a chance. Lord William had always been like the best of uncles to me and it was a joy to think he would become a real one now, and nothing could have been kinder than he and Aunt Lily were about it all.

In the afternoon everybody walked down to the Home Farm and coming back we managed to get right away from the rest of the party and had a delightful walk together. Oh, I was happy! It all seemed almost too good to be true and now I could show him how much I loved him, though I was still stupidly shy. He had to leave after tea, but I knew we should very soon meet again, as he promised to come up and see me as often as he could.

We returned to London the next morning and he came that day to tea, and again on Wednesday, Friday and Sunday, staying to dinner on the last day. On Wednesday 26th, Mother and I dined at the Bachelor's Club with him and, in order that the party should not be too much marked, he asked his 'Job' Trotter (2nd Lifeguards) to make a fourth. We always used to call the latter 'the gooseberry' after this; he was most tactful and talked to Mother all the time and took no notice while we strummed at the piano after dinner. Tyrone had a slight attack of influenza soon after, and it was nearly a week before I saw him again. Meanwhile, his sisters came home from abroad and were told of our engagement. Susie came to see me at once and was the greatest dear about it.

June ~ July 1897

The next day, June 1st, Tyrone came up for lunch and Susie and Clodagh joined us; T and I had a nice little *tête-à-tête* afterwards and then drove to Hampden House in a hansom, meeting several people, who all wagged their heads – and no doubt their tongues – after.

We settled that the engagement could no longer be kept a secret, so 'The Hose was let on', as T expressed it; I was left to bear the brunt of it alone, as T went off to Brighton with Susie for a change of air, and we were going to Bowood for Whitsuntide a few days later. I wanted to tell

Mademoiselle Berton (my old governess) the news myself, so went to see her next morning. She was very pleased, though she said:
'Il faut avouer, Chérie que j'avais espéré que vous épouseriez soit ce cher Lord Beachamp, ou ce bon Mr Charles Wyndham; mais enfin, puisque Lord Waterford est le neveu de ce cher Lord William, il doit être très charmant!'. The two gentlemen selected were brothers to her pupils, otherwise there was no reason that I should marry either of them!

Letters of congratulation simply poured in all day, and for many days after; and that night, at Lady Farquhar's dance, I was quite overwhelmed with congratulations, and everybody was so kind. Beasie Butler was there and was most charming, and I did feel grateful to her for not having wanted to marry Tyrone the year before, though it seemed very bad taste on her part.

That afternoon, we suddenly realized that nobody had thought of taking the news to old Lady Waterford, Tyrone's Grandmother. It was an awful moment and we didn't know what to do, as Mother, for some reason or other, couldn't go. So finally I went off to break it to the old lady, whom I was horribly frightened of; she had never liked me, though she was very fond of my sister, and devoted to my Father and Mother. My heart was in my mouth as I went upstairs at 14 Wilton Place and I could hardly speak when I got to the Drawing Room, and she stood looking at me as if I'd been a curious kind of animal. At last I blurted out 'I've come to tell you that Tyrone and I are engaged': 'Oh, you are, are you' said she, looking at me with some disgust; and then added 'Well, I always knew he'd do that – engaged to one girl for a month, throw her over, then get engaged to another, and throw her over'. This was fairly embarrassing, and I nervously said that I hoped he had made up his mind this time. 'Oh!' she said, with huge contempt, 'so you think you've caught him, do you?' This left me speechless, but after a minute she softened down slightly and said she liked my family, so with this faint praise, and a rather grudging kiss, I had to be content, and I was thankful to get away.

I may as well explain that Tyrone had had an affair with a certain Miss W. some time before, and had been more or less engaged to her, but he soon discovered that he did not really care for her, and so the engagement was broken off. He had a great many flirtations, but I think the only girl he really wanted to marry – except me – was Beasie Butler, and many people thought they would get engaged, but she did not care for him enough, although they always remained very good friends. His Grandmother always had a terror that he would be 'caught' by some designing minx; she was very devoted to him and gave him many warnings on the subject.

Two days later we went to Bowood and I did not see Tyrone again until after we returned to London. He came to luncheon on June 12th and we all went down to Deepdene in the afternoon, since Susie and Clodagh were also of the party. Little Billy Beresford was christened next day, Tyrone and Winston Churchill being his Godfathers. The latter was in great form and most amusing, though it made me rather angry to hear him lay down the law on every subject, and flatly contradict all the older men. T & I went for a walk and felt very sentimental over the place where we were engaged. He left that evening, and two days later I went to stay with his sisters at Remenham House, Wraysbury, which he had taken for them so that they might be near him at Windsor. I was there three or four days and had a very happy time, spending most of the time with T on the river. He had sprained his shoulder, so could not play polo, but we went over to Datchet twice to see his Regiment practice. All his brother officers were very nice to me, and Colonel Brocklehurst – who was a great friend of Tyrone's Mother – was particularly charming. The following Tuesday, June 22nd, was Jubilee day; T was with his regiment in the procession, but behind the Queen; and on Thursday, July 1st, he was Galloper to the Prince of Wales at the great Aldershot Review. On June 16th, he and I went down to Coates in order that my dear old Granny (Duchess of Abercorn) might make his acquaintance. She was delighted with him, and they became great friends and always remained so.

The Jubilee festivities kept us all pretty busy in London at that time. There was a Banquet for 92 people – nearly all Royalties – at Lansdowne House one night and a huge reception another night; the famous fancy dress Ball at Devonshire House, before which there were constant Quadrille practices and many other entertainments. All the same, I saw Tyrone pretty constantly; he was very good about coming up to see me and twice took me down to Hurlingham to see the Blues play in the semi-finals of the Inter Regimental polo, and again for the Subaltern's Cup. During all this time I continued to go to Balls as usual, as Tyrone was particularly anxious that I should do so, although he couldn't on account of mourning, but he said, 'I don't want you to sit and mope at home because I'm not there; you are to go and enjoy yourself'. I think some people were rather shocked at this, and H.R.H. went so far as to say so, which annoyed me very much, as I didn't care whether I went to the dance or not, and only went because Tyrone wished it.

I was not very sorry to get away from London, except that it meant going further away from Tyrone. I went down to Remenham again on July 17th for Saturday to Monday, and then went on to Bowood on the 24th. Mother and I went for the day to Stoke to see the Duke and Duchess of Beaufort, my future grandparents. They were most kind and the Duke wrote me such a charming letter next day. We came up to London again on the 26th for a few days, during which time Father chose a Tiara for me and Tyrone ordered a lovely pearl collarette and several other things besides.

T took me to luncheon with old Lady Waterford, who had by then got accustomed to the idea of me as his wife and was really very kind and pleasant, but I still felt rather frightened of her. Another day we dined at Princes and Mother, Charlie Bury, T & I, went to Earls Court afterwards, where we wandered to our hearts' content, and took especial interest in the Incubated Babies!

The next day, July 30th, we said goodbye for two whole months; it seemed an eternity before us and I went down to Bowood feeling thoroughly depressed.

August ~ September 1897

On August 9th we left for Derreen, crossing via Milford and Waterford, and I tried hard to make out the Curraghmore Woods as we passed them in the train, but it was too misty to see much. We were at Derreen seven weeks; Susie and Clodagh were with us for 2½ weeks. The day after they left came a wire from Tyrone to say 'coming tomorrow'; this was quite unexpected and was a great joy. He was with us for 8 days, September 16th to 24th – and it was very delightful. I always loved Derreen above any other place and it was such a pleasure to be able to show it all to him, and to know that he was enjoying the fishing and everything. He fished with Father most days, and then I used to go to meet him and perhaps take luncheon out to him. Other days we went sailing or rowing together and we spent one particularly blissful afternoon walking into Coomingeera, where we paid a visit to the old couple who lived at the head of the glen, and received many blessings from them. Tyrone was charming to all my old friends at Derreen and they all took a great fancy to him and always admired him very much. He left on September

24th, and I got up at 5.15am to see him off; I was going to see him very soon again, so did not feel so sad this time.

We left Derreen on September 18th, and went back via Dublin, where I had some of my trousseau gowns to try on at the Mannings. Tyrone had been at Curraghmore and I caught another glimpse of him at Kingsbridge Station on his way through; he and Father crossed together, but Mother and I stayed at the Royal Hospital and followed next evening, reaching London the morning of the 30th.

October 1897

The next 16 days were frightfully busy; presents came pouring in every day and they all had to be thanked for; then there were all my trousseau clothes to try on, and endless other things to do. Tyrone came up nearly every day, except when he was Orderly Officer, and one day he took me to the Aquarium to see the great Prize Fight between Corbett and Fitzsimmons on the Cinematograph. Mother was not at all well and had to spend several days in bed to avoid jaundice, but she came up to scratch all right and was wonderful through all this time, and so good to me.

How well I remember the last night at Lansdowne House; the feeling that the first chapter of my life was closed, and all the unknown before me, the sorrow at leaving Mother and Father and the great joy at the thought that tomorrow I should be with my darling and be his very own. I always wore a little gold locket he had given me just after we were engaged. It was one his Father had worn on his watch chain and contained a little head of Tyrone when he was only a few months old. I remembered the subterfuges which were needed to hide this, and a large photograph of him in uniform, when we were first engaged, and nobody knew of it, and how I used to pull them out from their hiding places at night and have a long and happy look at them and, before that, what anxieties and heart burnings there had been in that very room, when I had feared that he didn't really care for me. And now, I was really to be his wife the very next day and I went to bed feeling wonderfully happy and longing for the morning.

The 16th October was a lovely day and everything went off all right, though we were both very nervous. Tyrone was staying with his sisters at Ovington Square. Mr W. Perry and Mr C. Nugent Humble came to see how he was getting on, and finding him thoroughly shaky they insisted on his going for a walk with them, and Willie Perry always declared that Tyrone would have 'done a bolt' if he hadn't been firmly held on to. Then they met a hearse and he said that must mean very bad luck, but they assured him that it was the best omen in the world!

Meanwhile, I was being dressed up and gazed at by the family and the servants; I got on all right until the last ten minutes or so, when Mother had gone on. I was quite ready, but Father said it was too early to start, and so I had to wait with nothing at all to do! This was more than I could bear, so in desperation I had in all the maids and gave them my photograph, with many thanks for a most charming silver tea set they had all subscribed to.

At last we were off and then I got more nervous than ever and shook so much that I could hardly stand, but Father was a perfect dear and kept on squeezing my arm in such a comforting way. We were married at St. George's, Hanover Square; the Church was very crowded and at the door stood some of the 'Blues', who presented me with a lovely bouquet in a silver holder. Tyrone had particularly told me to say the N.C.O.'s name when I thanked him, which I did, but afterward discovered it was the wrong name. The 'Blues' also lined the aisle, and looked very fine. By some mistake, Tyrone was brought out of the vestry too soon and endured perfect tortures waiting before the whole congregation for what seemed to him a very long time. After the ceremony, he was so anxious to get away that he took me down the aisle at break-neck speed and my small page, after making several ineffectual attempts to pick up my train, tripped over it, and collapsed in the middle of the aisle, where we left him. We gained nothing by this hasty exit, as Tyrone's hat had been left behind in the confusion and we had to wait while the Best Man (Lord Crichton) fetched it. At last we got off, the crowd all waving and shouting good wishes. A man in the street put his head in and said something which I missed, but T sat back and got very pink. He afterwards told me the man had said 'Good luck in twins, My Lord!'

Hundreds of people came on to Lansdowne House and they filed by us in procession, all congratulating us, as we stood in the Ballroom. More than half of these I had never seen before, and we were both very glad when we were able to escape upstairs and get changed. I remember, when I was in my room, with the door on to the back stairs open, I heard the Housekeeper calling to my Maid, who was just coming down, and saying 'Miss Laws, where is your Marchioness?' I was very disgusted, and when my Maid came in, I gave her a good talking to and said I hoped she would never on any account refer to me as her Marchioness!

We had a later luncheon in Mother's Sitting Room and went off later to Coates, in Sussex, which my Granny had very kindly lent us for the Honeymoon. It was our fate that the day was to be early for everything and we had a long wait at the Station, which was very embarrassing, as we had to sit in a large saloon carriage which had been reserved for us; it had 'Engaged' on every window and, to make matters worse, the footman would walk up and down outside, with a large wedding favour in his buttonhole!

'Gyp', T's little fox-terrier, awaited us in the saloon carriage; she was very devoted to her master, but graciously accepted me as a friend and we were very glad to have her there to pass the time till we left the station. We got to Coates in time for dinner. We were thoroughly done up by then and were aghast to see that a dinner of seven or eight courses awaited us and didn't like to hurt the servants' feelings by cutting half of it out. However, we soon had to give it up, as we were so tired that we simply couldn't eat. So with many apologies to Mr Palmer (Granny's Butler) we retired.

The next day was Sunday, but Tyrone wouldn't hear of going to Church, so we just lazed away happily all day. We did not stay long at Coates as Tyrone was anxious to get to Curraghmore and we had promised to go to Bowood first; so on the 22nd we went up to London, where we lunched with Susie and Clodagh, and went on to Bowood in the afternoon. The employees there gave us a very hearty reception. It seemed so funny to be 'visiting' at Bowood and I was dreadfully shy that time, and almost wished that we hadn't come there. We left on the 26th, lunched with Granny Waterford in London, and crossed to Ireland by the night mail and luckily had a very good crossing.

We stopped a few hours in Dublin and got to Curraghmore in the afternoon. Fiddown Station was decorated and quite a crowd were there. In Portlaw, there were several pretty arches and every house was decorated with branches; the people gave us a great reception and we were cheered all the way. We drove in the Victoria, with a pair of grey horses, driven by A. Clark; a very smart turn-out.

At the front door we were received by the Agent and all the Heads of Departments. We had some lunch and then Tyrone came out and made a short speech to the people who were waiting there, and they received it with yells of delight.

I suffered very much from home-sickness during the first week at Curraghmore; everything seemed so new and strange. I missed Mother dreadfully, and I wondered if I should ever be able to adapt myself to the new surroundings, which were so utterly different from everything at Bowood. Tyrone had come home and returned to all his usual occupations, but I felt just a stranger with no interests and I got very depressed and shed some tears over my loneliness. Of course it was really only a kind of reaction after the excitement and strain of the last few weeks and it soon passed, as I found new interest every day and collected all my own little belongings round me. Tyrone said I was to invite some girlfriend to stay with me, so as not to be lonely when he went out hunting, but I remember Mother's wise advice about this and refused to ask anyone. She had begged me not to have friends to stay at first, but to remain alone with Tyrone for some time so that we might get to know each other better and learn to depend on each other's society, rather than on that of friends. I often afterwards felt grateful to her for this advice, for we made such a good start in this way and were always so perfectly happy alone together at Curraghmore.

The first Sunday was very trying! I had taken a 10/- piece to put in the plate and tucked it into a little pocket in my prayer book. Unfortunately, I turned this upside down about half-way through the service and the money fell out. Before I could catch it, it went clattering over the tiles as if possessed, and rolled down the aisle till it met a hot-air ventilator, down which it disappeared. The mere fact of walking into the front pew under the curious eyes of all the neighbours had filled me with nervous confusion, but when I felt all those eyes noting my awkwardness, I longed to sink into the floor. I stupidly never thought of asking Tyrone for some money, so when Mr Reynett came round with the plate I had nothing to put on it. I shook my head, but he waited patiently in front of me. I shook it again, but he never moved. At last, in desperation, I whispered 'it's down the pipe', but as bad luck would have it he was very deaf and, though I repeated the words in a louder whisper, he still heard nothing and at last moved off looking thoroughly disgusted, and evidently thinking that the new Lady Waterford was a very mean person. T enjoyed this incident enormously. Dr Staunton, whom I had met before, came to luncheon afterwards and they both chaffed me unmercifully about it.

November 1897

Many neighbours called on us during the following week, and several of them came to luncheon or tea. On November 3rd there was a Meet at Carrick-on-Suir and I drove there with T and got out at the Inn, whose Landlady, Mrs Phelan, was a great character. She introduced me to several people who came in and I was much entertained by Miss Mary Power, who took complete charge of me, drew up the blind, and chased away all the people who were standing outside the window, in order that I might have a good view of Tyrone on his horse. He did look very nice, and I felt very proud of him. I followed for some while in the phaeton, but saw nothing.

Our first visitor was Tyrone's great friend, Will Perry, who came over from Woodrooff in Tipperary. How well I remember his arrival! T and I were out walking when we saw the dog cart and went to meet it, and then Willie Perry got out and walked back with us. I had met him before, but we all felt decidedly shy and T did nothing but laugh at my cap (a red woollen tamoshanter made for me by Granny) till at last Will had to say he thought it was very nice and most becoming. There was a great deal of horse and hunting talk during the next few days, and on Sunday they spent the whole afternoon in the stables and I went for a tramp alone.

At that time Tyrone hated walking unless he had some definite objective and it was very difficult to get him to go for a constitutional. He sometimes took me out driving in the phaeton and other days he would potter about with a gun or rifle. He hunted two or three days a week then, and more later on. While he was out, I generally drove round returning calls. When hunting in Kilkenny or Waterford, he usually got home about tea time, but when he went to Tipperary he often started at 6.30am and didn't get home till 7.30pm; those days seemed very long to me and I always felt anxious about him when he was hunting.

Meanwhile, I was gradually getting to know the people round about and Miss Martin helped me a great deal with the poor in Portlaw, who were the most awful beggars and simply pestered me whenever I went down to the village, all of them wanting 'an order on the shop' for provisions, or coal or something or other. I always carried a little notebook and took down their names and addresses, so as to ask Miss Martin's advice about them.

Mr Humble was our next visitor, but he did not stay long. On November 18th we paid a formal visit to the town of Kilmacthomas. T drove me in the Phaeton. Before we got to the town the local band met us, also the Temperance Union, with a larger banner; and with the village lunatic dancing before us, the band playing and the banner waving, we made quite a state entry in the little town. Then followed introductions and speeches, and the presentation of a bouquet and we passed on under arches and banners to the Woollen Factory (which belonged to Tyrone), where we went through the rooms and saw all the machines working. T made a sketch of the entry, which may be seen in one of my scrapbooks.

The following week we paid our first real visit together, to the Perrys (Willie's parents) at Woodrooff. As a matter of fact, I was not able to go with T on the day arranged; he had to go on as he was hunting next day, so I followed all by myself. I went in ordinary travelling clothes and what was my horror, on arriving at Woodrooff, to find a large party assembled to meet me! T and Willie Perry were out hunting and I didn't know a soul there; it was most trying and as soon as I had had tea Mrs Perry insisted on my playing the violin to the assembled party, who had all been introduced to me by then. The next day, Mrs Perry was full of plans, all with the object of exhibiting me to as many friends as possible. It was a wet day, so we trundled round in the brougham; first had luncheon with her daughter, Mrs Platt, then coffee with the Bagwells at Marlfield, on to tea with Sir Charles & Lady Gough, and ended up with a visit to an old gentleman called 'Uncle Perry', who I was told would probably want to kiss me, but luckily he didn't! I was thoroughly tired out by the time we got back, but Mrs Perry's energy was unlimited.

Meanwhile, Tyrone and Willie hunted every day and when we went back to Curraghmore Willie came with us. We had a great day in Waterford soon after; we left Curraghmore at 10.30 and T drove me the 14 miles to Waterford where we inspected the Lunatic Asylum, T being their visiting Governor. We went all over the Asylum and it was most interesting, but I never want to go again! The faces of those poor souls haunted me for days afterwards, and I had awful nightmares that night. We lunched with Dr Atkins, who had been there for some years, though in the middle of this time he himself had retired into a private asylum for about 2 years, owing to some great trouble which had sent him temporarily off his head. He was a most pleasant man and had a great way with the patients, who were all devoted to him.

In the afternoon we took a car and drove miles, returning calls; it was cold work and by the time we got home we were fairly frozen and tired out. People have come from very great distances to call on us and many of the calls could only be returned by driving into Waterford, putting up and lunching there, and then driving sometimes 10 miles beyond Waterford on a hired car. I know one day I counted up the distance I had driven altogether and found it to be quite 70 miles. This was no joke before the days of motors, and in the winter too.

December 1897

On December 7th Susie and Clodagh arrived. Also Miss Gomme their Companion; they stayed with us, on and off, for about 2½ months. About this time, we had a visit from Willie Perry and 'Miss Dolly Boyce'. Some years before they wanted to get married, but the Perry family disapproved of the match and old Mr Perry, who was much feared by his family, would not hear of even an engagement. Willie was too much afraid of him to stand up to him about this and yet was determined to marry Dollie, so they managed to meet in London and got privately married at a Registry Office, after which they went to Tournaire (where Dollie's married sister, Mrs Wogan-Brown lived) and spent their Honeymoon there. None of the family knew of this, not even Dollie's own Mother. Dollie was only supposed to be visiting her sister and Willie's movements were unknown! After that, they returned to their respective houses, and only met when a convenient chance offered itself. Tyrone and his Mother knew of the marriage, and Susie and Clodagh were also told. Tyrone explained the situation to me before we married and said I must be kind to Dollie and help them to meet sometimes. It was a marvel to me how they could keep up this double life. I was always urging them to end it by owning up, but they knew there would be a storm when they did, and so kept putting it off.

About this time, I began to be seriously worried because there were no signs of a baby coming. We had only been married two months, but I wept bitterly over it and felt certain that I would never have any children! I remember well sitting one evening with my head on Tyrone's shoulder, sobbing over my failure, while he tried to comfort me, but I could see that he was quite as disappointed as I was, and was thoroughly depressed.

Nothing much happened during the rest of December. Tyrone had a scratch pack of Hounds – 9 couple – which he sometimes took out at Curraghmore. I didn't ride that winter, but generally followed on foot, and whenever there was a Meet of the real Hounds anywhere near, I used to drive out and follow for a bit. Then there was a bazaar and concert at Carrick-on-Suir, at which Susie and Clodagh and I were kept very busy, both selling and playing.

A small excitement at this time was the capture of a marten cat in the Portlaw Woods. It was a real beauty and was quite unhurt. Tyrone presented it to the Zoo in Dublin, where it lived for some years, but it was very wild and never could be tamed. In later years, these marten cats were seen fairly often by Tyrone and the Keeper and others. One day Tyrone and I were standing very still in the woods, listening for the deer calling, when there was a slight rustle, and two very big martens passed quite close to us. They were bounding along, and playing with each other, and did not see us at all, and we had a splendid view of them; they looked very dark, almost black, but this was no doubt owing to the shadow of the trees, for I believe they are really a brightish brown colour. Lately there has been some talk of a different animal, nearly black, which some suppose to be a cross between a black cat and a marten, and two or three people are said to have seen it in the woods.

The entries in my diary stop abruptly on December 21st, but the Visitors Book gives the names of our Christmas party that year: Evelyn & Norah Hely Hutchinson, Kathleen & Blanche Perry,

Lillian Nugent, Willie Perry, Mr Humble, Mr Reggie Chaplin, Mr Drage, Mr O'Hara, Lord Suirdale and old Colonel Reilly, and of course Susie & Clodagh and Miss Gomme.

What a cheery party it was, and what babies we all were! But there was nearly a terrible disaster! A few days after Xmas, we had left the men smoking in the Dining Room, after a very hearty lunch, when we suddenly heard shouts and then saw them tearing off towards the lake, some of them in such a hurry that they must needs jump out of the Dining Room window. We all dashed out too and arrived just in time to find Mr Chaplin preparing to swim the lake. Somebody had bet he wouldn't do it – I think it was Mr Drage – and in spite of the cold day, and the heavy lunch, he unhesitatingly took it on for the sum of £5. He gave me his watch and chain to keep and then ran round the lake, so as to swim towards home, while we waited to cheer him on landing. In he jumped and all went well for a bit. Then the swans seemed inclined to go for him and the men had to throw stones to keep them off. Then, little more than half-way across, he began to gasp and struggle and we realized that he was getting entangled in the weeds. Presently we heard him shout 'I can't do it', and it looked rather serious and several of the men were preparing to go to his assistance. But he was really in quite shallow water by then, only had not thought of putting his feet down, till Tyrone yelled to him to get up and wade in! They dragged him up the steps, but he was looking very bad and inclined to collapse; however, they kept him on the move and ran him straight upstairs, leaving a trail of water behind him all the way. They got him into bed at once, with five hot water bottles, and about nine blankets, but he was stony cold and his teeth never stopped chattering, and everybody got seriously alarmed. At last somebody suggested rubbing him with Eucalyptus, and Willie Perry, determined to do it thoroughly, poured out half a thimbleful and gave it to him almost neat to drink! This fortunately acted as an emetic and after that he gradually recovered.

That same night there was a sort of subscription dance in Portlaw at Mayfield, which was then empty, and we danced till all hours. Tyrone invented a bogus engagement between Tad (Norah) Hely Hutchinson and Mr Humble, which created great diversion; they sat under a palm tree looking unutterable nothings at each other, while T told Lady May Ponsonby – in the strictest confidence – that they were engaged, and of course it was soon known by everybody. Poor Tad got rather bored with it at last! It was at this dance that a middle-aged spinster, who had played the wall-flower for some time, and could stand it no longer, was heard to say to the Cloakroom Attendant, 'Give me my bonnet and my boots and let me go home, for no man will dance with me'.

On New Year's Eve we all dressed up. This was my idea, as we'd always done it at Bowood, but Tyrone didn't take at all kindly to it and refused to dress up at all. I was rather annoyed with him and I'm afraid I didn't improve matters by telling him that I noticed he was dressed as a wet blanket! I was obstinately determined to see the New Year in, but he wanted us to go to bed. At last, in desperation, Willie Perry got hold of the clock and moved the hands on half an hour so as to shorten the evening, so we drank in the New Year and sang Auld Lang Syne at 11.30 and went to bed!

January 1898

In January 1898 we paid visits to the Roberts at the Royal Hospital Dublin, to the Londonderrys at Mount Stewart and to the H. Bourkes at Hayes. We also had a visit from Lord & Lady Roberts at Curraghmore. I remember I had just learnt to drive a pair then, and one day took out Lord & Lady Roberts and Lady Nugent in the Invalid Phaeton, which had no brakes then. I took a wrong turning and found myself on the long steep hill coming down over Beaulough; the carriage was very heavy, the horses rather fresh, and I felt horribly nervous, but Lord Roberts, who sat next to me, hummed a little tune all the way down, which gave me great confidence, and we got down all right. I was afterward told that Lady Roberts and Lady Nugent were speechless with terror, and sat clasping each other's hands on the back seat; also it transpired that Lord Roberts only hummed like that when he was nervous. It was soon after this that I took Mother for a drive – with a single horse – she hadn't much faith in my driving powers. I knew this and, out of sheer nervousness, drove the trap right up on to a large heap of stones at a cross roads. Luckily we didn't upset.

While we were staying at the Royal Hospital I played the violin at a big concert given by Lady Roberts for the Soldiers' & Sailors' Families. The Concert was in the big hall at the Hospital; it was a very alarming affair. We stayed in Dublin a week. T went to a Levée and I made my curtsey at the Drawing Room (to Lord Cadogan). There were dances and a large dinner party at the Castle, at which the Lord Lieutenant took me in. I think it was at one of these dances that Tyrone and I were sent off to dance with Lord & Lady Cadogan, in the Quadrille, and so disgraced ourselves. Lord Cadogan, at the beginning of the 3rd or 4th figure, asked me what came next and I advised visiting, whereupon we started off to do it, but were stopped by the angry frowns of Lord Ashbourne, who was the one person who always did the Quadrilles correctly. Just after this, while Tyrone was doing a figure with Lady C, his cigarette case fell out of his sleeve (he was in uniform) and the whole of its contents were spread in the centre of the Viceregal Set!

The Dublin season was great fun in those days. The Cadogans were the best host and hostess imaginable and entertained delightfully. The staff did their work well and the dances were full of go. Besides this, it was always delightful to stay with the Roberts and we had most happy times at the Royal Hospital.

Mother came to stay with us after our return home; I remember how shy I was at first entertaining before her, when we gave a dinner party for the neighbours. Charlie was there at the same time, and other visitors later.

March to June 1898

Susie and Clodagh left us on March 7th, and two days later we went over to London. Tyrone's leave was nearly up and, as I was then happily expecting a baby, we were not to be back in Ireland for ever so long.

On March 11th Mother presented me at the Drawing Room; she managed to get the entrée for me on account of my health and I remember that some of the old dowagers were much annoyed at this, and looked very sourly at me. We paid a short visit to Deepdene and a longer one to Badminton. Between the two, there was the St. Patrick's Day Industries Sale at Lansdowne House; I helped Mother to sell and played at the Concert, and was so tired after that I had to stay in bed all next day. I felt rather ill all the time at Badminton too and couldn't enjoy the visit as much as I should have otherwise.

Mother had an operation while we were there – I did not know of it until it was safely over, but fortunately it turned out to be nothing serious, though of course it pulled her down a good deal at the time.

Tyrone returned to duty on March 31st and the next day I joined him at Rosemead, the little house he had taken for a month from Baron Campbell von Laurentz. T rode in a race at Hawthorn Hill that day and had thought of taking me there to see him ride, but being in some doubt whether it would be good for me under the circumstances, he asked the advice of Bone – our Admirable Crichton – who decidedly vetoed the proposition! I was allowed to go the next day, when he was taking no part. I felt very conscious, sitting in the Officers' Pew on the first Sunday, by special invitation of Colonel Brocklehurst; T rather disapproving. Our stay at Windsor was not exactly happy; I felt ill all the time, the house was stuffy, and domestic bliss was clouded by disputes over the Cook!! She was an awful woman, who wore a large auburn coloured false fringe and cooked abominably, but I stuck up for her, thinking she would improve, and T very naturally protested. Such are the teacup storms of early married life!

We often ran up to London. On one of these occasions we took Susie and Clodagh to the Play, Mr Molyneux & Captain Ricardo being also of the party. It was my first effort at chaperoning, and a very bad one too. I had to choose the Play and selected one which was described as a Screaming Farce, and of which the plot seemed to me quite innocent. But on the stage it was quite different and impossible situations, with bedroom muddles and unexpected babies, succeeded each other with alarming rapidity, till at last we could stand it no longer, so T and the other men murmured that they must catch a train and we all filed out, blushing furiously. It was a long time before I heard the end of that play!

Tyrone played polo a good deal at that time and, while at Windsor, I often used to walk or drive down to Datchet to watch the games. Later on, in London, I went to Ranelagh and Hurlingham fairly often.

The Blues came up to London early in May and then we took up our abode at 16 Mansfield Street, which he had taken from Mr Freddy Bentinck. T had a rather bad attack of influenza when first he came up and after that we went to Brighton for a few days. Then he had to return to duty, but was far from fit and soon got knocked up again by playing polo before he was strong enough. He was not at all strong at that time and I was often anxious about him, as he had influenza badly 2 or 3 times every year and always lost about a stone and was very weak afterwards. He also smoked much too much and his heart got very shaky. I never thought then that he would grow into the splendidly strong man he was later, with such broad shoulders, and a decided inclination to grow fat!

We stayed with Mr Astor at Cliveden for a Saturday to Monday in May, and later in the month I went to Bowood and T joined me on a week's special leave, as he was quite unfit for duty. The only other incident, besides the usual round of dinner parties and dances, was a musical evening which we gave with Col. Brocklehurst at our house. He produced Hollimann and I collected M. Emile Sonnet, my violin master, and we had some delightful music; but oh! the jealousies between those two and all the spiteful digs at each other! Hollimann refused the dinner; Sonnet accepted, and enjoyed it thoroughly (a Chef had succeeded the Lady of the auburn fringe!). Hollimann came as the professional and was so pleased with himself that he wouldn't give the other a look in for so long. Sonnet posed as the friend of the family and did not even bring his violin (knowing full well that I had a good one!) and only played to oblige us after much pressing. While Hollimann played, Sonnet murmured in an audible whisper 'Mais vraiment, ce garçon a du talent que c'est dommage qu'il joue une telle musique "Simple Aveu" mais c'est incroyable and so on a so forth while Hollimann glared at him, and in his turn looked thoroughly bored when Sonnet played. It was a wonder they didn't come to blows!

July to September 1898

In July, Tyrone went to Bulford with his Regiment for the manoeuvres, and I joined Mother at Bowood for nearly a fortnight, and then went on to stay with my Great Aunt Georgie – Madame de

Lavalette, at Lavington. T used to ride over from Bulford to see me at both places. How well I remember the first day he came to Lavington! I walked up on to the Downs to meet him; it was rather a climb for me just then, and also I felt rather lonely up there all by myself, so when I saw a tall horse and a well-known figure approaching, I was more than pleased and started waving frantically. To my horror, they went on past me at some distance, without paying any attention to my shouts of 'Tye – Tye' till I was nearly in tears. And all the time he was watching me out of the corner of his eye, and roaring with laughter at my discomfiture; and presently he swung round and joined me. He did love teasing me!

I was at Lavington till August 29th, and then came up to London for good; and then followed a time of weary waiting for the baby, in awfully hot weather. Tyrone came back on September 9th; he was Orderly Officer very often then, as several of the Officers were away on 1st leave. I often had tea with him in his own room in Barracks on those occasions. On September 22nd I thought the infant was going to arrive and sent for T to come back from Barracks early, but it was only a false alarm, of which there were several later, and we waited, and waited, and waited!

October and November 1898

On October 11th I felt rather bad in the evening, so paid my bills and set my house in order. Next morning, still feeling bad, I took a violent constitutional in Hyde Park, and then had the temerity (through sheer ignorance) to go and have tea in Barracks! I found Sir Owen Slacke there and I thought he would never go and give me the chance of telling T the state of affairs. He got off as early as he could that night and I was very glad to have him with me, as I had a pretty hard time for 25 hours after that, as the child didn't arrive till 11.15pm the next day, October 13th. Mother arrived from Bowood in the morning; the Irish odd man brought the telephone message to her himself, in the middle of the night, and she caught the first train up. I never knew when Blanchie was born, being under chloroform at the time, and I was so weary that I went straight off to sleep without realizing anything, and only woke two hours later. Then I heard a baby crying and could hardly believe that it was really mine. What bliss it was!

Blanchie was such a darling little baby and my only grief was that I couldn't nurse her properly, though I continued for a month to try and do it, but I believe she was always given a bottle as soon as she left me! This was the origin of a very ribald sketch T made of me in bed at that time; it is in the scrapbook. A few days after Blanchie was born, Tyrone had another attack of influenza and was packed off to Brighton after it. I have the letter he wrote to me from then. As a rule, he did not express his deeper feelings in his letters, which were in consequence rather stiff and cold, so I did not keep them, but this letter I always treasured, and so copy it here:

> *My Own Little Darling*
> *I have got here all right................... I feel the better for the change already, but I do so wish that my dear little wife was with me, as I am so lonely when I am away from her. Give little Angy a kiss and some pap from me, my darling.*
> *God bless you, my own little wifey, if we go on loving one another as much as at present, we shall be a very happy little couple.*
> *Your devoted Hubby*

When Blanchie was a fortnight old, I was carried into the Drawing Room for tea, and a week later I was allowed to walk from one room to the other. On November 8th I had my first drive, feeling very proud with the Nurse (Mrs Mitchell) and my baby beside me. Mother came up to London next day and we met her at the station. Next day (November 10th) Blanchie was christened, and I was churched, at St. George's, Hanover Square. Mother, Granny Beaufort, and Uncle Bill Beresford, were the Godparents, but Mother was the only one present, though several other members of the family were there. I took Blanchie to see Granny (Abercorn) afterwards; she always took the greatest interest in all the babies and was so kind to them.

The next day, Blanchie and I went to Brighton for change of air; the monthly nurse left and Mrs Brand took charge. We were there a little over a week, T being with us for two days only. I felt rather seedy most of the time, as the sea upset my liver and I was very glad to get back to London. Consuelo Marlborough was at Brighton, recovering after the arrival of her second boy, Tom, who was born the day after Blanchie.

On November 22nd we returned to Curraghmore, after an absence of 8½ months, and what a joy it was to get home, with the addition of a baby! The nurseries were the two centre rooms on the S.W. front and, as one of these had been Susie's and Clodagh's Sitting Room before, we gave them the use of the small (yellow) Drawing Room instead.

The diary has little to say here, but our Xmas party consisted of Susie and Clodagh, Willie & Dollie Perry, Kathleen Beresford, Captain 'Tubby' Morris, Blanche Malcomson, Captain O'Hara, Mrs Humble and Mr Drage; and I think Father and Mother came to us for the New Year.

January 1899

The second week in January, a Ball was given at Bessborough, and another at Curraghmore; so we gathered together a large party for these festivities. Lord Crichton was the first to arrive, then came Edwina & Freddy Roberts, Captain & Mrs Villiers Stuart of Dromana, Edith Perry, Mr & Mrs Platt (she was another Perry), Sir Owen Slake, Willie & Dollie Perry and Susie, Clodagh and Kathleen were still with us.

The first Ball was at Bessborough on January 11th; it ended with a Cotillon, and as W. Perry and I were to lead one at our Ball, we danced this together and made notes as to what was, or was not, to be done, Willie making audible criticisms all the time, with a Ponsonby Cousin sitting close by, much to my embarrassment!

How well I remember T at that Ball! There were three maiden ladies, the Misses Sadleir, who were not having a very good time of it and, though they were neither young nor beautiful – perhaps because of this – he led them out one by one and made them blissfully happy by dancing with them, and making himself thoroughly charming to them!

On the 13th, T's little Hounds had a Meet at Ballydurn (by arrangement with the Hunt), and that evening we gave our Ball. I don't remember very much about it, except that May's Band from Dublin played and we kept it up till nearly 5am. The whole neighbourhood from three counties was there, and I believe it was voted a great success. Willie Perry and I led the Cotillon; poor Freddy Roberts standing behind a screen, and passing us out the trays as we wanted them, and everything went swimmingly.

On January 30th we went up to Dublin and stayed first at the Castle, and then at the Royal Hospital. There was the usual round of Balls, until news came of Prince Alfred of Coburg's death, which put a stop to nearly everything. We came home on February 11th and had Aileen Roberts and the brother, Tilney, to stay with us.

On the 18th February T had another day outside with his own Hounds, meeting at Ballyneale on February 19th. Blanchie was short-coated – a great event! Later we spent a night at Woodrooff, where Willie and Dollie – having declared their marriage to the family, and gone through the religious ceremony for the benefit of the Public – were now installed in their own rooms. They came back with us on February 24th and next day Willie took me out schooling on Miss Florrie (commonly known as the Pipsqueak) to see if I showed any sort of aptitude for hunting. The pony was a beautiful jumper and I got on all right, but when we got home Willie told Tyrone that he was afraid it wouldn't do and that it would be better not to take me out. This was all a deep laid plot of Willie's imagining and I knew all about it, Willie having already told me I could go out hunting any day, but poor T took it very seriously and could hardly hide his disappointment. He was delighted when Willie told him the truth, and the following week I started hunting and enjoyed it enormously. I took a gentle toss on my 4th day out, but being quite unhurt, this gave me more confidence.

March and April 1899

On March 8th Tyrone and I hunted in Kilkenny, meeting at Newmarket, and had a good run from Carricktriss; this was my first serious hunt as the others had been only with T's scratch pack on his Hunt's Harriers. We had a long and weary ride back to get the carriage. It was cold and windy and pouring wet, and I got home very tired. Later in the month, I had two days with the Tips, but no sport either day – very disappointing, particularly as on the 2nd day Uncle Bill joined us (at Cahir Park) and he only had one day to spare.

On April 3rd 1899 we left Curraghmore for London. T went on duty next day and I went to Bowood for a week. Blanchie met me there and remained on with Mother for 12 days after I left.

We took a house in Rutland Gate that summer as the Blues were at Knightsbridge Barracks; very often we had one or two of the Officers to luncheon or dinner, and occasionally I had tea with Tyrone in Barracks when he was on duty.

On April 30th (Susie's birthday) the old Duke of Beaufort died and Tyrone went to his funeral at Badminton on May 5th. At this time, my diary shows a regular round of quiet amusements – people to lunch and dinner, dinner out, a good many plays, an occasional opera, and constant polo matches or practices at Ranelagh, Hurlingham, Eden Park etc.

Tyrone's brother officers were a very nice lot; those I saw most of were Lord Crichton, Mr Harold Brassey, Major Mann-Thompson, the Duke of Roxburghe, Lord Tullibardine, Sir Dudley Marjoribanks, Captain Ricardo and Mr Drage; Colonel Brocklehurst was in command and was always very charming to us, always having been a great friend of the family. There was also Mr Reggie Ward, to whom T was devoted, but who seldom came to see us, and Mr Edmond Charteris, Tyrone's great friend, who had a horror of all strangers, and most particularly of strange women, and who rose like a horse whenever he saw me in the near distance!

T played polo a great deal, and was in the Subaltern's team; he often drove me down to Ranelagh or one of the other grounds in his light buggy, drawn by 'Toby', an American Trotter. These were the happiest days. On others, I generally took somebody down with me in our Victoria, with a smart pair of grey horses – for in those days we always drove greys, and T took great pride in them. On one occasion, Miss May Power (of Mount Richard) came to luncheon and drove to Ranelagh with me. She was hugely fat and dressed in a loud purple blouse, and caused great merriment as we drove through the streets. She discovered that I was 'in an interesting condition', and embarrassed me dreadfully when we were in the grand stand, by constantly asking if I was tired, and begging me to put up my feet! Then she got wildly excited over the game and encouraged Tyrone, in a loud voice, 'Well hit Lord Waterford – go on now, hit it again' – 'Ah, look at that fellow pushing him, it's too bad now', etc. etc., till I nearly died of shame.

Tyrone and I had very strict ideas about the upbringing of our daughter and amongst other things, we resolved she should not go to many parties. I was inclined to make an exception for my cousin Bee Pembroke's annual baby party, but T would not hear of it when I suggested it. Then Evie came to see me and begged me to persuade T to let Blanchie go to this family gathering of babies, but I refused to bother him about it again and told Evie she must ask him herself if she was so keen about it. Evie promptly went round to Barracks and pointed out to Tyrone that if he never let his child be seen, people would be sure to say there was something wrong with her – whereupon he hurriedly gave his consent.

During that summer, my cousin, Katie Scott, married Tom Brand, and Elsie Grosvenor, a great friend, married Mr Aubrey Smith. Susie and Clodagh were living in Ovington Square, so we saw a good deal of them.

I made friends with a Miss Dundas, who played the piano beautifully, and with Signor Pezzi (a professional cellist) we played a great many trios during that summer.

May 1899

We spent two Sundays (in May and June) at Deepdene with Uncle Bill and Aunt Lily, and one Sunday we drove down to Ham to see Uncle Charlie and Aunt Nina. What a party that was! Long haired musicians, Poets, Art Critics, and the pet young man in a flower-embroidered waistcoat: all these Aunt Nina's friends – gabbling away in French, German and Italian, with much gesticulation at one table, while Uncle Charlie kept his naval and other friends in perpetual laughter at another, smiling indulgently the while at 'little Dot' and her outrageous foreignness. T selected a particularly greasy looking individual with long black hair and a diminutive white straw hat bound with black ribbon, and asked Uncle Charlie if that was one of his old shipmates. Uncle Charlie was much tickled by the joke and came and repeated it to 'little Dot' while I sat beside her; she wasn't a bit amused and turned away in great disgust!

Old Mrs Slingsby, a Leslie relation, died that summer and Tyrone and the Beresford Uncles went to the funeral. Mr Tom Slingsby, who was then quite blind, was heartbroken over his wife's death and cried bitterly in the carriage in which he drove with two of the Uncles. Unfortunately, he had just on his hat, which was furnished with a long streamer, wrong side before, so that the end of the streamer kept on tickling his nose. He thought it was a fly and tried to brush it away all the time till the Uncles (who were really very sorry for him) were convulsed with laughter and, of course, scandalized the passers-by. Not only this, but when the poor old gentleman himself died some years later, Uncle Marcus chose the most solemn moment, when several of the family were following the funeral procession to the Cemetery, to remind the others of the incident, whereupon they again went off into fits of laughter and caused a second scandal!

July to October 1899

*W*e hardly went to any Balls that season as we were in mourning for Tyrone's Grandfather at first, and later on Tyrone was not fit for much dancing. We both went to the Palace Ball on July 7th and to one at Derby House on the 14th.

I spent a week at Bowood and left Blanchie there rather longer. My Grandmother (The Dowager Duchess of Abercorn) was there, and a photograph was taken of the 4 generations, Granny (aged 87), Mother, myself and Blanchie – which is in one of my scrapbooks.

Blanchie was then 9 months old and the greatest darling; very bright and friendly and most intelligent. She was photographed by Faulkner on her return and there was a great excitement over these, the first proper photographs taken of her.

On August 4th we left London and arrived at Ford early next morning. This place had been let up till then, but Tyrone thought it would be nice to go there in the autumn, which we did for three years. It was a lovely place, but I never liked it nearly so well as Curraghmore. There was no park at all, only the length of the avenue on our side, and the width of the kitchen garden – beyond which was the Village – on the other side of the house. Though it appeared fairly large, it was very inconvenient and had very few really nice rooms in it. On the other hand, there was good shooting and T always like the place very much and generally felt well there, which I didn't! The people were all very pleased at the return of 'the family'. We went to visit most of the farmers and T gave them a big dinner, to which 20 came. Just after this, he had a very bad attack of influenza; he was in bed for 10 days and I was quite anxious about him.

We had a long visit from Kathleen Beresford, who was with us for 3 weeks, and my Granny paid us a fortnight's visit. T was always most charming to her and I loved seeing them together. He took such care of her and they were the greatest friends. She came to us every year, combining this with a visit to Fenton, only 4 miles away, where lived Freddy Lambton.

Amongst other visitors, we had Mr Harold Brassey, the Duke of Roxburghe, Beatrix Herbert, Aileen & Edwina Roberts, the Pembrokes etc.

Blanchie's first birthday was a great event and Beatie Lambton brought over Granny (then at Fenton), Aunt George, Violet and Joan for it. Blanchie sat in her high chair, smiling on all her friends, and enjoyed it all thoroughly. She was beginning to talk a good deal then and used to come into our bed every morning early and imitate all the animal's voices when shown their pictures. We had intended to return to Curraghmore at the end of October, but many things had been happening during those last few months and I must go back to the summer to show their special bearing on us.

Although our life in London seemed so happy, Tyrone was very restless, or restive? over it all the time. He really hated the Orderly Officer's duty in London and chafed at the dull regularity of it, combined with home ties and always said that us Subalterns should marry (he was the first to break that old rule!). He often talked of sending in his papers, but I begged him not to as I thought he was much too young to be doing nothing and felt that the life with the Regiment was really good for him. At that time there was much rumour of war with S. Africa. T was madly keen to see active service, but the Household Cavalry never went abroad then and he used to say, 'If there is war, and I do stay on in the Regiment, it's no earthly good, for of course they'll never be sent out'. Then we went to Ford and he came to the conclusion that if he were to look after Curraghmore and Ford properly, he must leave and, in spite of much protest from me, he sent in his papers.

Hardly had they been accepted when war broke out! He was awfully upset, but comforted himself by saying again, 'Of course the Blues won't go out'. Shortly after the Composite Regiment was formed, all his old brother officers were volunteering for it. Of course he would have gone, and I should have done nothing to prevent his doing so, but when he suggested volunteering now, I at once threw cold water on the idea as it did not seem to me to be his duty. We had no son, Tyrone had no brother, and the Uncles were only represented by one delicate little boy, Bill Beresford. So much depended on Tyrone and, hard as I knew it to be for him to stay at home, I felt that, having sent in his papers, it was his duty to abide by that decision.

I was to have had my baby at Curraghmore, and Mother would have come to me there, but Evie got fussed about this and said I ought to come to London. Father was Minister for War and was, of course, going through a frightfully anxious time and, besides this, both Kerry and Charlie had just sailed for S. Africa with their Regiments; Kerry from Gibraltar with the Grenadiers, and Charlie from London with the Royals. My one idea was to keep Tyrone out of London, where I knew the perpetual war talk would make him miserable, but I had to give in in the end.

November 1st 1899

*T*yrone went up on November 1st to make arrangements and came back a few days later in the depths of depression. Having seen all his old brother officers collecting their kit and full of their approaching departure, there was another sadly disappointed one – Mr Edmund Charteris, who, when looking through his kit, was cleaning a revolver without realizing it was loaded and let it off into his leg, which more or less disabled him for years.

We left Ford on November 11th 1899 and went to Mackellar Hotel in London, leaving Blanchie – oh! so sadly – to go to Curraghmore, where

T joined her a few days later. At the Mackellar we met Lord Roberts, whose only son had just gone out to the war. I was beginning to wonder whether I was right in not encouraging T to go out, as he was so anxious to go – though, indeed, he hardly ever said anything about it and did his best not to upset me on account of the infant that was coming so soon, but I always felt he was longing for me to say 'Go'. I knew Lord Roberts would give me an absolutely honest opinion, both as an old friend, and as the straightest soldier that ever lived; so I managed to see him alone and laid the whole case before him. To my intense relief, he said I was doing right and that he considered, under all the circumstances, it would be very wrong for Tyrone to volunteer. This eased my mind very much at the time, but in after years I often thought I had made a great mistake – though I know the principle as right – for T never got over the disappointment and vexation of it all, and had an idea he was a marked man because he hadn't gone out, and this idea embittered him for years.

I spent the next three weeks at Deepdene with Aunt Lily and Uncle Bill, when he wasn't away racing; they were very kind to me and I had a nice quiet time there till it was necessary to go up to London. T came over on the 5th December and I went up on the 7th, leaving him at Deepdene for another week. Meanwhile, the war was raging in South Africa, news of big battles arrived day after day and everyone was in a constant state of anxiety. Belmont, Graspan, Modder River, Magersfontein, and then the disastrous Chieveley. The day T came back to London we heard that Freddy Roberts was dangerously wounded and the next day – December 17th – came the news of his death. Oh, the awful sadness of it for Lord & Lady Roberts and my dear friends Aileen and Edwina; they were all absolutely wrapped up in him and it seemed almost impossible that he should be taken from them. His life made the sacrifice for a General's blunder. On December 19th we all went to a Memorial Service at St. Pauls; it was very beautiful, but terribly heart-breaking. Every day Mother used to drive to the War Office and scan the lists of dead and wounded, and I very often went with her.

In the middle of all this, Katie arrived. T had the influenza just before, but was luckily not bad and recovered just in time. He went to call Mother in the small hours of the morning and remained in her room impatiently waiting for her to come, and all the time keeping his eyes fixed on her. Mother, most modest of women, was waiting for him to go away while she got out of bed and into her dressing gown and slippers! Dr Handfield-Jones assisted Katie into the World (also Blanchie) and Mrs Mitchell, a monthly nurse of the ancient order, looked after me.

Xmas 1899

The next four entries in my diary as in Tyrone's writing:

Dec 22nd   Mrs Mitchell sent for.
Dec 23rd   Buonita II arrived 7.30am.
Dec 24th   Dairy started, quantity moderate.
Dec 25th   Dairy supplies still moderate, demand increasing.

We had two bulldogs called Koko and Buonita: Mother always said I oughtn't to look at them and was quite triumphant when Katie appeared with a very broad and squashed nose! She really was rather like a bulldog at first and was a very ugly baby, but such a dear little thing, and so persevering in her efforts to make the best of my very inadequate 'Dairy supply'. All the same, I got on much better with her than with Blanchie and, so long as I was quiet in bed, managed to nurse her fairly well, though the supplies diminished as soon as I got up, and at 3 months I had to stop altogether. On the 30th my diary records 'A tea party, consisting of Tyrone' and on the 31st the seeing in of the New Year with Mrs Mitchell and the baby!

Mother had influenza rather badly while I was laid up. I didn't see her at all for nine days and then she had to go off to Brighton for a change of air. T was away part of the time too, first on a visit to Halken, and then twice to Leicestershire, for a hunt. Much of my time while in bed was taken up in making a collection of 'Comforts' for the soldiers in S. Aftrica: it was for one particular regiment which was supposed to be very much neglected and I was able to send them out quite a nice collection of woolly garments and small delicacies.

A short time before I was laid up – it must have been about December 12th – I was walking down St. James's with Father, when we met Lord Roberts, who then walked on with us. He and Father talked anxiously about the war and the bad turn things were taking, and I remember hearing Lord Roberts say, 'I wish you would send me out there'. Very shortly afterward he went, in spite of the death of his son. Father had great faith in him and, though there were many who thought it a great mistake to send a man of his age, his opinion luckily prevailed and everyone knows how very thoroughly this choice was vindicated by subsequent events.

January and February 1900

I remember going to Church with Tyrone very soon after I got up – it was on January 28th – and the awful feeling of emotion which came over me there, till I felt I must howl. The prayers for the soldiers finished me completely and I had to come out, feeling an abject fool.

On February 1st 1900 we left for Ireland, arrived at Curraghmore the next morning, after an absence of 10 months – as far as I was concerned, it was delightful to be home and to see little Blanchie again, after being parted from her for 2½ months. She was then 15 months old and was running about everywhere with the aid of a chair – all our children were late walkers – she didn't much care about the arrival of a new baby and invariably worked herself out of the room when Katie was brought into it, and tried not to look at her when she was obliged to be near her. She took quite an interest, however, in Katie's Christening, which took place in Portlaw on February 18th.

At this time, Susie and Clodagh were established just outside the gates at Mayfield, which they had taken for a year; there had been rather a coolness between them and T the winter before, so they thought it best to have their own house. It was not a very wise plan settling so near and I did my best to dissuade Susie from it, but others advised them differently and the deed was done. It was not a success, for the friction still continued and was a perpetual source of worry and anxiety to me. I was always on perfectly good terms with S & C and did my best to bring them and T together, but it was no use and, though they constantly met casually, he hardly ever sought them out.

There was a great deal of snow that winter; on February 9th we had 9 inches and tobogganed gaily for 5 days. Down Sallyhene Hill was the favourite run. T made a rough bob sleigh on the lines of the ones used in the Engadine, and it worked splendidly. There was a queer little box sleigh put away in a shed. This was also brought out and we actually sleighed back from Church one day. Then there were some very sharp frosts – down to 26° – and we had just started skating on the Lake when the thaw came and we had quite warm weather again.

The knitting industry, which I had taken up the year before, was now growing and, as I had a very inefficient Secretary or Manageress for it, I was obliged to give a good deal of time to it and I used generally to go down to Portlaw once a week for pay day, so as to examine the work brought in. Tamoshanters were then the rage and we sold hundreds of them (besides socks and gloves) till I really hated the sight of them, but gradually we added more things to our stock list and the industry became quite a thriving concern; though this was not until later, when Irnia Ryan took over the Secretaryship.

March – July 1900

Meanwhile, things were beginning to look brighter in S. Africa. On February 16th we heard of the relief of Kimberley, on the 27th of Cronje's surrender at Paardeberg, on March 1st of the relief of Ladysmith, but it was not till May 19th that we had the news of the relief of Mafeking. Kerry was on Lord Robert's staff and Charles was with his regiment. Neither was wounded, but Charlie had a bad go of Enteric. We did not hear of it till he was virtually out of danger – the telegram came on June 21st, but one couldn't help feeling anxious all the same. T was out when the telegram came and I went to Mrs Brand (the children's nurse) for comfort and sympathy. She was very grim over it, and Job's friends were a joke to her. When I said I hoped he was over the crisis, she assured me that that was quite the most dangerous time, and a relapse then would be sure to be fatal! However, he mercifully did not have a relapse and on July 12th he was invalided home.

Nothing very particular happened at Curraghmore during those months. Tyrone generally hunted three or four days a week and on the off days we went for walks together, T usually carrying a gun or a rifle. Sometimes I would have a few shots too and T always used to tell the story of my first shot at a rabbit sitting in its lair, when I arrived at his tail and missed him clean! At that time, T hated walking for walking's sake and, except when he was hunting, he did not take nearly enough exercise and, in consequence, got very slack and sleepy.

He nearly always went to sleep after dinner and sometimes even dropped off in the Dining Room. I had great difficulty in rousing him enough to make him go to bed. In later years, he realized that exercise was a necessity to him and used to go for tremendous long walks and play violent games of squash racquets. The curious thing about him was that, even when he had been taking practically no walking exercise at all, he never became unfit and would take on a long walk or a mountain climb without seeming in the least distressed.

On March 29th 1900 we went to Woodrooff, where Susie and I played at a concert for the Soldiers and Sailors Families. Mother came to stay with us just after this and Susie and I met her at Clonmel on our way home. It was considered a great honour at Woodrooff to be sent anywhere in the family carriage, which old Mr Perry generally kept for his own use. He himself usually bustled off his guests very early, but on this occasion he said there was plenty of time – so what was our dismay on looking at our watches to find that we should most probably miss the train, with Mother in it! As soon as we were out of sight of the house, Susie said to the old family coachman, with her sweetest smile, 'We shan't mind being shaken, if you would like to canter', and accordingly we got on to the best grass verge and dashed down the avenue and arrived in Clonmel at a hard canter, only just in time. If old Sam could have seen us, he would have had a fit!

Mother went up to Dublin Castle on April 2nd and we followed on the 3rd, going to stay with the Iveaghs. On the 4th, Queen Victoria arrived in Dublin, where she had a most enthusiastic reception. Princess Christian and Princess Henry of Battenberg were with her and I remember that, while the Queen and Princess Christian looked thoroughly pleased with the crowd's welcome, Princess Beatrice looked quite miserable and wore a most strained expression, as if she expected a bomb to fall in the carriage at every moment.

On April 6th there was a big Banquet at the Castle and on the 7th we went to the Phoenix Park to see the children who had come from all parts of Ireland to look at the Queen. There were 30,000 of them and it was really a wonderful sight. The Queen drove slowly through them and as stands were provided for them all every child had a good view of her as she passed. We went down to see the fleet at Kingstown the next day, having been to the Chapel Royal in the morning, and on the 9th we returned to Curraghmore.

Little Worcester was born while we were in Dublin (on the day of the Queen's Entry) and there were, of course, great rejoicings in the family over his arrival, which took place just 9 months and 2 days before little Tyrone.

We had a succession of visitors after we got home – Bullens, Captain Forbes, Mr Adair, Sir Owen Slake, Rochforts, Captain Maxwell, Mrs Villiers Stuart of Dromana, Mr Palliser etc.

On the 21st there was a Hunt Meeting to decide on a Master for the Waterford Hounds, which were then just being started again. T wouldn't take them then, as he was not sure of the farmers and he was determined only to take the Hounds when they asked him to. He was very anxious that Commander Forbes should be appointed Master, but the Committee preferred a local man and Mr George Malcomson was chosen.

On the 23rd we went back to Dublin and stayed at the Castle for Punchestown – 24th and 25th. We dined with the Queen at the Viceregal on the 24th: she sent for each of us after dinner. I was very shy and stupid, but T and she had a long conversation and I remember how tall he looked, standing beside her low chair, in his black velvet court suit, in which he looked most charming, though he grumbled a good deal over its discomfort. The Queen left Ireland on the 26th April; we all went down to Kingstown to see her off and came home again next day.

A few days later, I heard of the death of my old friend, Captain Brasier Creagh, shot in S. Africa, where he had gone, broken-hearted after the death of his lovely young wife, a few months before. Their son, Brian was my godchild, and it was terrible to think of the poor little baby, left alone at about 6 months old!

In May, we attempted some Otter hunting with a scratch pack, but it was not successful. We did a good deal of clay pigeon shooting that summer. T bought 3 or 4 traps and had them set up, west of the Shellhouse Garden, which was then an open bit of grass. One day we had a competition, in which several of the neighbours joined and which was finally won by Mr MacDonald, the D.J. Mr Flemyng, our Vicar, also joined in the shooting and made us horribly nervous, as he would point his gun at everything and everybody, except the clay pigeons, and could not be induced to realize the danger of it. T and I did great execution among the young rooks that year and I developed an aptitude for rifle-shooting, which rather shocked some of my family.

We gave a good many dinner parties that summer. Portlaw was much fuller there than now and there were plenty of men about, though none of them were very lively. T used to take me out calling too and we did some long distance calls, even as far as Dunmore, where the good Greys carried us in fine style.

On May 19th, the day of the relief of Mafeking, the Duchess of St. Albans, and an artist friend, Mr Clifford, came over to luncheon. Mr Clifford did a sketch of T, which is in one of my scrapbooks, but it was not a very good likeness. He also did one or two sketches about the place, but when, after sitting near John's Bridge for over an hour, he produced nothing but two blue streaks and three green streaks (viz, Bluebells in the Grass) we came to the conclusion that he wasn't much good!

Mr Jennings – from Cork – brought his otter Hounds to Curraghmore in June and we had great fun with them. Mr Jennings was a real sportsman and insisted that the otter should have a fair chance. He had very good Hounds and was tremendously keen and the hunting with him was most enjoyable. His old friend, Mr Bob Dunscombe, who had taught him all he knew, generally came with him. He was a dear old man and loved to tell us of the charms of his daughter, Araminta, 'my little pet', whom he simply adored. She was a very loud young woman, with an enormous bushy fringe and a harsh voice, but he thought her lovely. In after years, when T went to stay with him, he embarrassed him sorely by asking whether he didn't consider her 'a little pet'. The Adams, Forbes, Villiers Stuarts, Mr Anderson and Mr Humble stayed with us for the otter hunting. Also Lady Gwendoline O'Shee and her daughter, Gwennie. We had three days hunting on June 7th, 9th and 11th and killed 2 otters, one of which we hunted for over 5 hours.

A deep sea Missionary came to preach in Portlaw on the Sunday during that party; Commander Forbes said he would like to hear him, as these men do such excellent work among the sailors. But, alas, this one thought it necessary to be nautical – besides which, he dropped his aitches – and the poor Mander squirmed and wriggled in his seat while he listened to anecdotes of 'Jack' and his breezy ways and the story of 'our Mrs Atkins' (she was a Matron), 'she 'as gone aloft – she 'as', etc. etc.

Our party left on the 12th and the only other little incident I remember that month was a picnic on the very top of the tower, at which T and I were joined by Phyllis, who was staying at Mayfield. On June 17th Tyrone went over to England to stay at Sandringham – I rather think for a sale of cattle. There was an accident in the park that day; Colonel Poë, with his wife, small daughter, and a 'lady friend' had been picnicking somewhere near the farm and, after lunch, while they were packing up, with the child strapped on to the back seat of the cart, the Colonel foolishly removed the pony's blinkers in order to adjust some part of the bridle. Just then, some deer came bounding by and off went the pony, upsetting the Colonel, whose head was cut by the step, and running over the friend's foot. The wretched child, who had very weak nerves already, was terrified and yelled distractedly as the pony bolted right down the farm hill. Luckily the strap broke then and the seat fell out with her, while the pony dashed on, and finally smashed into the gate at the middle lodge. The child was carried in to the house, followed by the father with a bleeding head and the friend with an injured foot, and T spent the afternoon trying to comfort the hysterical child and the absolutely helpless mother, till they recovered enough to return to Tramore, where they were staying.

On July 2nd, we went to Dunmore East, where T had taken the Villa Marina for a month. The babes and Phyllis Hamilton went over with me and Sue joined us next day. T arrived from England on the 8th by the Milford boat and I sent out a boat to take him off before she went on up the river to Waterford.

Mr Morley had very kindly lent us his little yacht, the 'Mavis', to use during our stay at Dunmore and we often went sailing in her. T loved sailing and was never so happy as when steering a boat. I was a very bad sailor, so never felt absolutely happy on the sea, but when I steered I forgot the qualms and really enjoyed it.

Beasie Butler came to stay with us for one night and went sailing with T next morning. I felt sure she would be a good sailor and was rather envious of her in consequence and I must own that I felt a secret joy when they came back after a very short sail because Beasie felt so sick – and was sick too!

Phyllis and Susie left us on the 9th. Before they went, we were walking on the outskirts of Dunmore one day, when we heard two women discussing us, and one, pointing at me, said 'I wonder, is that

Lady Waterford?' – to which the other replied 'Ah, now, can she be a mother at all?'

On the 14th, we came home for 4 days, during which time we had a treat for all the school children in Portlaw, of whom 380 came.

On the day after our return to Dunmore, we sailed round to Bannow (in Wexford) about 16 miles away. It was a lovely morning; I steered a good part of the way and enjoyed it immensely. We lunched with Mr Boyse and then brought him and the Perrys back with us on the yacht. The return voyage was far from pleasant, as the wind had got up meanwhile and the sea became very rough. Dollie Perry and I were both 'in an interesting condition', but we bore up bravely and were fairly happy as long as we remained on deck. As we neared the mouth of the river, however, the seas were breaking over the boat a good deal, so T insisted on our going into the cabin, a small and stuffy place where we spent a miserable half hour, tossing about and nearly suffocated. Our husbands were thoroughly brutal and merely jeered at us when they occasionally looked in to see how we were getting on. We were uncommonly glad to get off that boat and soon after we got in there was a violent thunderstorm; so we were pretty lucky.

Two days later, the Perry party left, and T took them over to Duncannon in the Mavis. They had a good crossing, but coming back it was very rough and stormy and T had rather an unpleasant time, as he only had one man with him and they had some difficulty in getting in the sails and nearly capsized.

On the 23rd, T sailed the Mavis against Mr Herbert Goff, who had a little yacht of exactly the same pattern. The course was 25 miles and I watched the race with great excitement and was very proud when T won by 2½ minutes. The next day they had another race, over half the distance, and T won it by 3 minutes. There was a very well-meaning clergyman at Dunmore, who was always trying to say 'a word in season' – which was more often out of season; when T was going down to the Harbour to see that his boat was all right, Mr Gilmore waylaid him and talked religion to him all the way down, much to his fury! After we returned to Curraghmore, Mrs Gilmore sent me a copy of *Daily Light*, which she begged that I would promise to read every day as she felt sure that one in my position never had time to read the Bible!!

On July 24th we left Dunmore; the children went to Bowood and T and I returned to Curraghmore, where we had another otter hunting party, Mr Jennings and Mr Dunscombe bringing the Hounds as before. Mr Wogan Brown, Mr Boyse, Kathleen Perry and her Fiancé, Mr Kirke, Col. Villiers Stuart and Mr Humble were our party, into which, for a short time, came also Lady Paul and her daughter, Lady Gwendoline O'Shee and two daughters, and Lord & Lady Iveagh with Mr Ernest Guinness and Mr Ward – a very mixed party altogether. The Iveaghs came in a big motor, which was rather a novelty (though we had been in Mr Goff's before this). They took us out for a drive round the country and we all thought it delightful.

I can't think why Lady Paul dropped into that party and I remember that she did not fit in at all well! She and her daughter drove over in a dogcart, driving tandem, the leader of which spent most of its time turning round to look at them. They had their luggage with them, packed in innumerable hand-boxes piled high above them at the back, and they had to stop constantly and eat buns while they rested the dear ponies. Lady Paul had a conscientious objection to bearing reins. We always used them, though they were left very loose, and she attacked T on the subject and implored him to give up using them. He was much annoyed and, with difficulty, refrained from being rude to her. She spoke sympathetically to me about the coming baby and said she hoped it would be a boy, and added, 'I think it is so sweet to think that there is a little title all ready waiting for him'!!

Beatrix on Lady Jane, Mademoiselle Berton in the Rickshaw, Simla, India 1893, when Beatrix's father was Viceroy.

Tyrone's sisters: Susie (left) and Clodagh (right) 1894.

Beatrix Waterford's first arrival at Curraghmore, September 1896.

Blanche, mother of Tyrone, who died of cancer in 1897 in the donkey carriage. She was the daughter of the Duke of Beaufort. This photo was taken at the time of Tyrone's Coming of Age party in 1896.

The Prince of Wales attends the marriage of the Marquis of Waterford and Lady Beatrix Petty Fitzmaurice, St George's, Hanover Square, London, 16th October 1897.

Beatrix's wedding at St George's, Hanover Square, 16th October 1897.

Poor Lady Paul, she was never without a mania of some kind. Later on she took up anti-vivisection violently, and did her best to convert T to her views, sending him piles of papers to read. His only answer was to ask her to take up the question of cruelty to oysters, which he felt a burning evil, and should be enquired into. She also started a crusade against the docking of horses and, in order to show her disapproval of it, she insisted that any of their own horses, which had already been docked, should be encouraged to grow a long tail. Poor Nellie Paul blushed with shame when she saw her long-suffering Father on his chestnut with the docked tail carried high and three dejected hairs hanging from it! T always derived vast amusement out of Lady Paul's vagaries, and drew her on about them whenever they met.

But to return to the otter hunting: we had four days hunting, but the sport was not very good, with the exception of one day when we killed a fine otter, weighing 23 lbs, near Whitestown. We drew the Mahon River one day. I was taking it rather easy and didn't want to walk very far and had been advised by old Mr Palliser (who was driving with his two cousins) to return to the road when I got to a certain point on the river. Lady Gwendoline O'Shee, also driving, got anxious about me when I didn't return, whereupon old Mr Palliser despatched the Miss Pallisers – who were dressed for show only, with long skirts and be-flowered hats – in search of me. When they had gone, he turned to Lady Gwendoline and said, with fiendish glee, 'I've sent the girls down into the bogs to find Lady Waterford, and they've got on Bond Street shoes!' Needless to say, the poor things never found me and returned a long time after in a most bedraggled condition, much to the old man's delight.

August 1900

We stayed at Curraghmore till August 11th as T wanted to go to the Clonmel Show. Then we went up to Glenbride for the first time. We stayed a night in Dublin and it took us five hours to get up from there, by train to Dunlavin, and then driving. We drove 'in state' in an ancient landau or barouche, which Mr Kane of Dunlavin had borrowed for the occasion; it was a very heavy old carriage, so we went at a snail's pace all the way and I thought we should never get there. Glenbride Lodge was very small then. There were no outhouses (except the men's rooms over the stables), so the Keeper and his family, and the maid-servants, were all squashed into the house, which contained only 7 bedrooms altogether. We always had to go through the kitchen, which was also the servants' only sitting-room, to get to the Dining Room. It was great fun for a short time, but all the arrangements were very inconvenient.

Captain J.G. Beresford stayed with us for nearly a week and he and T, with Mr Myles Ponsonby, and Mr Adair part of the time, had some quite good days over dogs, as the accompanying list shows.

3 guns	39½ brace
4 guns	25½ brace
2 guns	13½ brace
2 guns	22½ brace
2 guns	17½ brace

After that Mr Hall Dare and Mr Adair were with us. Also, Mr Grey (from Ford), Commander Forbes and a few other men came up for the day. They had three pretty good drives, getting 54½, 65 and 40 braces on the different days, and 84 hares altogether.

Commander Forbes stayed with us after the others had left. I had tried my hand at shooting, twice; the first day I got a grouse, a hare and a rabbit, and the second day 3 grouse, so T said I might have a try to drive grouse after the party had left. He had given me a lovely little single-barrelled 20 bore gun, made specially light so as not to tire me, and he liked me to join in the shooting when we were more or less alone. This was the last chance of a drive, so although it was a very wet day and I already had a cold I was determined to go out. We had a hare drive first, and I got three. Then, with the rain coming down in torrents, we had a small grouse drive. To my delight, I got a bird coming very fast. There were more coming and, in frantic excitement, I tried to reload, but alas there was the spent cartridge jammed in the barrel and I had nothing to get it out with, nor could I make anyone hear my frantic calls for assistance, for it was blowing a hurricane at the time and no-one was near me. I'm afraid I swore and Commander Forbes always declared he heard my awful language – though he was really much too far away; but it was quite exasperating. By the time somebody discovered my distress, the birds had all gone, so there ended my first grouse drive. T always delighted in telling this story against me and said that I was literally dancing with rage. Commander Forbes drew a fancy picture of the incident, which is in the scrapbook.

On August 25th we left Glenbride, drove to Blessington, and took the steam train on from there to Dublin, taking 3½ hours altogether to do the 30 miles. The steam train was a horrible conveyance; if you sat on the top you were nearly blown away by the draught and choked by the smell of sulphur, and if you went inside you were suffocated, so it was a choice of evils. T went to Leopardstown Races in the afternoon and the following night we both dined at the Castle. On the 27th T went to Curraghmore and I crossed to England, spent 3 days in London – where I saw Elsie Smith and her baby 'Pat' – and arrived at Bowood on the 30th, where, according to my diary, I found the 'Babies much grown'.

September and October 1900

Tyrone jointed me there on the 5th September and on September 7th we all went North, arriving at Ford on the 8th. I remember that, on both this journey and the one the year before, we had a saloon carriage to take us all together. T and I at one end and the babies at the other. Blanchie was very good, even when she was a tiny thing, but Katie cried a good deal and it must have been rather a trial for poor T, who was really wonderfully patient over it, though I don't think we ever did it again after this.

We only spent 6 weeks at Ford that year and it was not an eventful time in any way, except that shortly before we left we heard of Clodagh's engagement to Claud Anson, which was a great surprise to us – this was on October 12th.

We had a good many people to stay with us. Amongst others, Granny for 2½ weeks, Kathleen Beresford for 3 weeks, Charlie, Father & Mother, Mrs and Rose, Isobel Kerr, Capt. J.G. Beresford, Aunt Emmy Digley, Lord & Lady Cork, and Beatie Herbert. Also the Maharajah of Cooch Behar, to whom T had previously paid a visit at Selly for a shoot. T also went to Elveden for the Iveagh's shoot. The Greys were at West Learmouth and came over to see us sometimes. T also shot with them.

The elections were going on during the early part of October and caused the usual excitement. I drove a good deal that year and used to take Granny for long drives, which she loved, and sometimes I drove her myself (with a pair of horses), which I'm sure she must have hated, though she never let me see it. Granny found it rather difficult to get in and out of a delightful American Phaeton, which T had bought that year, so he had easily shaped steps specially made for her use and, if we were going anywhere she would have to get out, we carried them slung underneath the carriage.

On October 20th we left Ford, spent a day in London, and arrived at Curraghmore on the 22nd, just in time for the Opening Meet, which T went to. The babies arrived the next day and we were all very glad to be home again, as usual! T went to stay with Mr Dunscombe, near Cork, on October 31st and, while he was away, Miss Gomme, Susie and Clodagh's companion, came and stayed with me.

November and December 1900

On November 2nd Father was appointed to the Foreign Office, where he did such good work during the years that followed. On December 8th old Lord Donoughmore was buried and T went to the funeral. The Perry's eldest boy, Paddy, was born the day before. Claud Anson came to stay at Mayfield and on December 18th we gave a dinner party of 20 for him and Clodagh.

Our visitors during that time included Mr Adair, Sir Owen Slacke, Commissioner & Mrs Forbes, the Villiers Stuarts, Mr Humble, Willie Perry, Mr Vere Ponsonby and Charlie. Willie Perry was very full of his son and would talk about Dollie's bad time before me, which was hardly tactful, as my baby was expected in about 3 weeks time. However, I didn't really mind a bit, but T got perfectly frantic with him and kept on kicking him hard under the table to stop him. The whole table shook and I go an odd kick or two on the way, but dear old Willie went on gaily in spite of it all.

We had rather fun then, teaching my Italian greyhounds to course rabbits. T hated the greyhounds because they always shivered and one of them, 'Dante', (not named by me) familiarly called 'Danny', or 'the Poet', always yelled when Tyrone looked at him. Stella, however, was fairly courageous and much less shivery than the Poet, and it was a real pleasure to see her gallop. T often had a few rabbits caught up and then let loose to give the dogs a course. Stella took to it very kindly and killed the rabbits in fine greyhound style. I went on doing everything just as usual until within a fortnight of the baby's arrival. On December 22nd I went to a Meet at Rathgormac and drove about all the morning. I gave out all the Club tickets and on the 24th we had a school treat for about 400 children in the afternoon and a tea party for all the neighbours' children, in honour of Katie's birthday, on Sunday 23rd in the evening.

Susie and Clodagh had, meanwhile, left Portlaw and, as Clodagh was to be married early in the New Year, they had given up Mayfield for good.

January 1901

On Christmas Day 1900, dear Uncle Bill, who had been ailing for some time, got peritonitis; he never rallied from it and died 4 days later on the night of the 28th – 29th. This was a very great sorrow to us as we were both devoted to him. I had known him since I was 11 and loved him almost more than any of my own uncles. He was the kindest and most thoughtful of men and never forgot a friend. Added to which, he was most witty and amusing and had all the Beresford charm of manner. He was buried at Clongeen on January 3rd. Aunt Lily came over for the day only; she was so plucky and was determined to do nothing which could upset me and would not be persuaded to stay the night. Uncle Marcus also came over. I did not go to the funeral as my condition made it almost impossible and T had a great objection at all times to women's presence at funerals. We went up the following day to see the wreaths on his grave. There were over 70 and it looked like a lovely garden.

That evening Dr Handfield-Jones arrived. I went for a drive next morning and chose the roughest road and the most jolty carriage.

In the afternoon we went rabbit coursing and hunting on the race course and there I found a large horse shoe, full of nails! I walked home rather hurriedly and next morning little Tyrone made his appearance at '7.10am on January 6th, weight 8lb 14oz, a fine child', according to T's notes in my diary. Next day he added, 'Baby's length 22 inches – all well'. On the 9th, 'Jimmy thriving on his Mammy's pap', but this last entry was, I fear, rather sarcastic, for I could do no good with the nursing and had to give it up a week later. I think the shock of Uncle Bill's death had something to do with it. I cannot describe the joy it was to us to have a son at last; one could hardly believe it at first. It seemed altogether too good to be true. We had certainly thought of him more as a boy than as a girl – though he was sometimes 'Jem' and sometimes 'Jemima' and I hoped to make him a hardy fellow by doing a good deal of walking, shooting etc., but I always had a misgiving that it would be a girl after all. He was a very fine child, tall and big boned and, though not very strong at first, he soon picked up and got on well.

I suppose every woman feels that she is more or less of a failure, until she has given her husband a son who may carry on his name, and there is a wonderful feeling of peace and restful happiness when this is done.

The day after he was born, Lady Gwendoline O'Shee, who hadn't heard the news, came to see me. Archibald Goodchild, the Footman, commonly known as Henry, was on duty, and Lady Gwendoline asked him if I was at home. 'Her Ladyship is at home, but is not seeing anybody' was the answer. 'Oh!, but I *know* she'll see me', said Lady Gwendoline, whereupon poor Henry, blushing furiously blurted out, 'Beg your pardon, Milady, but Lord Tyrone arrived yesterday'!

There were great floods the following week. Over 2 inches of rain fell in one night. The river was over its banks in many places and John's Bridge was under water.

Mother arrived on the 8th and stayed 10 days. I enjoyed having her all to myself and altogether it was much nicer being laid up in the country than in London. Several of the neighbours came to see me while I was laid up – Mrs Villiers Stuart, Lady Duncannon, Lady G. O'Shee, Lady May Ponsonby, Miss Martin, Mrs Fleming, Irene Ponsonby etc. Captain J.G. Beresford was staying with us for 12 days and used to come and see me too. Dr Handfield-Jones left on the 14th. Some days before that Tyrone asked him whether he ever rode and the Doctor, wishing to appear sporting, said 'Oh yes', he had ridden a great deal at one time, so T at once offered him a mount, which he felt bound to accept. He got on with some difficulty and then only secured one rein, which he gripped tightly, while the horse went round and round in circles. T, of course, was in fits of laughter and the poor Doctor was horribly disconcerted. However, the other rein was captured and they proceeded on their ride, the Doctor trying to appear at ease, but really suffering acutely. He could hardly sit down when he came to see me afterwards and he declined to ride again, on the grounds that it might interfere with duties to me!

On January 19th 1901 Queen Victoria's serious illness was announced and the next day, being Sunday, there was a report that she was dead, so Mr Flemyng preached a funeral oration! The report was contradicted next day, but she died on the 22nd at 6.30pm. Poor old lady; the war had broken her heart and the worry of it was too much for her at her great age. We had a Memorial Service for her in Portlaw on February 2nd, the day of her funeral, but I didn't go to it.

I got on very well after the baby's arrival and was on the sofa at 14 days, down for tea and dinner (such a happy little tête-á-tête with T) at 21, out driving on the 23rd day, churched on the 24th and on the 28th little Tyrone was christened by Mr Flemyng in Portlaw.

Little Tyrone was doing well too and, after losing at first, had put on 15oz in a fortnight and 11½oz the next week, so Nurse was able to leave when he was a month old, at which time he was 24 inches long and weighed 9lbs 13oz.

∽✿∽

February 1901

On February 4th the Perrys came to stay; Dollie had had her baby – Paddy – a month before me, but had not been churched, so she and I went off to Guilcagh Church on the 10th to do it there after the service. Mr Flemying had no-one to play the organ (harmonium) for him and so I undertook to do it, but made an awful muddle of it, for I forgot all about the First Lesson and struck up the 'Te Deum' before Mr Flemyng had time to say a word. I never discovered my mistake until, hot and exhausted, I returned to our pew, where Dollie silently pointed out 'Then shall be read . . . the First Lesson!' There were always great discussions over the hymns at Guilcagh and I remember another Sunday when Mr Disney (the Curate) was officiating and he gave out a number and the Choir protested in audible whispers, 'We can't sing that, we don't know it'. Then he gave another number and again, 'No. no. We can't do it', till at last they agreed on a well-known tune!

T had a great surprise for me when I first came round to the opposite side of the house at Curraghmore. The bank above the terrace that was all choked up with scrubby trees and thick undergrowth, and I had often begged him to clear it as it not only looked untidy, but also made that side of the house so stuffy. He was very conservative then, and his invariable answer to such suggestions was, 'It has always been like that and it will do very nicely as it is'. So my surprise and delight were great when he took me to the Library window and showed me the place, quite clear of undergrowth and said he intended to take away some of the trees as well. This was the beginning of his interest in improvements and from that time he got more and more keen on clearing and planting, and developed a very great taste in landscape gardening. He never cared much for flowers and took very little interest in borders or bedding, but he loved flowering shrubs and trees and had a wonderful eye for effect in colour and grouping. But all this came gradually and that year – 1901 – there was little done besides clearing in different parts of the Pleasure Grounds. There were clumps everywhere – rhododendrons (mostly common ponticums), so tightly packed that they couldn't flower and, worse still, laurels, which grew in an untidy tangle all round the Shell-house Garden, the middle of it being overgrown with rhododendrons in three large clumps, while a few sad azaleas struggled for existence in smaller beds. All this was 'swept', the laurels rooted out, the rhododendrons put in their place on the outside, and all the ground in the centre levelled as far as was possible, and re-turfed. This, however, was not finished until 1902.

On February 14th 1901 the new Parliament was opened by King Edward VII. T was asked to move the address in the House of Lords and, after some dinner, he consented to do so. He was very nervous about it and spent much time composing a speech, and then rehearsing it. His little dog, Gyppie, and I used to act audience, but Gyppie could never bear it for very long and before he had reached his best period, she invariably slunk under the sofa with a look of utter misery. I was very sorry I could not hear T make his maiden speech, but was told by everyone that he got through the ordeal extremely well and made a very good impression. He only made one little mistake, which I believe caused a good deal of amusement, for he referred to 'Our Army........, which has so greatly distinguished itself on shore as well as on land'. Luckily it was reported as he had meant to say it – viz – 'as well as afloat'.

Father always hoped to persuade T to take more interest in the business of the House of Lords, and on this occasion he managed to keep him in London for 10 days – from the 8th to the 18th, but, although T took a great interest in all current events, he always disliked politics and hated the Party system. When he did appear in the Arena, he wanted to take a line of his own, but he always maintained that he could do his duty far better by living at home, giving employment, and keeping in touch with all classes over here, than by attending regularly at the House, and voting as he was bid, merely to swell an already overwhelming majority.

On the 15th I went to Cahir Lodge for one night to stay with Captain Charteris and Mr Wynne Finch; T was to arrive next morning and I hurried back to meet him and I remember scouring every carriage on the train and how disappointed I was not to find him there. He was always rather casual about his movements; he seldom bothered to think out his plans beforehand and therefore often changed them at the last moment and could not understand my preference for cut and dried arrangements.

The Perrys were still with us when he returned on the 18th. On the 20th Captain Charteris and Mr Wynne Finch came over for the day and the Perrys left that afternoon. When we were all out walking in the morning, we noticed a lot of branches in the river, jammed up against John's Bridge. 'What would you take to go in and clear them away', said T to Willie. 'Look here, I'll offer you 10/- to do the job'. Willie refused and said he wouldn't do it under £1.00. Then, 'Done with you', says T, just for the pleasure of seeing Willie's discomfiture. How we laughed at Willie; wry face as he took off boots and socks and turned up his trousers, disclosing the stick like legs and great flat feet, which T delighted to tease him about. The water was low and he had no difficulty in reaching the place, but some of the branches were so fairly wedged that he couldn't move them and, after spending some time at it, he had to give up without having carried out his contract!

On the 22nd, T left by an early train and joined a party of Tipperaryites who went up to have a hunt in Limerick. There was much jealous riding and some bad falls and T didn't get back till 12.40 at night.

At this time, we were a good deal worried over the arrangements for Clodagh's wedding. We thought it should have been very quiet on account of Uncle Bill's recent death, but Clodagh was anxious to have a big wedding and some of the family were rather busy seeing that T did everything right for her. In the end, the Abercorns lent us Hampden House and we gave a reception there after the wedding, entirely at T's expense, in spite of which I heard, with much annoyance, afterwards that most people thought they had given the reception and that T had done nothing.

We went over on the 23rd and the wedding was on the 29th, at St. George's, Hanover Square. Willie Perry travelled over with us on his way to Austria to look at a pair of white Hungarian carriage horses we had heard of, and which T wanted to buy. Willie's account on his return of his experiences in Vienna was very amusing. When he arrived at the Royal Stables, the horses were already harnessed and trotting around. They were a beautiful pair and moved well, but Willie was not quite satisfied about the legs of one of them, though assured by Count Kinsky that they were quite all right. After seeing them trot round a few more times, Willie said, thank you, and that they might be put in again, and then expressed a wish to see some of the other horses. Count Kinsky was most kind and showed him all over the Royal Stables, where, by the by, rather a curious thing happened. In one of the harness rooms there were rows of saddles, each marked with a name, which had been used by various members of the Imperial family. Willie lifted up the flap of one saddle, quite at random, and on it was written 'Waterford'! It was one which the Empress had used – either in Ireland, or on a hunter bought in Ireland. After this, Willie suddenly asked to see the white horses again and they had to be brought out, but meanwhile they had got cold, or rather stiff, standing still, and one of them was dreadfully lame! All Willie said, as he nodded his head in time to the horses limp, was 'Cloppety, cloppety, clop, cloppety, cloppety, clop', and poor Count Kinsky was dreadfully distressed and, of course, assured him that the horse had never gone so before etc. etc.

March 1901

The day after the wedding we went down to Badminton, where we stayed till March 7th and, while we were there, a window just put up in memory of the old Duke (T's grandfather) was dedicated. T had a few hunts and one day I drove after the Hounds with Sybil Codrington, who managed always to be in the right place, and we saw quite a lot of the run and a great deal of shirking! After three days in London, occupied by shopping, violin lesson, looking over houses, and going to plays we returned to Ireland on March 11th. T went to Cork for four days' fishing and I came home.

Little Tyrone had had to be put on humanized milk as he wasn't putting on weight well. It suited him splendidly and on our return we found him much improved and putting on weight steadily. He was kept on this milk for about 3 months.

On March 15th old Mr Congreve died. T returned the same day and Lord Donoughmore came to us for 2 days. The Perrys came on the

18th and stayed with us till April 4th; it was about this time that they took a little house in Fethard, which was christened (I think by Major Buldoo Bryan) 'Blue Lookout' and where they lived for some years.

On my birthday, March 25th, T gave me a lovely little spider wheeled American trap to drive myself in. It had pneumatic tyres and was wonderfully light and comfortable. The Meet was at Rathgormac and I drove him there, very proudly, also armed with a new whip given me by Willie. The only thing that spoilt my pleasure was anxiety over the Point-to-Point Races next day as T was going to ride in them. They were at Ballyhussa – our party consisted of Mr Bourke (the Tipperary Master), Mr Humble and his sister (Mrs Odell), the Perrys and Adams. It was a bitterly cold day and, as I drove Mr Bourke to the course, his only remark, in his usual sad, meditative style, was, 'A very cold day; east wind you know; terrible bad weather for shaving you know, what?' Our party distinguished themselves for T won the Heavy Weight race on 'the Drake' and Willie, riding for Mr Malcomson, won the Light Weight. Great was the excitement over T's win. 'The Lord, the Lord wins' was heard on all sides and he had a great reception. I got my first touch of sciatica after that day, but it never bothered me very much until five years later.

Katie's first walk, Tyrone's short-coating and vaccination, and the photographing of the family by Poole, were the chief events of the following week. Oh, that photographing. Poole would insist on waiting till all three children looked pleasant, and of course they never did, and only got more and more weary and cross, till at last Katie absolutely refused to sit at all and I had to be done with Blanchie and Tyrone only. I go so angry that I shook my fist at Poole when his head was under the velvet; quite forgetting that his eye was on me all the while.

April 1901

On April 8th T and I went to stay with Mr Burke at Grove, near Fethard, for the Cashel Races. What a funny visit that was! Mr Burke made much of our coming and, although he had a very good cook, he actually got down a chef and a waiter from Dublin. I believe it was entirely in my honour. We had no end of a banquet, starting with oysters, which I nearly refused, fearing their origin, till Mr Burke said he knew I liked oysters and had got them specially for me. I nervously asked where they came from and was not given any more confidence by his reply, 'Liffey, I suppose, Liffey, you know, what'!

Several people dined; amongst others, a charming person called Dan Maloney. An excellent fellow in many ways, but sadly addicted to the bottle. He was not at all in Clonmel 'Society' and I believe the senior Perrys and others were dreadfully shocked at his being invited to meet me. However, his behaviour on this occasion was perfect and his manners worthy of a foreign Grandee. Roulette was played after dinner and I had to join in, though I rather disliked it. The next day, Mr Burke drove us over with 'the team', as he always called his pair of horses, to Cashel Races; he was the worst driver imaginable and always had the reins hanging loosely on the horses' necks, while the ends were usually wound round his hands. I drove home the day after, while T stayed on another 2 days to hunt.

Mr Burke was a great character and T always delighted in hearing and telling tales of his queer sayings. He had a charming wife, to whom he was very devoted, but she died when the youngest child was a week or 10 days old – very soon after we married. I believe it was a clot of blood which went to her heart and she died quite suddenly. Mr Burke was heartbroken, but when someone came to see him a day or two later, he walked to the window and, looking out, murmured, 'A find hunting day, you know, a fine hunting day, what, and a corpse in the house'. He sent T a postcard after Tyrone was born. As far as I can remember, it ran, 'Congratulations, hope Mother and Son doing well. 10 days complete rest necessary'.

Willie Perry had a charming story of an afternoon walk with him, when Mr Burke brought out two pairs of wire clippers and said they 'should go in different directions cutting wire and meet at a given spot'. No sign of Mr Burke when Willie got there, so after waiting some time he went to look for him and finally found him sitting under a hedge with both boots off; his only explanation being, 'the chilblains, you know, William, the chilblains, bad – you know, what?'

Another story T loved was of Dan Maloney, who, after dining out, and dining much too well, was making his way home on a bicycle, and moreover trying to keep on the footpath. Somebody heard him, as he went along, murmuring to himself, 'Steady Dan, steady old man' – then crash, he missed the path and fell off, then up again and, once more, warningly to himself, 'Steady Dan. Steady old man', and so on, up and down!

On April 13th the last Meet of the season took place at Grouse Lodge; I saw the run fairly well from the carriage and then went to lunch at Gardenmorris with the O'Shees. I think it was on this occasion that Lady Gwendoline got into such trouble with Mr O'Shee on account of her unfortunate habit of interference. Mr O'Shee told me at luncheon that he had something to show me afterwards and he would not tell Lady G what it was, so of course she became terribly inquisitive! We left her in the Library and he ushered me into the empty drawing room, where, with a majestic wave of arm, he showed me a beautiful mezzotint print, which had a large bit of paper stuck over the name, so that one could not read it. 'Now,' said he, rather pompously, 'can you tell me who that is?'

Before I had time to reply, a voice came from behind me and there was Lady Gwendoline enveloped in a large shawl, and exclaiming, 'Why, that's Sir Henry Petty'. 'Oh, you stupid old woman, what did you come in here for', said the exasperated O'Shee, whose carefully planned surprise had all been spoiled and he was not the least appeased by my telling him that I really did recognize the portrait of my ancestor, and was just going to say the name. He very kindly gave me the picture, which is one of my most cherished possessions.

One day soon after, we went up to Coumshingaun Lake. T insisted on my riding up on the Wanderer, who pranced gaily among the rocks and heather, much to my alarm, and I utterly refused to ride him down again, my nerves being still decidedly shaky. Another day we had a stag hunt, or tried to, but the Hounds wouldn't pay any attention to the trail of the stag and picked up a fox instead.

On April 22nd we went up to Dublin and stayed with the Iveaghs at Farmleigh, for Punchestown. We had a wonderful little mare called Grange, who was running that year. She ran 4th in some race the first day and on the second day she was doing very well in the Conyngham Cup, when she unfortunately fell at the big double. The race was won by Covert Hack. After we got home I took to riding again pretty regularly and T and I often rode before breakfast.

Mr Jennings' Otter Hounds came to us again in the middle of May and we had a large party staying with us; Susie, Edwina Roberts, Emily Beresford, the Forbes, Perrys, Villiers Stuarts, Capt. J.G. Beresford, Mr Humble and Mr Gethin. The latter was then our sub-agent and usually lived in Waterford. We had 4 days hunting and a Bye, but the weather was too hot and the water too low and we had poor sport on the whole, though there was one good day on the Clodagh, where we killed at Whitestown. The temperature went up to 75° in the shade that week, though there had been frost only the week before. We had a very cheery – not to say rowdy – party and there was some consternation when we discovered that His Ex. The Lord Lieutenant, and Lady Cadogan, wanted to pay us a visit then. We made room for them somehow and got out our blackest clothes, for we had not been observing the mourning for the Queen as strictly as we might have, and some of the ladies had great difficulty in hiding their coloured trimmings for the occasion.

We were all on our best behaviour the evening of the Cadogans' arrival and when our bedtime came, and His Ex. retired to his room, I think the men breathed a sigh of relief and became somewhat uproarious. When Mr Dunscombe started off to bed, Captain Beresford said he would see him to his room and, of course, he began bally ragging on the way and was found by T, candle in hand, pouring hot wax on Mr Dunscombe's head; Mr D loudly protesting, and all this going on just outside the Lord Lieutenant's room. 'For God's sake, go to bed', said poor T, expecting every moment that Lord Cadogan would come running out to see what was the matter, and at last he got them off. We devoted ourselves to the Cadogans all the next day and Mr Jennings had a short bye-day – unfortunately unsuccessful – for their edification. Mr Victor Corkran and Lieutenant Athlumney were in attendance. They only stayed two nights and after they left we resumed the otter hunting.

I think it must have been that time that Mr Dunscombe, who was by no means young, got very tired after the long days in the river, failed to appear at breakfast on a Sunday morning. Capt. Beresford, having ascertained that he was still in bed, said we must take him his breakfast, so every lady seized a dish of some sort and we all proceeded to his room, led by Captain Beresford, who, as he threw open the door, shouted 'Ho, Mr Bunkscombe, here are the ladies with your breakfast'. The poor old man, who evidently had on a nightcap was much agitated and cried out, 'For God's sake, don't open the shutters', but no attention was paid to this protest and we trooped in and laid all the delicacies of the season on his bed.

May 1901

T had been busy for some time, designing and superintending the making of a flying machine – or land sailor- which he was very keen about and, after the party left, he took it out on its trial trip. 'Shamrock III' as we christened it, sailed very well when one could find a suitable wind, but the stays weren't quite strong enough and she unfortunately justified her name by the breaking of her mast, which snapped while T and James Fogarty were sailing on her, but luckily hurt no-one. James, who had built the machine, was very proud of his work, but terrified out of his wits going on her, and T always said he was telling his beads all the while.

Another mast was made and we had her out several times more and sailed her on the race course at Long Meadow with more or less success. Her shape was rather like that of an ice sailing boat, and she had three wheels; two smallish ones in front and a large steering wheel at the back.

There were donkey races at Milfort one day that month and T competed in some of them, but couldn't do much as he had strained his Rider's Muscle. There was a tug-of-war at the end and Mr Johnny Power of Mount Richard was very busy over it, trying to prevent the un-mounted people from catching hold of the rope. He had to get off his donkey to do this, and when he came back to look for it the ass was gone! T had removed it to the back and every time Mr Power got off, he did the same thing again, and then put on his most innocent face, as if he knew nothing about it. Mr Power thought the Village boys were doing it, and got mad with rage, till at last his sister caught T doing it!

June and July 1901

We went to London the first week in June and took up our abode at 35 Park Lane, which we had taken from Lady Grosvenor for the season. We went to a few dances, and I remember enjoying myself at one till 2am, whereas at another we were so little attracted by the company that we retreated down the back stairs about ¼ of an hour after we arrived there.

On June 15th I took Blanchie to Lansdowne House to see Queen Alexandra, who was paying Mother an informal visit. Two days later we went to Windsor to stay with the Fitzgeralds for Ascot. We had a very pleasant time there, with tennis, polo, riding and going on the river (I only did 2 days racing), and it was nice to see many of T's old brother officers again. We lunched with them in Barracks one day and watched a cricket match after, and that night we all went to a dance given by Lady Jane Coombe, which was great fun, but much too rowdy. One of the Grenfell twins, I think Mr Francis – took me in to supper and young Angus McDonnell, whom I did not know, afterwards squeezed in on the other side of me. Suddenly he said 'Do you know how to play "Bumps"'?, and before I could get out of the way he bumped on to my chair and others beyond him followed suit. Glasses upset, the tablecloth was dragged off the table and there was general confusion till T and some of the more sensible ones stopped the mad game. T was perfectly furious; he was no prude, but hated that sort of thing where women were concerned and, as it was 3am, we made up a party and returned to Windsor.

Next day we heard that Miss Chaplin, who had been with us to the Ball, had come back early, feeling very unwell, and it was found that she had the measles! Luckily no-body caught it from her, not even her partners.

Soon after our return to London, we went to see Lady Strafford (Cora) who showed us her Pianola; we were both delighted with it. I thought it a splendid thing for T, who loved music, but could not play a note. He bought one almost immediately and he got the greatest enjoyment out of it and soon played it very well.

We were made 'Knight & Lady of Grace' in the Order of St. John of Jerusalem that year – why, goodness only knows – and on June 25th we had to go to Clerkenwell, St. John's Gate and sign the Roll of the Order.

Bee Pembroke had her usual childrens' party and this time there was no question of refusing and I went with all three children, feeling frightfully proud of possessing them. One Sunday T & I took Blanchie to the Zoo for the first time – she was then 2 years and 9 months old and very observant and amusing. She was quite delighted with all the animals, but most of all with the porcupine, which she was most anxious to kiss!!

I exhibited my Italian greyhounds at the Richmond Dog Show that summer and T drove me down there. He was quite interested in the competition, though he had the greatest contempt for the Italians. Next day I took Blanchie to a tea party at Daisy Spicer's, and that night we danced at the Tweedmouths till 3am.

A few days later we went down to Ranelagh on Lord Shrewsbury's coach, and he gave a great luncheon there and also dinner, and between while T and I drove over to Wimbledon for a polo match. It was a great day out. We gave several big dinner parties that summer and went out a good deal, but I felt rather seedy all the time and it was a terribly hot summer.

On the 12th July, T played polo at Woolwich and went off to Ireland the same night to attend a hunt meeting. We met two days later at Wilton, where we stayed from Saturday to Monday with the Harry Whites; and on return to London, danced till the small hours at Mrs Adair's in Curzon Street.

I remember a very trying morning at the photographers that week; it was a grillingly hot day, 88° in the shade, and the children were all rather peevish and their Nurse still more so, and I expect I was worst of all for I was feeling dreadfully weary and below par then. In spite of all, Mr Speaight produced some excellent photographs, which may be seen in the family book.

I also had Blanchie's miniature done at this time, by Mrs Charlton. It was very like her, though it made her look much too old. We went to Deepdene for a Saturday to Monday. It was hotter than ever and done day, driving home in a hansom with Blanchie, I nearly fainted and quite collapsed after. The result was a strict regime prescribed by Dr Anderson, who said I must keep very quiet and stuff with milk, plasmon etc. for I was as thin as a rail then.

We began thinking of buying a house in London that year and went to look at a freehold which sounded tempting, but it was disappointing and the matter went no further.

We all went down to Bowood towards the end of the month and the children and I stayed there about 3 weeks.

August and September 1901

T spent 4 days at Badminton for their show, and he left a week before me to go to Glenbride. I was to have gone with him, but still felt very seedy, so it was decided that I should stay on a bit at Bowood, and then go straight to Ford. Mother was not at all well that summer either; she had been sent to Malvern in the early part of July, but got ill again in August. She had a nasty cough and one of her lungs was a little bit touched.

On August 16th the children and I left Bowood and arrived at Ford the next day. T did not come till September 1st. Violet and Lillian Lambton stayed with me part of this time and I often drove over to Fenton, which was only 4 miles away. Our old Clergyman, Mr Neville, went away on a holiday for some weeks and Mr Neligan, who had a large Parish in London, near Paddington, came in his stead. He was a most charming man and a very powerful preacher, and it was wonderful how he filled the big Church, which was usually so woefully empty. He was a sportsman too and, with a house full of nephews of all sizes, he gave the local cricket quite a fillip. T liked him very much and we saw a good deal of him and his nice little wife. He afterwards became Bishop of Auckland, where I believe he did excellent work, but unfortunately he taxed his strength too highly and had a breakdown, which necessitated his return to England and complete rest for a time. Later on, when Mr Neville died, he applied for the Ford Parish and though Ford was sold then T was instrumental in getting him appointed for it.

I drove myself in my little trap, with a trotter, a great deal that Autumn and used to go long distances calling on the neighbours. We went to a big bazaar at Berwick for the Lifeboat in September, and later on T opened a small bazaar to Crookham that was a most comical affair and T and I had great difficulty in behaving ourselves.

It was under the auspices of the Presbyterian Church, or a dissenting body of some sort, and the whole thing was desperately solemn and very prayerful. We found ourselves on a platform, singing hymns, and when the prayers began, we of course knelt down, not realizing that they stood for their prayers. This threw them into a great state of agitation as there were no hassocks and there was a desperate hunt for some for fear that our knees should wear out.

We had a good many people staying with us, on and off. Granny, as usual, paid us a long visit – over a fortnight – and we had Evelyn Harbord, the Villiers Stuarts of Dromana, the Hamiltons, Greys and Sybil, Roberts and Aileen, Susie, Charlie, Mr Harold Brassey, Sir Richard Stewart, the Hopes, Mother, Beatrix Herbert, Gerald Walsh, Ronnie Hamilton, Mr Kennaid etc. etc.

The Villiers Stuarts were only 2 days with us. The morning they were leaving, he went for a walk with T and forgot all about the time, so that when he returned there was no chance of catching that train. She was, of course, rather annoyed and I expected a storm when he came in, but she only looked sadly at him and said slowly, 'Piggy, Wiggy, Wiggy'!

When the Roberts were with us we were all lunching with the shooters one day, when we heard one of the retrievers whining a good deal. It was a young dog of Mr Grey's (the Agent) and he was training it by means of a spiked collar, a horrid contrivance. T had discovered this just before lunch and kept on threatening to tell Lady Roberts about it, till he had Mr Grey in a state of perfect frenzy! The Stewarts, who lived at Learmouth, were great friends of the Roberts family and we saw a good deal of them between their staying there and with us.

I remember one day, when T and I went for a drive, taking Blanchie with us, we went to see Mr & Mrs Jeffries who were tenants on an outlying farm called Gatherick, which had been won by a Delaval Ancestor at a game of cards. Mr & Mrs Jeffries were charming people of the working farmer type; quite different from most of the other tenants, who were very nice, but rather grand. They gave us a great welcome and made a great fuss of Blanchie, and just before we left Mr Jeffries asked whether she had a savings bank and insisted on giving her half a sovereign. I have it still and hope to give it to her when she is grown up.

October 1901

T spent a few days at Hornby in September and on October 14th he and I went via London to stay with the Crossleys at Somerleyton. I rather wanted to shirk this visit, as I still felt anything but fit, but Mother, who was staying with us at the time, wisely urged me to go as she thought it unwise to get into the habit of letting T go on visits without me. The shooting was very good and Crossleys were most kind, but I felt very much like a fish out of water there and we both found the evenings very tiresome, as everybody was mad on Bridge then – being a newish craze. As neither of us played, we were left high and dry every evening.

We returned to Ford direct on the 18th and the journey took us about 11 hours! We went to see York Minster as we were passing through. Grange won a £150 race at the Curragh on the 22nd October and won another race two days later.

When T was at Hornby, Leeds gave or sold him some greyhounds. I think it was 3 couple, which were not good enough for his purpose. We had great fun with them as there were a great many hares round Ford and we often went coursing with them.

Rather a curious thing happened to me one day when I was riding with the greyhounds. T had sent me up to a field where a lot of bullocks were grazing, to see if the hare broke on that side, and I was intently watching the hedge below me, when all of a sudden something hit me in the back and at the same moment 'Wanderer' gave a big lunge and kick. A bullock had jumped up behind me and, what with the start he gave me and the horse's plunge, I flew into space and found myself on the ground. I said very rude things to those bullocks when I got up! The greyhounds had to be got rid of some time after we left. One day the Keeper sent them out exercising in charge of a small boy and they all went for a donkey which a child was riding along the road. Luckily the child fell off, but they did for the donkey!

November 1901

On November 4th, T went to Fyvie for a shoot and I started for Curraghmore with the children. We had an awful journey! I had made out a very good cross country route, by which, leaving at 2pm, we should have go home about midday on the following day. But, unfortunately for us, there were thick fogs all that month and they were at their worst just then and caused us to miss every single connection. We had to change at all sorts of odd places and were turned out at miserable little wayside stations with no decent waiting room. The children were all miserably tired and frightened by all the strange voices – the eldest was only just 3 – Mrs Brand (the Nurse) was determined to take things as tragically as possible, refused to eat, and sat on the very edge of the seat by way of protest, and the two nursery maids spent most of their time being sick.

We arrived at Holyhead at 6.30am to find that both our boat and the North Wall had left and, after trying in vain to get taken over on a cattle boat, we turned into the hotel and crept wearily to bed. We took the afternoon boat over next day and the children went straight on to Curraghmore. There were more fogs all along the line in Ireland. Their train was late and they had to drive the 14 miles from Waterford at a foot's pace, owing to the denseness of the fog, and finally reached home at 2am, after travelling more or less for 36 hours. I slept in Dublin, as I had to see a doctor there, and got home at 12 midday. Dolly Perry came to stay with me and brought her little boy, Paddy. T arrived a few days later and started hunting next day.

December 1901

Early in December I began hunting again and had my first day on the Wanderer with the 'Bessborough Dogs', as the Ponsonby's little pack were always disrespectfully called; the Meet being at Castletown. The Wanderer was a delightful ride and I enjoyed the Hunt thoroughly. T was riding a young horse – I think a 4 year old – called the Monk; a beautiful jumper when he chose, but with the queerest of tempers. He also had a one-sided mouth, and had an unpleasant way of swerving back off a bank when you least expected it. He would also sometimes make a wild dash into a farmyard or shed, and absolutely refuse to leave it. He did this once or twice with T, but never got him into any real difficulties. Willie Perry always thought these tricks were exaggerated and rather made light of them. However, T gave him a mount on the Monk one day and in the middle of a fast run the horse suddenly nipped through an open gate (quite out of his course) and into a shed, where he remained for about 20 minutes, in spite of all Willie's blandishments. He could scrape along the wall as close as he could and, when Willie tried to turn him, he merely stood up and pawed the wall of the shed. Oh! how T chaffed Willie about that! T had another queer tempered horse called 'the Rogue', who at one time always had to be blind-folded and led in a circle, before he would go into his box, and sometimes he would bury his head in the straw – collected in one corner of his box – and stand there squealing like a naughty child!

On December 4th I went off to Manchester for the Irish Industries Sale, at which I had a stall for my knitting. I got to Manchester at 4am and went to the Hotel, where I found the sheets on my bed quite wet. Nobody was about and I was so weary that I tumbled into bed wrapped in a shawl. I already had a slight cold and was quite voiceless next day, with a heavy cold which lasted for days. Aileen came up to help me and we had a capital sale. On the third day, after selling for 3 hours, I went off the Holker, where I stayed with Evie for about a week. Dick and Moyra were there; also Lady Frederick Cavendish, whom I thought a most attractive person. I crossed back in an awful gale, slept in Dublin and went on to Limerick the next day for another sale and exhibition, at which I was called upon to present the prizes, after a large luncheon party at the Palace with the Bishop and Miss Bunbury.

I came home that evening and was soon deep in Xmas work: Knitters' Tea, School Treat, Children's Party and flannel distributions.

Xmas 1901

Mr Charteris paid us a short visit and for Xmas we had Captain Beresford, Mr Humble and the Perrys. We all hunted at Gardenmorris on the 27th, but after 30 minutes on a hunt the Hounds had to be taken home as the ground was too hard from the frost. We had better luck at Gracedieu four days later; it was my first experience of that fluid and boggy bit of country, which I thought detestable, but I enjoyed the hunting very much all the same. We had to hurry home for the 'Steward's Tea', then, as now, a standing institution on New Year's Eve.

I think it was that Xmas that I first went, with Miss Martin, to the Workhouse treat at Kilmacthomas. It was, and still is, the most depressing affair imaginable; all those rows of old people, many of them quite doddery, sitting down to tea, the stolid children singing melancholy little songs or hymns, the awful 'Casuals' peeping through the door and, saddest of all, the poor old people in the Infirmary, nearly all bed-ridden and just waiting to die. To these it was decreed that we should give whiskey, as it was the only thing they really cared for and it was pathetic and rather awful to see the poor old things gulping it down, generally neat for choice, spluttering and choking over it, but determined not to lose a drop of the wine glassful allowed.

There was one old lady, Mrs Foley, who was a sort of pensioner of the O'Shees and had special privileges. I saw somebody in front of me give her the tot of whiskey, so was going to pass her by, but the 'good Nun' in charge told me, with gentle pressure on my arm, that I should give her another glass as she was 'such a great old pet'. 'But, Sister', said I, 'she'll surely be drunk if she has so much', but the gentle little Nun merely replied, 'Ah, well now, the poor thing, she's in bed, and she can't fall out.' Of course, I had to give her the glass and, to my horror, when leaving the Ward I saw somebody else give her a third! When we passed that way again a little later, the 'old pet' was singing at the top of her voice.

There was a young woman there – about my own age – who had been paralysed since she was about 15. She couldn't move hand or foot, and could do absolutely nothing for herself, but she was always bright and cheerful and kept everybody happy around her. I saw her only last year, still with the same bright and happy face, and it made one wonder how one could ever be wicked enough to grumble over small troubles and ailments.

There was an old man called Cooney, who danced jigs for our edification that year; he had been a famous dancer and was still quite nimble, in spite of old age. The next time I was there, he insisted on dancing again, but had to support himself on two chairs in order to do so. When I went again, I found the poor old fellow in bed. 'Ah, Lady Waterford' said he, 'I'm real sorry I couldn't dance the jigs for you today, but I'll tell you now' (sinking his voice to a confidential whisper), 'it's owing to the dirty chronic impediment I have in my legs that I'm not able to dance at all'!

'Ping Pong' was very much the fashion that winter and we used to play it a good deal and have great contests. I remember one day that Dollie Perry and I rode through Portlaw Woods to Coolfinn to play a match there. Another day I rode – also through the Woods, to Mount Congreve, for luncheon. I think it was that year that we got rid of the old Orchestrian, which used to stand in the Inner Hall, and to the ciphering strain of which we had so often danced. It was a constant trouble to keep in tune, and took up a great deal of room and now we had the Pianola to supply the music if we wanted it.

Memoirs
Notebook Two
(begun April 1914)

January 1902

The year 1902 opened with great gaieties in and near Curraghmore. There were Balls at Bessborough and Curraghmoare, and both houses were filled with guests. Our party consisted of: Susie, the W. Perrys and Edith Perry, the Frank Wises, Kerry, Lord Crichton, Kathleen Beresford, Emily Beresford, Major Blacker, Major Askwith, Major 'Buldoo' Bryan and Mr Humble.

On the 8th January we danced at Bessborough for Vere Ponsonby's coming of age, keeping it up until after 4am. On the 10th we had our own Ball, which was in fancy dress, and masked till 12, after which we had a Cotillon. Oh! what excitement there was over that Ball and the fancy dresses to be worn at it! One of the Miss Sadleirs, meeting T out hunting some weeks before, approached him with a grim face, and said, 'Is it true, Lord Waterford, that you are going to give a fancy dress Ball'? 'Yes Miss Sadleir', he answered, and I hope you'll come to it', to which the lady merely replied with a groan, and 'Oh Lord.'

Major Buldoo arrived without any attempt at a fancy dress, trusting that we would rig him out in something out of the property box. This, however, contained nothing suitable and we finally made him a 'Boulogne Fish-Wife' costume of red twill and white muslin. Mrs Wise made most of it and the evening before the Ball we arranged that Major Bryan should slip out of the Dining Room soon after the ladies and come and be fitted in my Dressing Room. This he did, but unfortunately the other men got wind of it and, just as we had got the Major into a filled petticoat of mine, with his evening shirt showing above, and an experimental cap on his head, we heard the tread of many feet in the passage. Hastily, we locked the doors, but by a subterfuge the party presently forced their way in. 'Buldoo' skipped behind the curtain, on the window seat, where he was

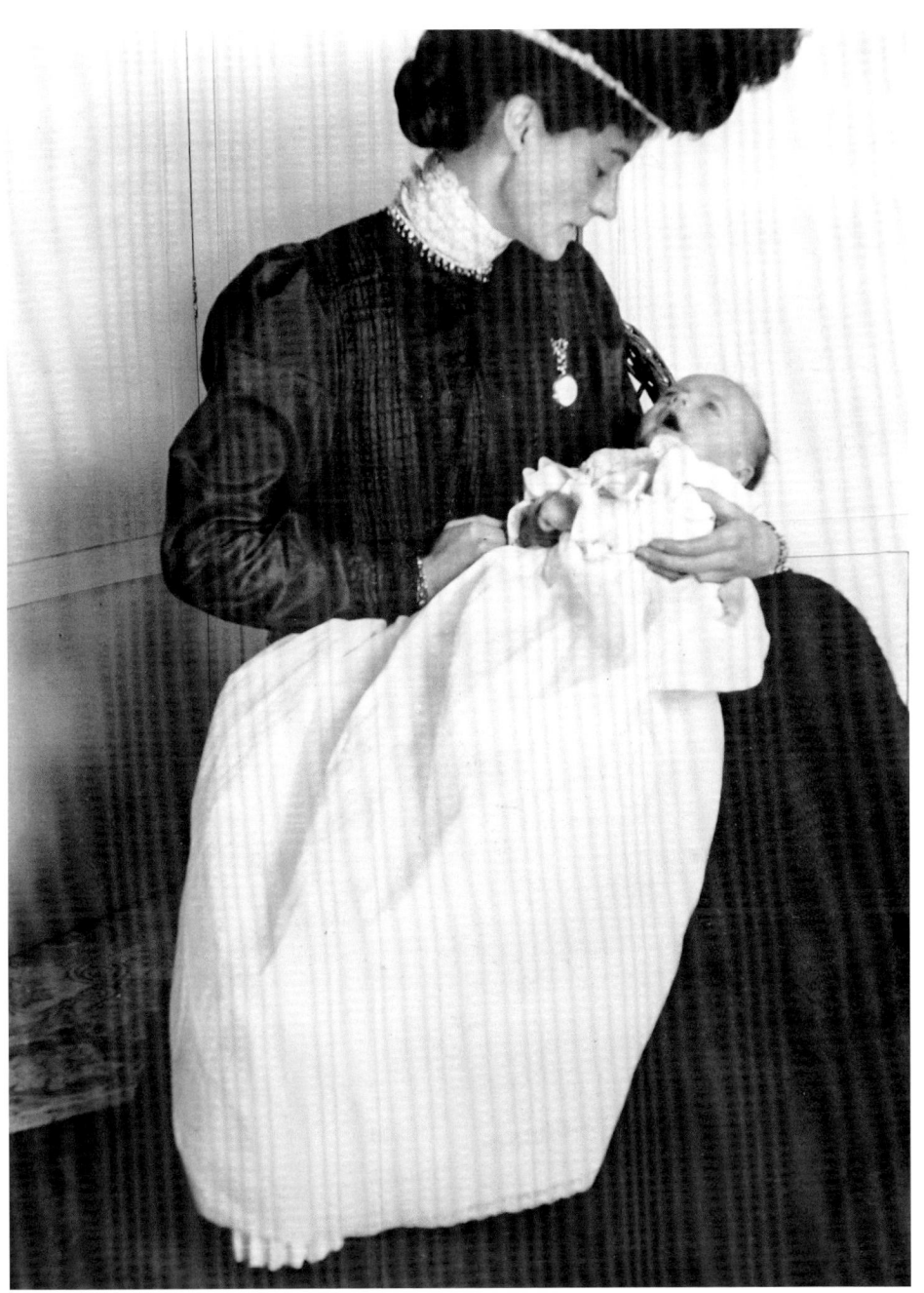
Beatrix and Tyrone (taken by D.Perry).

The Four Generations at Bowood, 1899.
(LEFT TO RIGHT) *Beatrix, Granny, Blanchie, Mother.*

Beatrix and Blanchie.

Tyrone's sister, Clodagh Anson with Clodagh Blanche and Vicky.

LEFT TO RIGHT: *Tyrone, Blanchie, Patsy, Katie.*

presently discovered and then proceeded to recite 'Friends – Romans –Countrymen' from his niche, till we nearly had hysterics. His costume was ultimately a great success and though his feet should have betrayed him, he took in quite a lot of people, as long as the masks were on.

Mr Richard Burke, Master of the Tips, had not the courage to don either of the three fancy dresses which we heard he possessed, and came in his red coat, with the smallest possible little mask. Major Bryan sidled up to him in the middle of the Ballroom and standing on tip-top- whispered his name, tried to kiss him, which Mr Burke, much flustered, drew away, murmuring 'You have the advantage of me, Ma'am, you have the advantage of me.'

Some of us wore dominos and exchanged them at intervals so as to further mystify our friends, but the heat of them, added to the masks and wigs, was something awful and we were very glad to cast off the disguises when midnight struck. T was dressed as his great-grandfather, the 2nd Lord Waterford, as he appears in the Lawrence picture; he was at that time, having shaved off his moustache, remarkably like him and he looked very well in the high stock and dark blue coat with the faux wig. Unfortunately, however, he found the wig very hot and uncomfortable and kept on taking it off and, as it was put on at a different angle each time, it assumed a somewhat rakish appearance. I wore a beautifully embroidered dress we found in the property box and I was supposed to be the wife of the 1st Lord Waterford and had a grey wig just like her picture.

We received our guests in the Inner Hall and Eileen Flemyng, who was then about 14, stood near us, dressed as a Vivandière in bright red, distributing programmes. Miss Sadleir dressed as Night, still looked very mournful when she arrived, but cheered up later. Mr Johnny Power of Mount Richard dressed as a Toreador and, wearing a mask, walked up between his two sisters, whom no fancy dress could disguise, and when accosted by someone, 'Hello Johnny', whispered 'Sh-h-h, Shush – don't be giving me away like that'! Miss Mary said she was after Gainsborough and wasn't it 'very hot'!

On the whole, the dresses were remarkably good and well thought out, and the Ball was quite a pretty sight. Kathleen Beresford, dressed as Grace Darling, rolled her eye most wickedly behind her mask in the early part of the evening and when someone asked the Carrick D.J. whether he knew who she was, he replied 'I don't know who she is, but she has the eye of a divil, and I'd say she knew more than her prayers'!.

We had ordered dozens of Cotillon favours from Paris, but they didn't arrive until some days after the Ball, so we had to make up favours as best we could to supplement what we had fortunately got from London, and we had a good many fancy figures, which caused great amusement. Amongst others there was the balloon figure, in which two men pursue the lady trailing a balloon after her and try to burst it by stamping on it. An old lady, describing this to a friend later in the evening, was heard to say, 'Well, the funniest thing that ever I saw was Mr Burke trying to stamp on Mrs Murphy's bladder'! In another figure, a sheet was stretched across the room and the ladies had each to show a foot underneath it, by which the men would choose them. One of our house party caught hold of the foot of his choice, whereupon the fellow to it came sharply down on his hand, stamping furiously, while the hidden lady screamed, 'Let go of my foot, let go at once. I won't have it, let go'!

We danced till 5am and would not have stopped then, but that Clark Barry's band, which played so splendidly, had to catch a train.

There was a Meet in the yard the next day and all the men, and a few ladies, turned out. The latter, I was told, caused great amusement by their anxiety to show they were still full of go, which caused them to ride very jealous of each other and one of them finally collapsed into hysterics.

I thoroughly enjoyed that Ball and was never tired of telling stories about it and the subsequent happenings of that night – or rather, the next morning. Refreshment was provided for the waiting coachmen, and evidently some of them partook too freely of it, for in the small hours of the morning Mephistopheles and a Romany Lady, with several others, found themselves at the foot of the Comeragh mountains, when they should have been 8 miles in another direction and it was said that several other strangely dressed parties were found wandering about in muddy by-roads, many miles from their proper destinations. The body of the family brougham, which bore Miss Mary Power and her sister on their homeward way, completely collapsed under the strain when crossing Carrick Bridge; and the poor Gainsborough Lady was left sitting in the back part of it, while the horse, relieved of the extra weight, went gaily on its way to Mount Richard.

That was a very happy winter. T seemed to have nearly forgotten his great disappointment over the war and was taking a great deal of interest in affairs at home. We were very proud of our three children and everything seemed to be going well. We had a quiet time after the Balls, only Mother, Charlie and Willie Perry coming to stay with us. One day that T went out hunting with the Tips, the Master didn't turn up and he was asked to take the horn. They had a good day's sport and he came back as pleased as punch over this – both at having been asked to hunt the Hounds, and at having done it so successfully. I remember that when he came home from the next day's hunting, he said it was very dull work merely following Hounds, after having hunted them, and it made him keener than ever to have his own pack some day.

February 1902

A hard frost came on the 31st January and he went off to fish with Mr Dunscombe in Cork, till February 3rd, when we met in Dublin where we were to take part in the first week of the Season, staying with the Cadogans at the Castle.

Then came the event which, though not so very great in itself, really altered all the rest of our married life. There had been, for some time, talk of the raising of one or two Regiments of Yeomanry in Ireland – a very doubtful question, for, though it was intended as a compliment to Ireland, the idea might very probably meet with much opposition on account of the bad name acquired by 'the Yeos', Cromwell's butchering yeomanry of old. However, those in authority decided to risk the experiment and the day after we came to Dublin the Duke of Connaught, then Commander-in-Chief in Ireland, sent to T and asked him whether he would undertake to raise the first Regiment in the South. After some hesitation, T agreed to do it, but only on condition that he might first go to S. Africa – where the war still continued – for he said he could not possibly think of commanding men who had been on active service until he himself had seen some fighting, even if only for a short time. The Duke quite fell in with this view and promised that he should have leave, but meanwhile the work of raising the Regiment was to be started at once.

This time I did nothing to prevent T from going, for I felt that he was perfectly right and I knew that he never would be happy unless he went to the war, but I was very miserable at the thought of losing him and I found it very hard to keep a smiling face through all the entertainments we had to go to. I remember one night being thoroughly over tired when I got to bed in the small hours, that my misery quite got the better of me. I managed to smother my sobs in the bedclothes for some time, but at last an extra big one reached T's ears. I was afraid he would be angry with me for being such a coward, but he was so gentle and kind and did all he could to comfort me. I really felt much better after this outburst and had a good talk with Mother when she passed through Dublin on the 7th. She was a real Spartan and said she was very glad he was going as she knew how he had suffered from staying at home before.

On the 6th we had tea with the Connaughts, who were both quite charming and kindness personified; in fact, everybody was good to me and I was much touched by all the kindness shown to me. Of course, I was very proud that T should have been chosen to raise the Yeomanry, for it was a job which would require great tact and only a really popular man could have attempted it.

The Northern Yeomanry was quite a different business, for there you were dealing with people who were much more generally loyal, and mostly Protestants. There would therefore be no difficulty about the recruiting; also, it would be much easier to keep in communication with the units out of training time, as they would be recruited from a much smaller area. Lord Shaftesbury was subsequently asked to raise the Northern Regiment.

Meanwhile, gaieties and entertainments were the order of the day: a Drawing Room on the 5th February, a big Banquet in St. Patrick's Hall, followed by a dance in the Throne Room on the 6th, a big Dinner Party and a Ball in St. Patrick's Hall on the 7th.

On the 8th, there was a Concert at the Royal Hospital for the S.S.F.A. and I played a violin solo, accompanied by Miss Sybil Palliser. That evening we dined with the Connaughts and I danced afterwards.

On the 9th T went to the Curragh, where Lord Longford was in Camp with the Irish Horse and hoping soon to get off to S. Africa.

T asked him to take him as Galloper, as there was no other vacancy and Lord Longford agreed. Later on, however, objections were raised to this plan, as the authorities said it would not do for T, as a Colonel, to go out as a super-numerary. Later on, an old friend, 'Brasspot', Major J.G.Beresford, who was taking a Regiment of Scottish Horse out to the war, wrote and offered T a Squadron in that, which he accepted, but this wasn't until March 10th.

In the meantime, there was more dissipation in Dublin, for we were asked to stay on longer while T started on the preliminary business of raising the Regiment, finding out what officers would be likely to join etc. etc.

On February 10th we all watched a hockey match at the Royal Hospital. T was playing and unfortunately hit Princess Patricia somewhat violently on the leg! That night there was a dinner of 70 people and a Ball after, but I was too done up to stay up for it. On the 11th, T and I spent a peaceful and happy afternoon together at the zoo and in the evening there was another banquet – 110 people. I remember that Prince Arthur of Connaught took me in and told me how he loathed Germany and all Germans, which struck me as odd considering his parentage.

On February 12th, we at last got home and it seemed an eternity since we had left. Three days later, T was inoculated against Enteric. He was very miserable the next day and had rather a high temperature, but was quite well again in 3 days. During the next three weeks, he made excursions to Limerick, London and Dublin in connection with the Irish yeomanry. Hundreds of letters were sent out to likely people all over the South of Ireland, asking for their co-operation, and every day, when the answers came in, we entered them on lists of 'those likely to join', or 'likely to help' etc., till, in a few weeks, T had matters fairly well advanced and helpers scattered all over the South and West of Ireland.

On February 19th 'Shot' Malcomson was married to Mr McClintock, much against the wishes of her parents, who were quite brutal to her about it, but as far as the character of the bridegroom was concerned, they were certainly right, for he turned out to be a most unprincipled man, and finally died of D.T., or a form of it, about 8 years later, leaving her with two boys and almost penniless.

Major Buldoo Bryan and his great friend, Lord Southampton, commonly known as 'the Sinner', came to stay on the 22nd. T was returning from London that evening and was mounting them both; the day was wretchedly wet and they came in at three o'clock. An hour or so later, to my amazement, I heard that Lord Southampton was leaving and by 6.30 he was gone, saying he had to get to England, and looking thoroughly miserable. It afterward transpired that he had been scheming for some time to go to S. Africa, but that his wife always prevented him from going; they being at that time exactly in the same position as we had been 2½ years before. At last Lord Southampton arranged to go and stay with his old Regiment in S. Africa and had just written casually to Lady Southampton to tell her of his proposed pleasure trip. Needless to say, she was not in the least taken in and wired to say she was coming over at once to talk to him about it! To prevent her from doing this, he immediately started off to England; they met somewhere half-way and no more was heard of the S. African trip, but I believe he was heart-broken at not getting out there.

On February 26th 1902, Susie was engaged to Hugh Dawnay. The news came as a complete surprise to us; I had never met him at all and I don't think T knew him either. Two days later came the news that Clodagh had a daughter – so there were many excitements in the family.

March and April 1902

On March 3rd, T was made a K.P., much to my delight, and I think he was also very pleased, though he pretended not to be. On the same day, we each planted a tree in the recently cleared ground above the circular balustrade. In later years we always used to quarrel – in most friendly fashion – about those trees, each claiming that our own tree was the finest; 'Yours may be taller', I said, 'but it isn't nearly such a strong grower as mine', then he would laugh and say, 'Oh, yours is a foolish stumpy little thing, just like you'! The winter after he died, I went to look at the trees and his was gone! It had failed gradually for some time and then died; such a strange coincidence.

On March 10th he definitely decided on joining 'Beresford's Horse' and on the 14th we went up to Dublin for his investiture, again staying at the Castle. There was a big dinner that evening – 110 people – and the next evening another dinner – specially in T's honour, at which there were speeches and compliments to him. After dinner came the investiture, a most impressive business, and I felt very proud of my dear one, who looked splendid in his robes and insignia. My brother Charlie acted as his Esquire, and Captain Mark Fraser as his Standard Bearer. Lord Roberts was there and Aileen sat near me. T caused great amusement by trying to rise from his kneeling position too soon, with the result that his head met the Lord Lieutenant's sword with some violence, as it was being lowered to 'dub him knight'.

The next day being the Sunday before St. Patrick's Day, we had 'St. Patrick's Breastplate' in the Castle Chapel – the first time I had heard that beautiful hymn. Charlie would have it that it was being sung for T, who was thus called on to renounce the devil and all his wiles – and I am afraid he took it in a somewhat ribald spirit. We dined at the Royal Hospital (with the Connaughts) that evening, and Norah Dawnay sang most deliciously afterwards.

On the 17th we saw the Trooping of the Colours and then went home once more, but only for a very few days, before going to London. T did not expect to be home again before leaving for S. Africa, so we went round paying farewell calls to all the Heads of Departments etc. This was rather trying, but most of the people did all they could to make it easy for us. Mrs Johnny Ryan, however, was an exception, for she melted with tears at once and enlarged on all the dangers T would be incurring, till I could hardly bear it. But, in the end, she made us laugh for, as she clasped T's hand, with the tears streaming down her cheeks, she said 'Oh – My Lord, there is only one thing I beg of you. If you see any of those dreadful Boers, pray keep clear of them'! Lord Methuen had been captured by the Boers only 9 days before.

T went straight to Aldershot when we arrived in England (on March 20th) and set about getting a house there, so that I could be with him till he sailed. After a week spent at Lansdowne House, during which I made the acquaintance of my niece, Clodagh, and of our brother-in-law to be, Hugh Dawnay, I joined T at Woodlands on the Farnborough Road, Aldershot, where we lived for two months. It was quite a nice little house and, as the Yeomanry were in North Camp, it was very handy for T.

There were three Beresfords in the Regiment; Col. J.G. Beresford (afterwards Lord Decies) in command, T, and Captain H. Pack-Beresford. Among the other officers were Captain Goodfellow, Captain Clarke, Mr Hardy, Mr Paulett, Mr Moroney, Mr Rowe, Captain Ramsay, Mr Gresson. We saw a good deal of the first three and some of them generally dined with us.

On the 30th, T paid a flying visit to Curraghmore in order to ride in the Point-to-Point races next day, and he won the Heavyweight Race on the Drake. It was at this meeting that Willie Perry described rather an amusing incident. T and he were strolling about, when suddenly they caught sight of a dog-cart, in which the horse was plunging and kicking, till finally the whole thing turned clean over, scattering food and drinks all over the field. T was convulsed with laughter and said it was the funniest thing he had ever seen, till Willie pointed out to him that it was his own dog-cart and his own luncheon that was lost!!

While T was away, I went to Shillinglee, the Winterton's place, where Mother was then staying, but got back before he returned for I would not miss one moment of him. A few days later he got a heavy cold, which turned to influenza later on. I was also out of sorts; however, we had plenty to do indoors for letters were pouring in about the Irish Yeomanry and all had to be answered and many lists made etc. All this we did together and I loved helping T with the work. It was lucky that there was plenty to do, for he was chafing very much at the delay in starting for S. Africa. The Regiment were ready to go, but the marching orders didn't come and they were getting very impatient.

I used often to go out riding with the 'Highland Horse' on Ash Range, Dust Heap and other places round there, and one day I assisted at their cooking and camping experiments on Pyestock Hill, when they made 'Sea Pie', and some kind of 'Plum Duff', which was so hard that they finally used it as a football.

While T was laid up, I was taken to see Broadmoor Asylum: Colonel Beresford had arranged this visit with the Doctor through a mutual friend. Four or five of us went and I drove with Prince Alexander of Teck. We went to the wrong house and were received with great coldness and scant civility by the Superintendant, who knew nothing of our coming and only thought he was being hoaxed when he was presented to Prince Alexander. At last we found our way to the Doctor's house, where we were warmly welcomed and then shown round some of the wards. I was the only woman and was presently left all by myself in the Doctor's quarters, while the men went to the more interesting wards where no ladies were allowed. Every time I heard a step in the passage, I expected a patient to walk in and from the windows one saw nothing but patients in the garden: I was thankful when the men came back and very glad when we took our departure.

General Hildyard and a Colonel Godley were then at Aldershot. I got to know their wives and made great friends with Mrs Godley and we used to meet a good deal at Field Days when we rode together. I also got to know the Careys, who were very kind. T and I were going to the Iveaghs for Punchestown, but two days before I was laid low with influenza and had to take to my bed, so T went without me, attended a Levée in London on the 21st and on the 23rd saw our little mare, 'Grange', win the Conyngham Cup at Punchestown. I believe she was the smallest mare that ever won the Conyngham Cup and at the start everybody was laughing at the idea of a thing that looked like a polo pony competing at all.

T was back on April 24th and on the 25th and 26th we went up to London for Susie's wedding. It had been hurried on a great deal as Susie was very anxious that T should be there and she didn't want to be married in May.

Lord Downe was away in Australia or somewhere, so no settlements could be made and I think Susie and Hugh rather suffered afterwards for being so precipitate. The wedding was on the 28th (T's birthday) at St. Mark's, North Audley Street, and Uncle Hamley lent us Hampden House for the Reception afterwards. We went back to Aldershot that evening and the next day there was a grand inspection of the 10th Battalion of Yeomanry by Lord Roberts; a big luncheon with the Hildyards and a big – no, not very big – tea at our house afterwards.

On April 30th we crossed to Dublin and went on next day to Cork for the opening of the Great Exhibition there. It was a curious business, as the Exhibition wasn't nearly ready and half of the most important exhibits were still wrapped up so closely that we could see nothing of them. Nevertheless, there was a procession of trades through the streets and how well I remember one of the cars on which two stout men in pink woollen tights represented Adam & Eve under a fig tree, and a grand opening ceremony, with speeches and recitals in Irish, which nobody understood, and bands playing and everything complete – except the Exhibition!

May 1902

We were back at Curraghmore that evening, May 1st, really for the last visit this time. The place was looking lovely and how I longed that we might stay on there. My diary says, 'Children very well, and much grown'. Blanchie was then 3½, Katie not yet 2½ and Tyrone 1 yr and 4 months, and they were all great ducks. We got out an old goat carriage which belonged to T and his sisters and got first one goat, and then two, to drag them along in it. This was of course a great delight to them, but their Nurse 'Mrs Brand' was terrified of the goats and absolutely refused to have anything to do with 'the nasty things'.

Claud and Clodagh Anson had then taken Woodhouse, near Stradbally, and from there they drove over to see us. On the 11th May Susie and Hugh Dawnay arrived from Stoke to spend the last part of their honeymoon at Curraghmore, but T had already left then and they were soon left in sole possession. Aunt Lily Marlborough came over for three days and Willie and Dollie Perry paid us a flying visit, to remove their son, Paddy, who had spent all the winter with us while his Mother was doing an open air 'Cure' in Wales.

T left on the 10th, but I had to wait till the 13th as I had another slight attack of influenza. The children came with me to the station and I remember going off very miserably, feeling ill, and knowing I must part from T very soon, and Blanchie, for some unknown reason, clinging to me and sobbing on the platform as the train carried me off.

Patsy was 'en route' then and I was feeling wretchedly tired and overstrained. I kept on having little feverish attacks, but I was determined to keep going as long as T was there. I was back at Aldershot on the 14th May; on the 19th Colonel Beresford took 260 of his men on an excursion to Slough, and thence to a place belonging to his sister-in-law's (the Decies) people, where they were fed and entertained most kindly. T & I joined the party and it was most amusing, as the Highland Horse were thirsty souls and were always trying to bolt off to Public Houses, whence they were hurriedly chased by their officers, only to bolt off again the moment the latters' backs were turned. It was the same at each station and on the return journey it was worse than ever. By then a good many had been successful and the noise they made was deafening. However, they enjoyed it and it was their last day out.

We made another trip up to London on the 21st and went to the Academy and saw Edwina, who had lately been operated on for appendicitis. On the 24th I drove with Mrs Godley to see an Inspection of Volunteers & Presentation of Colours to 3rd Manchester Regiment by Lord Roberts, and that night we gave a dinner party, including the Careys, my cousin Henry Anson, and Colonel & Mrs Pritchard, old Indian friends. The next day was Sunday (25th) and, as the Highland Horse were going in a few days, they had a big parade before Kirk and I went with the officers to their service. The minister gave a most charming address and, though it made me feel horribly gulpy, I was very glad to have heard it.

The next day I presented Pipes to all the men of C Squadron (T's) and promised that they should find the tobacco to fill them on board ship.

The heavy luggage had gone three days earlier and now everything was ready and they were to be off next day, 27th, quite early. T got up about 5am. I said goodbye to him then, but was to have another sight of him when the Regiment marched by. This was to be at about 7am or later, but at 6.30am, when I wasn't half dressed, to my horror I heard the band approaching. I was in a perfect frenzy for fear of missing them and threw on a coat and skirt, fastened a hat on my dishevelled head, and dashed out, only just in time, as the Regiment appeared round the end of our wall. The Highland Light Infantry Band played them off. The C Squadron men saw me and gave me a hearty cheer, while I took a parting snapshot of them. T fell out and gave me a big hug – and then they were gone and I felt the loneliest person in the world!

But there was a comic incident even then, for I saw a sergeant, who had been acting as orderly and often came to our house, fall out near our maids and embrace them all, not even omitting my maid, who was elderly and forbidding and who looked frightfully taken aback when he threw his arms round her neck.

Dear Aileen Roberts had left London at cock crow, and appeared just when I most wanted help, like a true friend; and after luncheon, having cleared up all my belongings, we went up to London together and I took up my abode at Lansdowne House, where the children joined me three days later.

For the first few days after T left, I felt dreadfully tired and found it very difficult to settle down to anything, but the children's arrival made things much easier and I was greatly cheered and encouraged by a letter from T, in which he said 'I am very proud of the plucky way you behaved yesterday. I could hear the men cheering you behind me, but I couldn't look back. Bless your dear little heart, the little book and photos are charming and I value them ever so much'. This referred to a small New Testament I had given him, with photographs of myself and the children stuck in on the fly-leaf.

The Highland Horse went out on the S.S. *Orotava*. T wrote me a diary letter, beginning on the 20thand posted on June 1st at Las Palmas and another one posted at Queenstown, which I will give later on.

T was very much interested in the coming Polo Match, England v America, and told me to be sure to go to see it and write and tell him all about it. In fact, we had even arranged a code in order that I might cable the results. Accordingly, I went with Charlie to the three matches, which spread over three weeks, the goals being as follows:

May 31st	England 1	America 2
June 9th	England 6	America 1
June 21st	England 7	America 1

The first match was a most exciting one and we much feared we should lose the whole thing, but subsequent wet weather made the ground very soft and the Americans, not being accustomed to this, were taken at a great disadvantage. At that time, they did not ride at all well and constantly tumbled off, but things have changed since and they have improved steadily, while I fear our teams have decidedly deteriorated.

June, July and August 1902

On June 1st 1902. Peace was declared and on the 2nd 'Peace Day' was observed and we went that night to the Alhambra, where there was a special performance. Of course, everyone was thankful that peace was declared at last, but in my innermost heart I ached with disappointment for T, who I knew would feel it most dreadfully. He wrote from Capetown, for they just missed the news at Las Palmas – 'We are very disappointed over peace being proclaimed and I have wired you to say that we go to Queenstown in the North of Cape Colony and I don't suppose shall do anything worth doing there, although there may be some rebels. Best love, my darling, from your devoted but very disappointed Hubby' (June 16.02).

T's diary letters were very interesting and I have kept them all, so I won't quote much from them here; they will all be put away with this record. On June 18th he says 'If we had only been here (Queenstown) 2 months ago we should have had any amount of fighting, as the stiffest fighting in these neighbourhoods was then. I see that none of this lot of Yeomanry are to get the medal. I am glad I am not to get it myself, but think it hard on the men, considering that lots of people who have never been in S.A. have got it'. In the same letter he writes, 'Mind you do all you can about getting the Green Uniform for the S.I.Y. They have not given us one concession, although it is the most difficult Yeomanry to make a success of in the whole Kingdom'. This question of uniform had been, and was still to be, a great worry. The fiat had gone forth some time before that all Yeomanrys were to wear khaki and no fancy uniforms were to be allowed.

Now this was all very well in England, and even in the North of Ireland, but in the South of Ireland, where the British Army was generally unpopular, and many prejudices against the Yeomanry had to be overcome, it was most important that we should have a different coloured uniform. Any Irishman would understand this, but the War Office, with its usual obstinacy and stupid red-tapeism, refused to see that there was any difference in the conditions and said we must adhere to the English rules. It was very little T asked for, only a green tunic instead of the second khaki one, so that they need never parade in the khaki. There was no extra expense whatever, and the same breeches were to do and the green would be the same serge as the other and could be worn alternately with it.

The Duke of Connaught was early enlisted on our side and did all he could to support T, but Mr Broderick was in opposition, as were most of the War Office people. T had a complete outfit, as he wanted it, made. This was not done until the middle of July and I then sent it to the Duke of Connaught, who had expressed a wish to see it and at the same time wrote (July 19th) to him, once more repeating T's claims for a concession on the question of colour. He wrote back most kindly (July 21st) and said the uniform was 'certainly very neat', and that he was 'prepared to support this colour for the South of Ireland Yeomanry as a special case', though he knew that there would 'be great opposition, especially from the Adjt General'.

There was another great difficulty in connection with the Yeomanry, viz – having settled to raise it, and matters being well forward with respect to the enlisting of men, the authorities then discovered that the raising of such a force in Ireland was illegal! It was therefore necessary to introduce in the House a clause, or short Act, legalizing this measure, but the matter was allowed to drag on from month to month, and nothing was done. Meanwhile, the uncertainty over it all was doing a lot of harm in Ireland, where enlisting was at a standstill and there was great danger that the enthusiasm of our supporters would cool off, and that the whole movement would be prejudiced. T got desperate about the delay and was always writing to beg me to push the matter, 'Do try and get your Father to agitate about the Irish Yeomanry being made legal, it merely wants a short Act of Parliament for the purpose and it seems a thousand pities to risk the success of what I am sure is an important thing for Irish loyalty, on account of a mere technicality' – and other words to the same effect.

At last I determined to take the bull by the horns, and so wrote, August 15th, a long letter to Mr Broderick, begging him to support us, both over the legalizing Act and the green uniform. I put both matters very strongly to him, told him of the growing 'discontent amongst officers and men already enlisted for S.I.Y. on account of the delay', and the danger that the Nationalists might take up the question and make endless trouble for us; also of the objections to khaki – including the new form of Lovat Mixture – and the strong reasons for allowing us to have green; and at the same time I offered to send him the whole kit to see.

His answers on both subjects were very unsatisfactory; he gave no hope of the passing of the Act before November and refused to see that we had any special claims to a different uniform, and thought we should be content with, 'a nice serge…with green facings'! He ended up, 'Please try and meet me about the uniform'. But, of course, I refused to give way one inch about the uniform and wrote again (August 28th) telling him I felt strongly, 'that in the case of the English Yeomanry, the wish' (for a colour) 'is only a fancy, or desire for smartness; whereas in Ireland it is a case of expediency' etc. etc. and I pointed out to him that 'Green facings hide so very little of the khaki'! I ended up, with some sarcasm, 'How can I meet you by suggesting khaki facings'?

I was tremendously anxious to get the uniform settled before T came home and the want of success of my efforts was a great disappointment to me. However, in the end, T got his own way, but not until he had really badgered the War Office people till they were sick of him. Lord Shaftesbury then joined in the agitation and the N & S Irish Yeomanry were granted the special favour of green tunics, with red facings for the South and white for the North. The legalizing Act was also passed in due course and, though the delay had caused great inconvenience, I don't think it did any permanent harm to the Regiment.

But to return to London – and the month of June – there was a great Thanksgiving Service at St. Pauls Cathedral on the 8th and we all went to it. On the 13th I attended a Court and being then, 'in delicate health', and very easily tired, Victor passed me in as his wife by a private entrance and thence past all obstacles to my seat and the same coming away so that I did it quite as comfortably as if I had had the entrée. On the 22nd I dined with Lady Roberts to meet Field Marshal Count von Waldersee, the German Commander in Chief. Charlie told me beforehand that it was polite to bow and to say 'Mahlzeit' to one's neighbour at the end of dinner, so, accordingly, I turned to Col.von Rauch and said 'I believe, in your Country, it is customary now to say Mahlzeit', at which he hummed and hawed and looked much embarrassed. When I told Charlie afterwards that I had carried out his instructions, he exclaimed, 'You didn't. Good Lord'! Of course it is only done in the most middle-class families and Col. von Rauch was no doubt scandalized! So much for brothers and their advice to credulous sisters!

On June 15th the King got a chill and his condition caused some anxiety as the days passed by and the date of the Coronation (26th) approached. The rehearsal took place on the 23rd, but it was pretty obvious that the date would have to be postponed. The next day the King's condition became very serious and he was operated on for 'Perityphlitis'. Thousands of people had already come up for the Coronation – which was not actually postponed until that day – decorations were going up, illuminations prepared, and London was all 'en fête'.

The state of gloom and anxious foreboding which followed is indescribable and I shall never forget the endless stream of carriages passing up to the side entrance of Buckingham Palace, where we studied the latest bulletins, and all wrote our names. On the 26th, instead of a Coronation, there was an Intercession Service at St.

Pauls, and the news was decidedly better next day and continued satisfactorily after.

As the King was so much better, and many of the foreign and colonial representatives had arrived, and could not possibly return again later, a good many of the festivities did actually take place. Amongst others, the Review of Colonial Troops on July 1st and a big party at Lansdowne House that same evening for the Colonial and Indian representatives, with a good many Royalties thrown in, also a Review of Indian Troops on July 2nd and a Reception at the India Office on the 4th. I missed these last two events, being laid up again with a sort of influenza cold, which left me very weak for some days.

On July 8th, being Granny Abercorn's 90th birthday, Mother had an afternoon party for her and collected about 40 of her descendants, mostly children, in honour of the event. Queen Alexandra looked in for a short time, bringing Princess Victoria and the Duchess of Aosta with her, and three or four Wales children came to the party.

On July 12th, Lord Kitchener returned from S. Africa and had a great reception. Mother, Aunt Georgie and I went to Constitution Hill to see him pass. The following day, being Sunday, I went to St. Stephen's, Paddington, to hear our friend, Mr Neligan, preach. I lunched with the family after and was joined later by the children for his Children's Service, which was quite delightful and attended by hundreds of children.

A dinner to the Crown Prince of Siam and a luncheon to some Naval Americans – both at Lansdowne House – were the chief excitements after that, but I don't think I cared much for any of these entertainments, my great excitements being letters and cablegrams from T, which I was always eagerly looking for.

On the 23rd June I took the three children to Speaights to be photographed. I was very pleased with the result, but T, when he saw the photographs, only commented on the length of Tyrone's hair, which, he said was much too long and should be cut at once. Tyrone was a great duck then. He had been very backward, but was beginning to wake up and become more enterprising. I remember one day, when Mrs Brand was away on a visit (a very rare event) that we took him out in the garden at Lansdowne House and let him run on the grass for the first time. He was wildly excited and delighted and gurgled with joy and of course I photographed him and the result is among my snapshots.

After spending nearly 2 months at Lansdowne House – including a few days at Bowood – the children and I took our departure on 21st July for Llanbedrog, Near Pwllheli, in N. Wales, where we had taken a little house for 5 or 6 weeks. We had quite a pleasant time there; our house was quite close to the beach and we went down there every day, the three children on a donkey, often taking our tea with us. Blanchie and Katie loved running about barefoot and B delighted in the paddling, but Katie screwed up her queer little nose, grasped her little knickers, and complained that the water was too wet! The little girls were terribly naughty and quarrelsome in the Nursery at that time; I think the sea air made them irritable, besides which, Blanchie had a very bad eye, supposed at the time to be a stye, but which, we came to the conclusion after, must have really been a little ulcer. It was years before she got over the effects of this and no doubt it must have hurt her very much at the time and made her very cross. She loved building castles and Katie equally loved knocking them over. Then Blanchie slapped her. Katie returned the slaps with interest and finally they both howled and Tyrone joined in the chorus. It wasn't altogether a peaceful time!

I saw a good deal of the Wynne Finches while at Llanbedrog; their place, Cefuamwich, was only about 10 miles off, though I lost my way and made 20 of it the first time I drove there, and we used often to drive over to see each other. I had my American 4 wheel trap, with a nice quiet mare ('Miss Fuss') and the children had their new Governess Cart, so we were quite independent. Once we went over en masse to stay at Cefuamwich for a few days. Another time they came to lunch – bringing Captain Charteris and Colonel West – and we all went for a sail. I enjoyed this so much that I went out another day with a very nice Admiral Wodehouse, living near us, but this time the result was disastrous and I was very sick! I also exchanged visits with a charming Mrs Lloyd Edward who lived in the neighbourhood, at Nanhoron.

On August 9th we celebrated the Coronation of King Edward as best we could, by going to a Coronation service and singing 'God Save the King' in Welsh and English! I was very sorry to miss the Coronation, particularly as I had my gown and all, but circumstances made it impossible for me to go when it was postponed.

On August 29th I left Llanbedrog, stopped that night in Dublin and saw Dr Macan, who was to come to Curraghmore for my confinement in December. I had great difficulty in finding a room for I had entirely forgotten that it was Horse Show week and that every hotel would be full. I at last secured a very dirty room in a third-rate hotel called Tarprey's, and gladly departed at 10am next day, arriving at Curraghmore in the afternoon (August 30th).

September, October and November 1902

Curraghmore felt very lonely without T, but a wire from him that day cheered me up and I was thankful to be home again. The children arrived two days later.

Another three months passed before T came home, but my friends were very good to me all that time and never allowed me to be alone. I went to stay with Claud and Clodagh at Woodhouse for three days – September 2 – 5, driving myself over – and bringing back Kathleen with me. Later on, Claud and Clodagh paid me two visits and, finally, on November 3rd they brought their little girl over with them and left her with me next day when they went off to Texas. We kept her at Curraghmore all that winter. Elsie Smith and her son, Pat, were with me for 9 days; they should have been there longer, but departed rather suddenly on receipt of a telegram and it wasn't till years after that I heard that Elsie had caused this telegram to be sent, as Pat was so naughty (he was a very high spirited boy) that she couldn't bear to stay any longer. Edwina Roberts was with me for nearly 4 weeks, on and off; Aileen for 10 days, Evie (her first visit to Curraghmore) for 2½ weeks and I had shorter visits from the Perrys, Susie and Hugh, Mrs Villiers Stuart, Miss Martin, Mother, Kerry, Beatrix Herbert, Alex Beauclerk, Tad Hely Hutchinson, Mrs Flemyng, and also from Phyllis Hamilton for 10 days.

While Evie was with me (on October 22nd) we had a scare that the baby was going to arrive as I felt very unwell for 2 days, but I kept very quiet and got all right again. Curiously enough, T felt so anxious about me just before then that he sent a runner to the Coast, about 100 miles, with a telegram to ask how I was! Except for this little upset, I kept very well and did a good deal both of walking and driving. While Phyllis was with me, we went to a Meet at Guilcagh and followed Hounds all the morning. Gladys Wicklow's boy, Clonmore, was born just before Phyllis came to me (October 30th) and 2 days after Gladys got very ill and nearly died, but mercifully pulled through all right. Bone's little girl, Mary (who died some years later) was born on November 15th; the Castlereaghs' son on the 18th and Hubie McClintock on the 20th. Mrs Medlycott's Johnnie, and Onie Aranmore's Kathleen, were born about the same time as Patsy.

I was very full of a new scheme of charity organization for Portlaw that winter. We had several meetings about it and everybody talked a great deal, but in the end it came to very little. It seemed to me that we all overlapped so much in our gifts that there were many 'Old Pets' who got much more than they wanted, from everyone, while others, quite as deserving, got nothing. So we divided the Village into districts, each of which was apportioned to some lady and we promised always to let that lady know when we gave to people in her district, at the same time making it our special business to look after our own district. For a while this worked fairly well and I found it a great help for my Xmas charities, but, like everything started in Portlaw, it gradually fizzled out, till, in a few years districts were entirely forgotten.

I must now go back to T's letters, so as to show what he was doing during all these months.

On June 29th, writing from Queenstown, he said that he wanted to go to Rhodesia, if he could get leave, and after seeing something of the country, to return by the East Coast; this plan, however, did not come off. In this and subsequent letters he said that the H.H. had horses for all the men and did a good deal of drilling on an enormous plain, four miles long, near Queenstown; after a time he said the men drilled splendidly and that sometimes he himself drilled them as a whole regiment, which was 'great practice for me', and I know this was a great help to him when he took up the command of his own Yeomanry.

On July 12th he wrote 'Many thanks for your letters which I get with clockwork regularity, and you can't imagine how much I look forward to getting them'. He told me of two shooting expeditions nearby, with quite good sport. Rey Buck, Guinea Fowl, Partridges and Dikkop, a bird like a large Plover, and in the next letter he tells of a Gymkhana at the Remount Depot, in which his C Squadron won several events. He said that the Peace was progressing well and the Boers were behaving very sensibly; and in another letter he says, 'All the men who have been here in S.A. for a number of years think that the next big war will be against the Blacks, and that it will be a very big war indeed and take us all our time to come out on top'. Talking of Lynch, the Irish M.P., who fought with the Boers, he says, 'I hear that he was sjamboked when out here for cowardice and disobeying orders; this was told me by a Dutchman, a cousin of Commandant Smuts'.

On July 9th he says, 'I shall be back before December 1st all right, and how nice it will be to be together again', and a week later, writing of the babies, he said he was, 'Longing to see you and them again... however, we shall appreciate it all the more when we do meet'.

On July 28th he went on a shooting expedition up the Fish River, trekking for 4 days – 35 miles a day – and returning 115 miles in three days to Tarkestad, 40 miles from Queenstown, to which the regiment had meanwhile moved. He had a great disappointment on this trip; he was most anxious to get a Koodoo, which was the best thing to be got there, and he actually got within good firing distance of one – and a real beauty – when a cur dog sprang from nowhere and scared it away. He never saw another and he was very sick about it.

On August 18th he wrote from Johannesburg and on the 23rd from Pretoria, whither he had gone to see Colonel Lawley of the 7th Hussars about a trip to the Shire River – a tributary of the Zambesi – in which he was anxious to join him, if he could get leave. He added, 'Don't think me horrid to go up the Zambesi instead of coming home, but it is the chance of a lifetime to see the Country and I shall be home, bar accidents, by December 1st, as originally intended; in time to support your deal little back (!!!) my dear little mouse, and then never no more babbies on any pretence whatever!!

I am looking forward more and more to seeing your little face again, and when we are once home and settled, we will have such a happy time in our own little home and never go away any more. Well, God bless you my darling, mind and take care of yourself, and take things easy you dear little creature, and not fuss'.

He said there would not be much chance of my getting letters after this, as they would be so far up country; however, I got three more letters – one from Pretoria, one from Lourenço Marques, and the last from Chuide, or near there, written on September 3rd. These letters gave more details of the trip – he had cabled to say it was all arranged – which he was to make with Col. Lawley and Captain Dalgetty, both of the 7th Hussars, for which regiment he put Tyrone down at that time – he said they were, 'both charming fellows and old experienced hunters', and his experience certainly justified his first impressions of them.

The trip was to take about 6 weeks and they would go via Delagoa Bay, up the Zambesi, first by ship to Chuide thence by river boat up the Zambesi, then up the Shire River to Chiromo, where they would start their shooting. Meanwhile, T had resigned his Commission in the Highland Horse; he was taking with him our groom, Mark Purser, who had been with him in S. Africa, and the outfit included '50 Blacks and plenty of comforts'. He also said, 'I have got your dear little letter, the one in which there is no news except the babbies howling'! This was evidently written during the stormy time at Llanbedrog.

They sailed from Lourenço Marques on August 31st, by S.S. *Kaiser*, to Beira; there they changed ships and T's last letter (September 3rd), after which I was entirely without news of him, except for a telegram from Chiromo – sent down by runner – on October 16th, and another from Aden on November 18th. It was a very anxious time, as I knew that on the shooting trip he would be running into a good many dangers, and there never was a more welcome telegram than the one which told me that he was on his way home.

Colonel Lawley kept the 'Staff Diary' and a few extracts from it will give an idea of how they spent those 2 months.

'September 1902 – got nearly to Beira before daybreak, but hung about all morning on a/c of fog and tide. Fairly warm. Arrived at Beira about noon. W & I went ashore... a hot night...

Tues 2nd Remained in Beira taking in cargo all day. We all three went ashore in p.m.....

Sept 3rd. Left Beira 5am and got off Chuide about 4pm, where we transferred to the adjutant and expected to get into Chuide the same night, but having run on a sand-bank she stove a hole in her bottom, and they had to keep the pumps going hard, all to keep the old tub afloat, and we therefore cruised about in a rather nasty sea all night.

Sept 4th. Got into Chuide about 7am.... Put up at Keiller's Hotel.

Sept 5th. In pm went and called on H.M.S. *Herald*, the Zambesi Gunboat, Commander Stevenson and the Dr Geogaghan pulled out three of W's teeth – poor T, he told me of the agonies of these extractions; he had violent toothache from abysses in three old stumps which he ought to have had out ages before, and when he consulted the Naval doctor he said the only thing was to take them out; there was no chloroform and, of course, the stumps had to be dug out, and T was so near fainting after that he had to have a very stiff brandy and soda to pull him together.

I omit all the details given by Col. Lawley as to people they interviewed and how all the arrangements were made at the various stations. They started up the River (Zambesi) on September 6th about 4.30pm on the

Empress, the 'best boat on the river. Everything most comfortable and all the A.R.C. people doing all they could for us. Steamed on up the river till nearly 10pm and then tied up for the night'.

Sept 7th. Got off at daybreak.

Sept 8th. About 9am passed Jesuit Mission Station where Mrs Livingstone died... Tied up at night just in the Shire.

Sept 9th. On up the Shire... A very hot still night.

Sept 10th. Navigation getting exceeding difficult and our rate of progress becoming slower and slower...keep on running on to sandbanks and have to perform the most involved nautical manoeuvres in order to worm our way up the river at all'.

After this, the *Empress* stuck; Col. Lawley and Capt. Dalgety seem to have chartered some sort of houseboat, borrowed a crew from a German trader at a wooding station, also an Ass Cart, and at last reached Chiromo at 7pm on the 12th, while T, who evidently preferred to rely on the *Empress*, or some other river boat which took her passengers on, arrived there on the 14th, at the same time as the baggage. At Chiromo they stayed with Mr Macdonald who, T told me, was most hospitable and kind to them.

On September 15th they made up their loads and got everything ready. On the 16th they 'got off at 1pm and trekked 8 miles to Malolos along East bank of Ruo'. In the evening 'H.B.D. and W going after Guineas and killing 3.' On the 17th they reached Manganillas and on the 18th Siadzi; H.B.D. got a young Bushbuck one day and a Hartebeest and 2 Duiker the next. On the 19th 'W got a Waterbuck and H.B.D. a Quagga.' Next day, September 20th, after 'a long hot march' they reached Masamba's, and on the 21st two of their dogs went off into the jungle and 'evidently met a leopard. "Satan" we never saw again and "Micky" crawled back into camp at Masamba late in the pm with two very nasty wounds in his back... about 11 got to Chirombo's, where we held a 'Kriegsrad' and as the country in front seemed so hopeless decided to turn back'. So they retraced their steps as far as Chiromo. Thence, after some delays they started again on September 27th, crossed to the West bank of the Shire and travelled in Machillas (a sort of hammock slung on a pole) to Chisamba, and thence on the 29th to Lalanges, where a Chief called Makwira joined them.

They don't seem to have been very lucky with the game just then, though they got several buck of different sorts between them. On October 2nd they went on to Mount Charlie and on the 4th to Makwira's village. There they 'used the indaba hut for a mess house and another empty hut for a kitchen', and camped close by. Game had been more plentiful the last few days – Reedbuck, Quagga, Hartebeest chicken, Waterbuck, Bushbuck and 'gnondo'. 'Camp plenty full of meat', and on October 5th H.B.D. got a good lion.

On October 8th they decided to go south again, and before leaving Makwira's village, H.B.D. took a delightful photo of him in a blanket and top hat (this is in my scrapbook).

On the 9th they (Col.L. & W.) had a long stalk after buffalo, but W. missed his shot; afterwards 'spotted an ngondo which, thinking it was a bull, I persuaded W. to shoot, he killing it with a good galloping shot. W. got a small warthog...(later)... a herd of waterbuck out of which W. killed one, a galloping shot, but it was only a moderate bull'.

October 10th...'shooting our way to next camp, we each got an ngondo and W. a reedbuck'. The shooting of various buck is recorded in the next few days.

On the 14th, 'Comr Sharpe, having given us permission to shoot one bull buffalo each in the Elephant Marsh, arranged to go for them tomorrow morning and Makwira sent men out in pm to locate them'. Accordingly, on the 15th they went out and, after walking and stalking all day, they each succeeded in getting a bull buffalo. W's was 'quite a nice head', but Capt. Dalgety's was the best, 'an exceeding fine head'.

On the 17th they went back to Malolos, shooting as they went, and on the 18th: 'W. had a galloping shot at distant ngondo..., and killed a doe gwape, galloping shot thro' the head at 140 yards; a rather fancy performance!

On the 19th, 'Moved camp to Manganillas' and on October 20th W. and Mark went back to Chiromo while H.B.D and I started on our way for Chugilla'. After this, the Diary, though full of interest, concerns us no more and as W. never kept a diary himself there is no further record of his travels. I know, however, that one of the boats he went down river in was very nearly swamped and that he all but missed the German Steamer which was to bring him home and was in a great state, thinking that after all is promises he would be too late for 'the event'. By some lucky chance, the boat stopped at some port where she had never stopped before, which enabled T to get to her. He was very ill on the journey home, with malaria – contracted in the swamps near the Shire –, and his bunk being much too short for him, and the weather grillingly hot, he had a most miserable time.

The Shire River must have been a most unhealthy hunting-ground and simply teeming with malaria. T was dreadfully ill after he came home. Col. Lawley has been a perfect wreck ever since that trip and Capt. Dalgety was very bad for a time. The weather was very hot and stuffy and even the nights were suffocating; it must have been a most trying climate. I was horrified at T's appearance when he came home, for he was as thin as a rail – his clothes literally hanging on him – and quite sallow and hollow-eyed. All the same, he always spoke of that trip as one of the most enjoyable times of his life; it was his first experience of anything of the kind and he not only loved the sport, but delighted in the freedom and the wandering irresponsibility of the life. He was wonderfully quick at picking up languages, and although only in the country for 6 or 7 weeks, he could speak enough Chinyangi (?) to get on perfectly well with the natives.

One night, after he came home, I was awoke by very odd sounds beside me, and there was my friend hunting in his sleep and talking fluent Chinyangi in a mysterious whisper to his gunbearer, Kasamcha, with every now and then a few very forcible English words thrown in when (he was going over an incident which had actually happened) his Machilla boys popped up and ruined a long stalk after waterbuck – this trip awoke quite a new element in T's nature and he was always restless after and longing to be away again. Certainly, the 'never go away any more' feeling which he wrote of in S. Africa, disappeared after the Central African trip.

December 1902

Now, to return once more to Curraghmore, my spirits rose by leaps and bounds after I got T's telegram from Aden (November 18th) and another from Turin on the 19th; then, on December 1st, came one to say he's be home next day and on the 2nd, he actually arrived and I felt all my troubles were over. At the same time, his appearance caused me a good deal of anxiety and he was evidently far from well and in very bad spirits. During the 6 months he had been away, much business and correspondence had of course accumulated; I had done my best to keep it down, by answering all the letters I could and docketing all the rest in such a way that they could easily be tackled, and it had been my great anxiety to keep down expenses for him while he was away and to have everything in as good order as possible by his return.

Big game shooting in a warm climate, one of the most fascinating pursuits in the world, is undoubtedly one that is also to a certain extent demoralizing, from its inherent selfishness and the want of responsibility in the life, and I know from later experience how difficult it is to settle down to humdrum every day business after it. T found it most irksome and being in bad health as well made it all the more difficult. Add to this that I was within a fortnight of my expected confinement and therefore could not be of much use to him, and I'm sure my monstrous appearance was far from cheering!

There had been a good deal of talk of stopping hunting that year and in September some very violent letters were written to the papers, but luckily the agitation had blown over and Mr Malcomson, who was the Master of the Waterford Hounds, was still hunting away. T had been asked several times to take the Hounds, but the request had not been unanimous from all classes and he always refused to consider it for that reason and said that only when all the farmers, as well as the gentry, asked him to hunt the County, would he consent to do so.

He was much hampered at this time – and for the rest of his life – by his Rider's Muscle, which he constantly strained. Two days after his return, he went out hunting and strained it badly; he ought to have had treatment for it then, but hunted again as soon as he could and made it worse, so that even his hunting was no real pleasure to him. The weather was very cold then; he felt it very much after Africa and it did not improve the state of his liver.

My Nurse arrived (Nurse Monk) on December 9th and Dr Macan on the 13th, and after that followed a weary time of waiting, with Dr Macan's bill rolling up at the rate of £20 per day, which nearly drove me to despair. In vain did I take long walks and drive in the old pony

Granny Beaufort with (LEFT TO RIGHT) *Diana Somerset, Blanchie Beresford, Katie Beresford, Blanchie Somerset at Badminton.*

Invitation to the Fancy Dress Ball.

Meet of the Waterford Hounds at Curraghmore the day after the Ball.

Beatrix and Tyrone in fancy dress. Beatrix as Catty de la Poer, Tyrone as the 2nd Marquis.

Bowood, Beatrix's childhood home, Old House and Portico in 1902.

Upper Terrace and Big House, Curraghmore.

carriage – with bad springs – over the roughest roads; in vain did I take pills and pray for the speedy arrival of the baby – day after day passed and still I was as well as ever. I begged T to send Dr Macan away and wire for him when the pains began, but he refused to do this – very naturally – and the result was a bill of 200gs before anything happened at all. I used to think every day of all the useful things we could have done with that money; it made me quite miserable to be the cause of such waste! Mother arrived on December 18th and, at last, on December 22nd there were signs that the time of waiting was over and Patsy arrived at 8.55am next morning.

December 23rd was Katie's birthday and at about 7.30am Mother brought her down to see me, so that I might wish her many happy returns and give her the Doll & Teaset I had for her. She was three years old that day and the little sister was presented to her later on as another special gift for her birthday, with which she was much delighted.

Patsy weighed 8lb 14oz when born and measured 21 inches; she was a funny gollywoggish little thing, with masses of long dark hair, large blue eyes, a small mouth and a big nose. Her eyebrows were well marked and her eyelashes long and curling. She had a yellow skin at first, but her complexion soon became quite good.

Meanwhile, T had been hunting fairly regularly again – the muscle having improved. Will Perry had been down for a few days and T had hunted at Fethard and also had a day's shooting at Cahir Park. He seemed better, though he had several slight attacks of malaria, which made him rather wretched while they lasted. On the 27th December, however, he felt very ill out hunting and had to get off and lean against a bank in the middle of a run; then he went on again, but by the time he came home he had a highish temperature, and after seeing me for a few minutes he retired to bed. The Doctor pronounced it to be influenza with malaria; there was not much change in the next 2 days, but then he got much worse and they feared that it might be Blackwater Fever.

January 1903

A night nurse was sent for and on January 1st 1903 Dr Smith came down from Dublin and diagnosed it as jaundice, complicated by malaria. The temperature had been over 104°, but after the jaundice came out (it was suppressed at the beginning) the temperature went down and matters gradually improved. I was not supposed to know how bad T was, but I had a pretty good idea of it and felt very anxious. There we were, in rooms next door to each other, and unable to meet for nearly a fortnight; it was most tantalizing. At last T devised the setting up of a telephone between our rooms and we used to converse through this. I knew at once when T was better for he started teasing me through the telephone, pretending he didn't hear me, and making me shout louder and louder and also accusing me of eating onions!!

We had various visitors, the Duncannons amongst others, and here I must tell rather an amusing episode of Lord Duncannon's visit, though it is hardly a drawing-room tale. It was most important that T should have plenty of water to work off the jaundice. The quantity passed was measured twice a day, but it was not nearly enough and the Nurse and Doctor were rather worried about it. But on the day that Lord Duncannon came there were loud jubilations for the quantity was splendid and the quality much improved. Everybody was delighted and it was thought that T was really on the mend, till it transpired that the extra quantity had been contributed by Lord Duncannon!!

On January 6th I got onto the sofa, Mother left next day, and on the 8th I was put into a chair and wheeled in to see T. He looked shockingly ill; thinner than ever and as yellow as a guinea, and of course he was very weak. However, he always had the most wonderful recuperative power and once he started getting up he improved rapidly. We made the Blue Bedroom into a sitting room and met there in the evenings, but he was soon down and out and got on his feet long before me.

A propos of this time, Blanchie, dictating a letter a few days after Patsy's birth, said, 'We have got a new little baby sister and our Mother is ill and Daddy has got a sore finger (i.e. fever) and our Mother isn't very well, but she doesn't feel ill, she has got a cold! She was only 4 years old and was much worried at our both being laid up. I saw both her and Katie on Xmas day and they and Tyrone used to come and see me regularly after, but Blanchie was rather nervous and felt there was something going on that she couldn't understand, and she would never stay with me long while I was in bed.

Patsy lost weight steadily for the first fortnight after she was born, but after that she improved and soon did quite well. I didn't attempt to nurse her as the wherewithal was entirely absent.

I went downstairs on January 16th and drove with T on the 18th. Willie Perry stayed with us, also Capt. Burns Lindow, T's Yeomanry Adjutant, who had much business to settle with him. My Nurse left on January 20th and next day T and I went for a little walk together. Oh! how I enjoyed that; it was good to be out again, and with him, and I remember even now what a lovely day it was.

On January 24th T left for London, en route to St. Moritz, where he had been ordered for change of air and where I was to join him as soon as possible. He arrived there on 29th and I joined him on February 14th.

On January 28th Patsy was christened, 'Beatrix Patricia de la Poer'. T had insisted that Beatrix should come first, though there was no question of calling her by that name. Beatrix Herbert, Elsie Smith and Major J.G. Beresford were her godparents, but none of them were present. Before I left my bed, Nurse Monk took a photograph of me there, with Patsy beside me. It came out wonderfully well, considering that Nurse Monk could see nothing in the finder except the pink ribbon at my neck. I photographed Patsy myself before I went away; she was only 6 weeks old when I left and I hated having to part from her so soon, but I was longing to be with T.

February and March 1903

I broke the journey in London, staying with the Roberts for a few days, and it was during this time that Beatrix Herbert's engagement to Nevile Wilkinson was announced – on the telephone by herself! Also, Lord Crichton's engagement to Molly Grosvenor. Talking of Lord Crichton, who was always a great friend of T, and habitually called him Waterbugs (his usual name in the Blues), caused much amusement by writing to T just after he was made K.P. and addressing his letter to the Marquis of Waterford. K.P... BU.CES. etc.

I left London on February 12th and travelled via Boulogne, Basle, Zurich, Chur, and Thursis, from whence there was, in those pre-railway days, a 2 hours sleigh drive to Tiefenkasten (where I slept) and 6 or 7 hours drive on again to St. Moritz. T met me about 2 miles from St. Moritz, where we arrived about 4.30pm at the Palace Hotel. I was, in those days, painfully shy and awkward in any public place and this was my first experience of staying in a big hotel. I simply hated it at first, but I really think it cured me of my self-consciousness in a great measure and gave me more self-assurance than I should have had otherwise. T warned me that everybody would stare at me, as they did at every new arrival, 'but', he said, 'for goodness sake don't look silly and wriggle into the room sideways; just stare back at them if they stare at you and you'll find they'll soon stop it'! At dinner in the restaurant the ordeal really began and never have I seen such staring. At last T said, 'Now look here, there is a dark-faced girl over there who has been staring hard every since you came in – ill-mannered brute; we'll stare at her for a change – both together – now'. We tackled that girl most successfully and really made her uncomfortable at last. A very nice young couple – Captain & Mrs Bingham, had been misguided enough to go there for their honeymoon, thinking that nobody there would know them. Unfortunately, a few days after their arrival, there appeared a *Gentlewoman* paper, with their photographs in it. T spotted them at once and, having already made their acquaintance, he teased them unmercifully about this, and went into the restaurant, *Gentlewoman* in hand, and proceeded to study the pictures with one eye on them, till they became nearly frantic.

There was a great deal of gaiety at St. Moritz and we had quite a nice time on the whole, though I felt far from fit and got dreadfully tired, and T had a nasty attack of influenza the week after I arrived. He had already taken violently to tobogganing when I came and had had rather a nasty spill, the steel-shod toboggan following him and giving him a blow in the liver, which kept him doubled up for 3 days, but he was soon on the Cresta again and I used to go and watch him flash down the Church Leap with my heart in my mouth every time.

I skated every day and he generally joined me for a bit, but he didn't really care about skating and preferred tobogganing and bob sleighing. There were quite a lot of nice people that we got to know and a few queerish ones as well. There were various 'intrigues' being carried on and it was an awful place for gossip. The most discussed people there were the Baron & Baroness de Forest (she was widow of M. Menier of chocolate fame), for he was carrying on perpetually with Lady Gerard's daughter, while the disconsolate little Baroness consoled herself with 'Mr Sugie de Bathe', who, handsome and attentive, was always at her beck and call. Their little daughter, one of the most beautiful children I have ever seen, seemed to get very little attention from anyone. I sometimes went to see her undressed and longed to take possession of her. It was not long after that the unscrupulous Baron made his wife divorce him – under threat of divorcing her if she wouldn't – he then married Ethel Gerard, who, some years later, ran away with another man.

Pleasanter people were the Comte de Bylandt, Mr Haughton – a delightful Irish American – Mme O'Connor and her daughters, Miss Hall, a charming Canadian girl, Dr Holland, Mr Strutt, Mr Hoare, the Dudgeons, Count Schönborn and his daughters, Maja and Johanna, Count & Countess Czernin etc. etc. These Austrians were charming people and I was very sorry that we only got to know them towards the end of our stay; however, we renewed acquaintance later. T stayed with them all in Hungary and the Schönborns stayed with us at Curraghmore. Poor Maja, a very nervous girl, suffered very much from her eyes as she had recently lost one from a bob-sleighing accident, when she had fallen on to a partly buried post, which ran into her eye.

Miss Dod and Mr Doherty were staying up there and once we saw them playing tennis, which was a real joy. The Bots were great people up there, though not at all popular. Mr Bot was the best Englishman on the Cresta and his wife and sister the only local ladies who went down it. They wore bloomers and looked far from attractive, but they were very good at it and, though Miss Bot was the best, I was lost in admiration of Mrs Bot when I heard that she usually had a baby in the summer and won the ladies toboggan race in the winter!!

The weather was very unsettled and a bad thaw made the going slushy and the Cresta Race an impossibility on the day fixed. However, it took place on March 6th amidst the usual excitement and the three first in it (the Grand National) were Thoma 1, Bot 2, Bylandt 3. A year later Bylandt was killed on that run. The men in charge left a plank across it and he, being the first to go down that morning, met it with his head and fractured his skull.

We dined several times with friends at the Kulm; also at our own hotel, where we ourselves gave a dinner party too. There were also several dances and some entertainments, at one of which I was made to join in a minuet, which I danced very badly, and one day we all went to Belvon where the de Forests and O'Connors entertained us to a sumptuous luncheon.

The frost broke up very early that year and the place was becoming unbearably dirty and slushy when we took our departure on March 9th. Nevertheless, we had a bitterly cold drive over the Pass and were very glad when we got over to the other side. After Muhlen, where we lunched, we got our wheels again and reached Chur in the afternoon. We spent one night at Innsbruck and four at Munich, and did a good deal of sight-seeing at both places; the Hofkirche, National Museum etc at Innsbruck and at Munich the Alte und Neue Pinakothek, the Basilica, Church of our Lady and National Museum. At the hotel we met an old acquaintance, Baron Campbell von Laurentz who, with his friend General le Bret, took us under his wing and was most kind to us, taking us first to Bernheuniers, the big Dealers, where we bought a very pretty little gilt shrine for a miniature case and a small fountain (boy with swan) for the Shellhouse Garden, which, though it pretended to be bronze and was only cast-iron (the bronze paint came off when the water was turned on), was quite a successful purchase.

Then we were taken to tea with Mrs le Bret; rather an alarming affair; went to the play – *Die Puppe* and afterwards, personally conducted by Baron C, ate sausage and sauerkraut and drank delicious Munich beer at the Hofbrau Haus. The next morning we were taken to see the Scriver Reiter's Cavalry Barracks, and most kindly received by Gen. le Bret and his officers, with whom we had to drink sherry before parting from them! The day we arrived there had been a parade of troops in honour of Leopold, the Prince Regent's birthday and we were much struck by the fine appearance of the men and the careful way they were matched for height in each regiment. We went to two operas – *Fidelio* and *Der Fliegende Hollander*. The latter is supposed to be done better in Munich than anywhere else and it certainly was perfect; nevertheless, T, who never could keep awake through an opera, went sound asleep after the first act, much to the horror of our German neighbours, who looked absolutely scandalized.

We left Munich on the 15th – though we would have gladly stayed there another week to explore its wonderful picture galleries and other treasures – and arrived at Karlsruhe that evening. We stopped there on purpose to see my old Governess, Fräulein Noedel, who had a sort of 'pension' there and T was so kind about it and so charming to her, though he had never seen her before. She and her friend, Miss Stewart, dined with us that night. They were both quite fascinated by T, who had the art of making himself charmingly agreeable to people and had the most delightful manners. We both went to tea at Fräulein Noedel's house the next day and in the evening we went to a concert (Isarge playing) where we sat in a front row, with rows of 'my girls' in white frocks sitting behind! I had been introduced to those same girls that morning as 'my best pupil', which embarrassed me terribly, particularly as I knew there was no truth in the statement!

Next day we were at Strasbourg, where we watched the famous monster Clock strike at twelve o'clock and on the 18th we arrived in Paris. Mme Carême was on, the crowds in the streets were rather overpowering, and we came in smothered with confetti. T was tired of sight-seeing and though we wandered round the Louvre Museum and the Musée de Chien, we were not in the mood for sights or art. We went to see Sarah Bernhardt in *Werther* but didn't see it out and thus missed the excitement caused by a lady who pulled out a revolver in the middle of an act and tried to shoot herself. We also went to the Opera and heard *Samson et Delilah* and *Pagliacci*, but I think T, in his frivolous mood, preferred the 'Cirque Nouveau', which we visited on our last evening.

We were back in London on the 23rd March and T left for Curraghmore on the 25th while I followed a few days later, after having done some shopping, had my photograph taken by Lafayette, and seen something of my friends and relations.

The Irish Land Bill was brought in at that time. Also Father was examined by the War Commission.

April 1903

Getting back to Curraghmore was, as usual, a great joy and my diary records, on April 1st, the day of my return, a 'delightful evening with the babies'. Little Tyrone, aged 2¼, was promoted to tunics and short knickers that summer and a great duck he looked in them, with a manly panama hat. He also took to riding the ass on a special saddle we had had made for the children – a real boy's saddle, with a little rail round the back to give them support and safety.

We had done a good deal at Curraghmore the year before in the house – the two halls had been done up in their present colour – before that the ceiling of the lower hall was picked out in blue and buff, and the walls were blue. I think it was about then that we put down the crimson pile carpet on Front Stairs and 1st floor landing and passage. Also we had put a new bath in our bathroom, which was then the only big bath in our part of the house and had made the two new bathrooms on 1st and 2nd floor, out of what used to be tiny dressing rooms.

Outside, the clearings had been gone on with and the Shellhouse garden – which was a very drear and untidy spot – had been entirely cleared in the centre, the whole of the turf re-laid and then all replanted with Azaleas, and many choice shrubs; when we came home the Munich fountain was put up there. T loved this little garden, which was his first venture in shrub gardening. Everybody used to be taken to see it and he was immensely proud of it. He did not care much for flowers, except the wild bluebells which he loved, but was very keen about flowering shrubs, bamboos and trees with good foliage. Red was his favourite colour and, though there was not much of it in the Shellhouse garden, nearly all the rhododendrons he planted later were red and he always said we couldn't have too much of it here.

The other great improvement made at that time was in the herbaceous border below the terrace, which formerly had but one narrow flower border on the terrace side, the other side being turfed like a bowling alley, but broken near the middle by a solitary Irish Yew. This we removed – with the turf – and by putting the gravel path in the middle, made two flower borders of equal width. The Yew Hedge, which was lower than at present, and quite straight, we allowed to grow to its present height and also to grow out at intervals, until it formed bastions to match those in the Terrace Wall.

A few days after our return, Claud and Clodagh came back from Texas and after spending a couple of nights with us, they carried off little Clodagh, who had been at Curraghmore for four months, and all returned to Woodhouse.

We had a great time hanging all T's central African heads when they arrived from Rowland Ward. T made a record catch of trout in the lake that month, getting 52 to his own rod in 2½ hours.

One more day's hunting and a Point-to-Point Meeting near Kilmacthomas – at which T rode the Drake, but fell – finished the season – and on April 20th we went off to stay with the St. Leger Moores at Killashee, for Punchestown. We had a horse called Boundaway running in the Conyngham Cup that year and he did very well till he came to the big wall, where he fell. 'Bumpabout', as some ribald friend called him, was not a lucky horse and never did much for us. Col. St. Leger Moore, with whom we were staying, was 2nd in Command of T's Yeomanry and a charming man, but gifted with the most powerful imagination! With a guileless face, and the most innocent blue eye imaginable, he would calmly relate stories which hadn't one particle of truth in them, but which I really think he believed in himself. On this, my first acquaintance with him, I believed them all, but soon discovered that what was commonly known as 'a Dick Moore' had to be taken with several grains of salt. He had been in S. Africa during the war, but it was said that, through no fault of his own, he had never been near the firing line. Yet he had the mark of a wound on his hand (it was said that he painted it blue every morning) and in a bottle he showed the fragments of the shell which hit him. Out hunting, when thrown out of a run, he would get off his horse when he thought nobody could see him and roll in the mud, even going to the length of spoiling his hat; and then he would come back and say he had had an awful fall. Several people had, at different times, actually seen him do this. And yet he was a clever man and a plucky one too, and good at everything he took up!

Once, after staying with us, he met Edwina Roberts and Commander Forbes in the train, and told them a harrowing tale of how he had just seen a little child run over on Waterford Bridge and killed; and he put his hands over his eyes and said the sight haunted him still. Edwina was much distressed, till she caught the Commander's eye, with a large wink in it, and realized that as they had driven over the bridge just after Col.Moore, they could not have failed to note the accident, if there had been one. Sure enough, it was an entire invention, a typical 'Dick Moore'.

From Killashee we went up to Dublin for Phoenix Park Races, where we met the Dudleys, who persuaded us to go and stay with them at the Viceregal Lodge. We drove from there to Leopardstown the next day and saw Grange run 2nd in a flat race and on April 25th we caught the early train (6am) home. Count Schönborn and his daughters arrived in the afternoon. Also the Doynes (Mr Robert and Lady Mary), Capt. H. Pack Beresford and Captain Clarke – both of whom had been in the Highland Horse with T. The Schönborns were loud in their praises of all they saw and thought it all most beautiful, so lovely, so delightful. We took them all out riding. One day we rode a party of 8 and they bought three or four horses from Willie Perry and Mr Stafford.

May and June 1903

On May 6th Kathleen Villiers Stuart was married to Col.Gale; a dreary wedding on a pouring wet day. Everybody looking bedraggled. Mr Haughton paid us a long visit after that, staying with us, on and off, from May 9th to June 4th. He was a very pleasant man, simple and straightforward, and had some delightful American expressions. Anything he liked very much was 'just crack-a-jack', and once, when expressing his approval of a certain young lady, he said 'Well, I guess she can just pack her clothes in my trunk right-a-way'. Towards the end of his visit, however, he got himself into terrible trouble with T, who also blamed me a good deal for the incident. Kathleen Beresford was staying with us. Haughton obviously admired her very much and she was flattered by his attention and went about with him a good deal, so that no-one could help noticing it. One night after dinner, the ladies being alone in the Billiard Room, Haughton, to my surprise, walked in alone, long before we expected the men. Kathleen, with a very pink face, was playing the piano and he went up to her and said, 'Well, Miss Beresford, have you asked Lady Waterford?' Pinker still, Kathleen blurted out 'Oh, Beatrix dear, do you think we might go out in the garden' and I, very much taken aback, gave my permission – on condition they didn't stay out too long. So off they went, and I immediately regretted giving leave, for Kathleen, though then nearly 24, was a very scatter-brained creature, and one never quite knew what she would be up to. 'Where is Kathleen'?, said T, when he came up, and he was perfectly furious when I told him, called Haughton many names and roundly abused me for not preventing this really harmless little escapade. We had a miserable evening and, as time went on, I really got quite nervous. Bed time came and still no sign of Kathleen and we waited on in glum silence, broken now and then by angry ejaculations from T. 'What do we know of this man – a nice pie you've got me into – of course they'll get engaged – what shall I say to my Uncle Charlie' – etc. etc.

At last, just as we had made up our minds to go to bed, in walked the truants, and I whisked Kathleen off at once, ascertained that she wasn't engaged, and was not a bit in love with Haughton, gave her a bit of a talking to and packed her off to bed. Before long I heard T bring Haughton to his own room and give him a tremendous blowing up, and his voice was so loud and angry that I couldn't help hearing the words now and then and was quite nervous for fear there should be a row; for Haughton, being much older than T, might well have resented being thus spoken to by him. Luckily, he took it very well and was genuinely distressed at having upset us, and particularly at having, as T thought, given cause for gossip (among servants etc.) about Kathleen. T was certainly not a prude, but he was most tremendously particular about his women folk, or anybody entrusted to his care, and this incident shows how very strong his feelings were in such a case.

But to return to May: I remember we had a short visit from Dr Spurrier, whom T had met in Central Africa, and a happy day stands out in my memory when, in lovely weather, with the gorse in all its glory, T and I drove off with the Trotter and paid a few long distance calls, having our tea at the Tramore Hotel overlooking the sea.

On May 23rd, Captain Sheppard brought his otter Hounds to Curraghmore for a week's hunting in the neighbouring streams; he had with him a long man called Harford, who sang comic songs, and a little man called Gape, both of the King's Royal Rifle Corps – to which Regiment the Hounds nominally belonged.

Aileen Roberts, Miss Hall, Kathleen, the Perrys, the Forbes, the Wises, Col. Villiers Stuart, and Mr Jennings stayed with us and we had quite a pleasant week, but poor sport on the whole: 5 days hunting and 2 kills. One Meet was at Woodhouse, when the Ansons gave us lunch and where a certain pole across a narrow part of the river caused great diversion, several of the men trying to walk across it and most of them falling into the river.

This reminds me of two incidents at the otter hunting of 1901, which I forgot to put down: The Piltown D.J., Mr Mercer, was always getting his leg pulled and one day, when we were walking over garlic after the Hounds, T persuaded him that it was the smell of the otter: 'Don't you smell it', said he, 'Oh Yes, I'm sure I do', said the unfortunate man, after sniffing about for some time. The other incident was a disgraceful trick of Capt. J.G. Beresford's, who, having discovered that Susie and Edwina used hot water bottles in the middle of summer (in grillingly hot weather) went up to the room they shared after dinner and loosened the screws of both the 'Judy Bags', as he called them, so that when they went to bed, they found everything wet, and had to sleep in the blankets as best they could. It was a horrid trick and I sternly forbade any meddling with beds in future and only mention it here in order to explain the lines 'To a brass pot from two Judy Bags', in one of my books.

On June 1st there was a match between Lord Dudley's Flying Swallow and our Grange. T was quite certain she would win it, but she was defeated. It was run at the Ballydoyle Race Meeting and he, Willie Perry and Mr Haughton, went up to see it; Miss Hall left the same time. We had had great fun with Miss Hall and Mr Haughton, who had known each other at St. Moritz, but were not aware that they were going to meet at Curraghmore. Haughton was there first and the morning that Miss Hall was to arrive we dressed him up in the most fanciful way – an ordinary tweed coat, riding breeches (without gaiters), silk stockings, and evening pumps. He also had his hair curled and wore a sham moustache and imperial. In this guise, we presented him to Miss Hall as Count Crackajackowski, and privately informed her that he was rather queer and she mustn't mind his odd ways. She was completely taken in and gazed at him with a face of horror, which increased when he started making eyes at her and paying her compliments. We all laughed so much that we could not keep up the hoax very long and poor Miss Hall was much relieved when the eccentric foreigner declared himself!

Father and Mother paid us a short visit after that and while Mother was still with us T had to go in to Waterford on business and was brought back by Mr Goff in his motor car. We all went for a drive in her after; I think it was the first time any of us had motored and we were very excited over it. I had no wish for a motor then, but T soon hankered after one; we had great discussions over it for I loved our grey horses, which had been driven at Curraghmore for so many years and it seemed to me that people with motors became so restless and always wanted to be on the road. How T laughed at me about all my objections, when the motor was an established fact and I was even keener about it than he was. 'What about those nice horses now', he would say, whenever I wanted to use the car. We paid a visit to the Dudleys at Rockingham in June; Lord Dudley had a birthday while we were there and it was pathetic to see Lady D's devotion to him and her joy when he came for a drive with her. She simply adored him and he so little deserved her love, being thoroughly weak and self-indulgent; he was always getting into scrapes and she forgave him again and again until, at last (1913), she had to part from him.

We came home on June 16th and a few days later we lunched with the George Malcomsons at Rathmore and went to Piltown Races after. What a race meeting that was. The result of every race was practically arranged before-hand, and it was too comical to see the efforts of the jockey on the horse that wasn't 'meant' to keep far enough behind! In one race there were seven starters and they <u>all</u> fell. In another, there were only two and the best horse wouldn't jump without a lead. One race was won literally at a walk – and the excitement over all these races was immense and any amount of advice to the jockeys was continually offered by the crowds. A local squireen, courting popularity, was giving free drinks in an enclosure on the course and, of course, everyone was anxious to show how much his kindness was appreciated, and by the end of the meeting there were very few sober men about.

Croker, the photographer, came out one day that summer to do some old pictures and miniatures we wanted reproduced, and we let him do a family group at the same time. It was the only time that T ever consented to be photographed with the family and I was very pleased at his being taken with us. They came out very well and one of them is almost my favourite photograph of him.

July 1903

There was great excitement that summer over the Gordon Bennet Motor Race, and we went up to Fenagh (Co. Carlow) to stay with the Denis Pack Beresfords for it. It took place on July 2nd 1903. We saw it from the Carlow stand, opposite which there was a fairly sharp corner; the competitors had to slow down there, so we had a very good view of them; and more than that, two or three of them mistook the turn and instead of swinging round it, they came full tilt up the lane where we stood, causing great consternation. A wire was stretched across the lane and the first man who made the mistake merely flattened the wire down and was able to back onto the road without any damage, but the next got mixed up in the slackened wire, which wrenched off of his wheels and turned his car over. Jenatzy won the race. The Englishmen were all lucky. We had a most dangerous drive with our host, who drove his own motor – a very new possession – and never used more than two wheels going round a corner, and we were not sorry when it was over. A delightful story of Mr Beresford's cure for a motor shy horse was told us some time later: he assured the owner that he would very soon cure it of all nervousness, if he would bring it to Fenagh; he then set a feed of oats on the silent car and when the horse was accustomed to that he said 'Now, we will start the engine'. Unfortunately, when he did this, the car gave a kick and a plunge, hit the horse and broke its leg, and the poor brute had to be shot. It was never frightened of a motor again!

These Pack Beresfords, having been disappointed in their hopes of having a child some years before (she expected an imaginary one for 10 months), had gone off to Norway for change of air and come back with a little fair-haired girl whom they had adopted; we were all expected to think that it was actually theirs and Mrs P.B. went so far as to ask me who I thought the child was like. It was most embarrassing and I didn't know what to answer.

There were motor speed trials in Dublin the same week and we managed to see them before returning home. The Villiers Stuarts, Mr Vere Ponsonby and his friend, Mr Lionel Rothschild, came to stay with us for a few days; Mrs V.S. to practise and play with me at a charity concert at Whitfield, the others passing by on a motor tour. Rather a curious incident occurred at luncheon one day: T received a little parcel, which he opened, showing a small bottle of which none of us could possibly see either the contents or the label. 'What on earth is that', we all cried, and T laughed and answered, 'I bet you a thousand pounds that nobody will guess what it is'. Fortunately, nobody took the bet, but the astute Jew guessed right the very first time and when he said 'Liquid coffee', poor T went quite pale for a moment.

T went up to Dublin with the two young men; Mr Rothschild's car was a 60 horse power and they only touched the ground in spots. T came back quite thrilled by it and determined to waste no time before getting a car and, shortly afterwards, we were in possession of a neat little Gladiator, only about 10 – 12 horsepower, but a little marvel at hill-climbing and quite fast enough for us in those days. T very soon picked up the art of driving, though he was a bit dangerous at first and we had several pretty narrow shaves, notably one in Portlaw Woods when only the weight of three men sitting at the back prevented our turning turtle coming round a corner.

'Daidai', my own dear old Nurse, spent a week with us that month and the only other excitement was the news of the arrival of Susie's first baby (David Dawnay) on July 10th.

On July 21st King Edward and Queen Alexandra paid their first visit to Ireland and we went to stay with the Iveaghs for their Dublin stay. They had a most splendid reception and there was tremendous cheering wherever they went. We saw the procession from Dame Street. T's Yeomanry were on street duty for the first time that day and they looked extremely neat and smart in their khaki breeches and gaiters, and the much discussed green tunics and green caps. I believe they were the first regiment to have these caps, of the 'staff pattern', which have now become general throughout most of the army and they all had khaki waterproof covers for them, which was an idea of T's, both to preserve the caps in bad weather and also to make them match when the khaki tunic was worn.

T took off his officers to the Levée on the 22nd and I heard that they made a very good impression there in the all green uniform worn by officers only. T looked particularly well in his, with the K.P. ribbon and star and I felt very proud of him. There was some agitation in Royal circles because the S.I.Y. had no full-dress head gear; T considered it an unnecessary expense, but the idea of officers attending a Levée with a cap tucked under their arms offended all Royal ideas of propriety and T was in terror that he would be forced to have some ornamental and unpractical head-dress of the inverted coal-scuttle order. But, though many designs were made and the matter was much discussed, it never came to anything in his time. The Northern Yeomanry had a headdress and such an affair it was; a kind of Bersaglieri hat, with no added plumes, so that the Regiment was described somewhere as 'them of the Cock's plumes', and our Southerners called them 'The Barn doors' and, I regret to say, once plucked one of them.

On July 23rd we went to Phoenix Park Races, dined at the Royal Hospital to meet the King and Queen, and then attended a Court at the Castle, not getting home until after 2am. The next evening we went to a party given by the King and Queen at the Viceregal, got to bed at 1am and were up again at 5am to catch the mail train. T, accompanied by Charlie, was going home for a few days before going to the Curragh for his Yeomanry training and I was bound for Co. Kerry to meet the children and had been persuaded by Lady Fitzgerald to spend a day at Valentia on the way. I was shown the Slate Quarry and other curiosities of the Island; also the American Cable Station.

On the 27th I drove on to the Butlers Arms at Waterville and saw the children and nurses established at the house of Mr Fahy, the Clergyman (as lodgers) that evening. After a happy day messing about with the children, ending in a visit to a certain Mrs Butler, famous for having had 5 children in 2 years (twice twins and a singleton in between). I went on my way to Derreen, where I was to help Mother in preparing for a visit from the King and Queen. I drove the 40 miles from Waterville to Kenmare on an outside car – in pelting rain most of the way – and then the remaining 18 on to Derreen in state in the old landau, which was always looked upon as the proper conveyance for the family.

Mother was very excited over the approaching visit, which was only to be a luncheon party, but she was most anxious to show all the beauties of the place to their Majesties. Unfortunately, the morning broke foggy and drizzly – a horrible day – and after a bit came a telegram to say that owing to the fog it would be impossible for their Majesties to carry out the original plans and that they would only be able to come in the afternoon. Great was the disappointment of the poor Cook (the Gardener's wife, formerly cook to the Miss Keysers), who had prepared an appetising luncheon and we were all disappointed. At 4m the party arrived by motor and after eating a large tea, at which I insisted that Mother should give them prawns and periwinkles, they were shown all round the grounds, caught some prawns off the boathouse pier, planted some bamboos in 'the Ousie' and, after expressing themselves highly delighted with all they had seen, departed at 6.30. They left Ireland the next day (August 1st) after a most successful visit, which they promised to repeat before long.

August 1903

I joined T at the Curragh the same day and stayed for over a fortnight with Capt. & Mrs Greer – the kindest of hosts – at Crotanstown, where we had a delightful time. T was, of course, in camp with the S.I.Y., but he and the other officers often came down in the evenings and we used to ride out for field days etc., and sometimes lunch or dine in camp. Mrs Frank Wise, whose husband commanded the Limerick Squadron, was also staying at Crotanstown with her little boy, Billy. The Greers had two sons, Eric and Frank, who were about 9 and 7, or 10 and 8, at the time and both very good riders.

The Duke & Duchess of Connaught were living at the Headquarter Hut and we saw a good deal of them; they took a great interest in the Yeomanry and often rode out to see them at their field days. Soon after I arrived, they both rode into Crotanstown one morning and told me they had been watching the Yeomanry. 'I hope they got on all right, Sir', said I anxiously, 'Well', said the Duke, 'some of the men got out of line'! 'Yes', said the Duchess, 'and they did not get back into line very well'. The poor Yeomen, they had only been in training for a few days and some of them had never sat on a horse before!

T had his new motor at the Curragh, at Crotanstown, and it came in very useful and did a lot of work.

On August 5th we dined with the Connaughts; next morning, at about 8.30am, I happened to look out over the Curragh and saw a horseman galloping towards the house. I wondered who would be in such a hurry and then realized that it was T, who was evidently much agitated. I dashed down to the front door in my dressing-gown, fearing that one of the children was ill, and he told me that he had just had a wire, 'Curraghmore on fire', and was going to motor there at once. The children were away, so there was no anxiety for them, but it was dreadful not to know how serious the fire was and, of course, we imagined the whole place being burnt to the ground.

T and Captain Wise went off together in the motor as soon as they could. T had given various points to which telegrams could be sent on his way, but he drove at such a rate that he just missed every telegram and didn't know how matters stood until he got into the yard, where he found most of the furniture and pictures piled up, but the fire out. It had started through some carelessness over plumbing operations, at which the gasoline lamp was used, which evidently set some bit of timber in the top W.C. alight. It must have smouldered all night and burst out at about 6am when it was discovered, almost at the same moment, by the head housemaid inside and the night watchman outside. A fire extinguisher nearly put it out, but there was a tin of the same gasoline standing in the W.C. and when this caught and flared up matters became serious. As bad luck would have it, Mr Gethin, Bone and Clark were all away and the only person in authority was the Office

Clerk, who completely lost his head; and after bicycling to Portlaw in his pyjamas (to the consternation of the Post Mistress, who felt she really oughtn't to look at him) and sending the same vague telegram to all those that were absent, returned to the house and threw out everything he could lay hands on – pictures, mirrors, china etc., which were a good deal damaged in consequence. It was some time before the hydrants round the house could be got to work, as nobody knew whether to turn on the water from the main supply. At last, however, they were working properly, but even then the fire was gaining and matters looked very serious. Luckily somebody – I think it was Crombie – thought of cutting away the roof in front of the fire and, by doing this, saturating it with water, the progress of the flames was stopped and they were soon got under control. There were really only three rooms badly damaged – the W.C. and the two next bedrooms, but the water spoiled a great many other rooms beyond and below and a great many things were smashed in the scrimmage. T came back that evening and something happened to the motor on the return journey, for I remember that he and Captain Wise arrived back in the middle of the night on an outside car and they were so tired that they simply couldn't keep awake and had to link arms across the well so as not to fall off.

On the 9th, T made a dash over to London to vote on the Irish Land Bill, but returned next day. At the end of the Training, the unfortunate Yeomanry were inspected by three Generals on three consecutive days! On the 12th by General Baden-Powell, on the 13th by the Duke of Connaught, and on the 14th – just before they broke up – by General Rimington. I think they acquitted themselves pretty well, but it was a severe test for a regiment only just formed (General Morton also had a look at them). There were some delightful men among the officers that year; Col.St. Leger Moore was 2nd in command, Major Wise, Major Villiers Stuart (of Dromana) and Sir Kildare Borrowes, commanded the Limerick,

Cork and Kildare squadrons respectively. Captain Burns Lindow was Adjutant and amongst the subalterns were: Mr Aylmer Somerville (commonly called Skibbereen, brother to Miss Somerville, the part author of *An Irish RM*), Mr O'Grady Delmege, who was a great talker and generally made the butt of Skibbereen and others; the Knight of Glin, Captain Stopford – famous for his untidy appearance and big feet – Messrs Furlong, Hewson, Warren, Moore and O'Connor. Then there was Dr McCabe, a funny little man with a round face, who divided his time between medicine and race horses and wrote various pamphlets on Hygiene for man and beast, and Mr Bayliss, the Quarter Master. I must also mention my friend, Sergeant Major White of the Limerick Squadron, who took a leading part in the organization of the sports etc., besides being a very keen soldier. Skibbereen, the Knight and Major Wise were an irrepressible trio, and most amusing, and poor old Mr Delmege had an awful time with them. After B.P.'s inspection, we all had lunch in camp and sports after. It was on this occasion that I was introduced to Lady McCabe, the Doctor's mother, a very comical old lady, who continually put her foot in it and spoke with a terrific brogue. Her comments on the sports were very odd and made her son and daughter most uncomfortable.

At last, when the tent pegging started she turned to the Dr and said, 'Tell me now, Jim, do they do that in real warfare'? 'Well, no, Mother, not exactly, but sometimes they charge'. 'Well then', continued she, 'is it at the tents they charge'? That evening, there was a sing-song in camp and we came over for it – likewise the Connaughts – and all sat round a large bonfire, listening to the songs and other diversions.

On the 14th, the Training ended and we went to Kildare to see the Yeomanry off; after which T joined me at Crotanstown and we departed on the 16th, motoring home via Rathwade, where we had luncheon with the Forbes. It was our first long drive together and went none too smoothly for we had rain most of the way and got very wet, besides losing our way several times and also having various contretemps with the motor. We had a newly trained groom chauffeur then (Mark Purser) and when anything went wrong he had to try at least six different parts of the motor before discovering which was amiss – and this took time! T soon found that plan too trying, both for the motor and his temper, and engaged a fully trained chauffeur called Honeysett.

Lord Dudley had business in Waterford on the 18th and spent the night before at Curraghmore – unofficially – and on the 19th I dashed up to Dublin to try on clothes and met T at Crotanstown, whence we motored up to Glenbride.

The Field Trials took place there on the 20th and 21st and we had Mr Lowe – one of the Judges – staying with us. Later came Mr Adair, Col. Moore, the Wises and Gen. Rimington. At the end of the month Mr Hall-Dare and Major Nugent, but the birds were very scarce that year and there was very little shooting done.

On August 25th we went down to Dublin for the Horse Show, staying at the Viceregal for it. Other diversions were a polo match at Castletown, a delightful dance given by Lady Grosvenor at the Chief Secretary's Lodge, and a very good play, *Monsieur Beaucaire*, in Dublin.

On the 29th we slipped off early, lunched with Major Beresford at Jammet's and all three motored up to Glenbride in the afternoon. Talking of Jammet's – which was then the fashionable restaurant – I had rather a funny experience there a short time before. I was alone in Dublin for the day and thought I might as well go to lunch there, so I walked in by the first entrance I saw, and asked for a cold luncheon. I thought the room was rather plain and bare and was surprised to see no-one else there; one or two cooks were hanging about and an occasional waiter put his head round the door, and looked at me with some amusement, sometimes whispering and winking to the cooks. I felt very shy and uncomfortable and thought Jammet's was an odd place, but after a time an excellent piece of cold beef with salad was produced and, having devoured this and paid a very moderate bill, I went on my way. It was not until I came back to Jammet's in August to lunch there with T that I discovered the restaurant was upstairs and that I had had my cold beef in some grill room or bar, where ladies never went at all!

On the 30th we went to afternoon service at Hollywood – a most dreary barn-like Church – and then motored on to Barretstown, near Ballymore Eustace, to have tea with Sir Kildare and Lady Borrowes. Sir Kildare received us, looking very serious, and told us that his wife would come down presently, but she was just then rather upset about the death of a favourite little dog which had met with an accident. Presently poor Lady Borrowes appeared, red-eyed and tragic, and when I consoled with her about the sad occurrence, the tears ran down her cheeks and between her sobs she said, 'Poor little fellow... he disappeared...yesterday...we searched everywhere for him...and only about an hour ago...he was found...in the Cess-pool'. Somehow, it was very difficult not to laugh, though I really did feel dreadfully sorry for her, for she had no children and adored this little dog.

September and October 1903

In September we went to the North of Ireland. First we stayed with Sir John & Lady Constance Leslie at Glaslough for the Dedication of a Memorial window to the Beresford Primate in Armagh Cathedral. There was a great ceremony for this; a fine service in the Cathedral and afterwards a big lunch given by Primate Alexander at the Library and many Beresford relations turned up.

It was during this visit that I first realized the possibility that Elsie Hope might become my sister-in-law. Kerry, it appeared, had been very attentive to her for some time, but she was very young – hardly eighteen – and her Mother was most anxious that she should see a little more of the world before committing herself.

From Glaslough we went to Baronscourt to stay with our mutual Uncle and Aunt, the Abercorns, and thence to Crom – the Ernes – for one night. We were not much impressed with the latter place; it rained nearly all the time we were there and there was a certain kind of fooling and ballyragging in vogue in the Crichton family, which we found very tedious and tiresome.

On September 8th we were at Rossmore for the Monaghan Show, and after that we went South again and arrived at Kenmare on the 11th. The next day several of the family were in from Derreen and we all met at luncheon. Afterwards we went on by motor to Parknasilla, to which the children had lately been moved. We found them very well and happy and little Tyrone, who always loved the sea, very much improved. He looked a great duck in his knitted jersey and knickers and we felt he was becoming quite a man (2½!). Blanchie used sometimes to bathe, but it never suited her and both her bad eye and her little inside always went wrong at the sea. Katie was all right, but got a pain when she bathed.

After spending a very happy day with the children, we went over to Derreen; Mother and Louise Beaufort coming by boat to fetch us. We stayed there 12 days, T fishing most days and I going on long walks and paying visits with Mother. Father, Kerry and Charlie were also there most of the while and it was a very happy time.

We went to Kenmare on the 24th to see the children off and to pay a visit to the good Nuns at the Convent. On the 26th we went home. A few days later, T went off again, to Austria this time, to pay a visit to the Schönborns. He went first to Styria to the Jagdhaus Brun, where he went chamois shooting and also got some deer; he enjoyed this very much and did some great climbs in pursuit of the deer. He went again the following year and, on his return, Comr Forbes persuaded him to write an account of a day's shooting in Styria for the *Country Gentleman*; this is in my scrap-book, with photographs he brought back with him. After leaving the Schönborns he went on to stay with Prince Auersperg at Pardubice, where he was most kindly received and he was very much struck with the fact that, although he was the only Englishman present, the whole family and others staying there spoke nothing but English at dinner etc.

Meanwhile I was at Curraghmore with Clodagh and her little girl, who stayed with us for a fortnight, I went up to stay with the Perrys at Fethard for one night to try a little thoroughbred horse Willie had got for me called 'Jack Tar', and I went out cubbing on him. Kathleen came to stay, also Aunt Emily Leslie, and T returned on October 17th. I remember the night after he returned. we were sitting in the Blue Drawing Room and he strolled off into the Yellow Drawing Room to play the Pianola, at which he was rather adept. Presently Aunt Emily looked up sharply and said, 'Who is that playing'? 'It is T', I answered. 'But I didn't know he played' – 'Oh, yes, he is very fond of music'. 'Can he read, or does he play by ear'? 'He never has any music'. 'But it's wonderful – wonderful – I had no idea of it', and so on and so on! The poor old lady was completely taken in and we kept her away from the Pianola by telling her that T was very nervous if anyone came near him when he played. He always swayed his body a good deal when playing and his expression and movements really looked as if he were playing the piano. It gave him great pleasure as he was very fond of music and had been very anxious to learn the piano as a boy.

One day about then, T and I went out in the Portlaw Woods to look for deer. There were some fine big fallow stags there, which had long ago escaped from the Deer Park and T had heard one roaring another day, and this time went armed with a rifle to stalk it. We crept noiselessly into the wood and waited a long time, but neither saw nor heard any deer. We did, however, see a very find pair of marten cats – great big ones, with beautiful dark fur – which came bounding past us, quite close, without seeing us. T was very keen on the preservation of these martens, which only now exist where there are big stretches of wood and are often wantonly destroyed by ignorant people (I find this actually occurred in October 1908).

The Opening Meet was at Kilmacthomas that year on October 22nd and I rode Jack Tar. He was a wonderful jumper and very fast. When Hounds were really going he was a joy to ride, but he was much too flippant for this country and very often I was quite unable to hold him.

On October 24th we heard that Kerry and Elsie were engaged – so they hadn't taken very long to think about it after all! We were all very pleased, for we had begun to fear that Kerry would never marry as he was then 31 and had never cared for any girl, or shown any inclination to look about for a wife. Elsie, though 13 years younger than him, was a wonderfully self-possessed girl and, in most ways, very old for her age.

On the 26th I played at a Concert in Waterford for the Nursing Fund and had tea at the Palace after. T very seldom came to hear me play on these occasions, and that day he was engaged in an extensive deer hunt in Portlaw Woods, where the deer were becoming rather a nuisance; so he borrowed some old Hounds and tried to get at them by hunting and shooting. They only got five deer. One hound disappeared and we feared it had got killed, but it returned a day or two later, having run down a wounded deer, and remained gorging it after it died.

A few days later Miss Martin invited me to meet Father Henebry at her house to hear him discourse on Irish music. He was brother to the Grocer in Portlaw, but had been away a great deal and had, for some years, been working up a theory on Irish music and its peculiar scales and 'tonality'. He was very anxious that I should take this up, so as to play the old Irish music correctly on the 'fiddle', but, though I was much interested in it, I saw that it would put one out very much for modern music and that it would be almost impossible to play correctly in both styles. Father Henebry came up to Curraghmore the following week, bringing with him an Irish Piper called Byrne, whom he had picked up off the roads, a really wonderful player. T was delighted with the music and Byrne played to us for ever so long. These were, of course, the 'Peace Pipes' with the bellows under the arm and the extra notes for accompaniments, a far more melodious instrument than the Scottish Bag Pipes, and really suited to playing indoors. It is said that the pipes really originated in Ireland.

November and December 1903

In November 1903 we went to Scotland. We first motored up (on a Sunday) to lunch with the Perrys at Fethard and then on to Thurles, where we caught the Mail. We arrived at Fyvie (the Forbes-Leiths) on November 9th and shot there for four days and went on from there, a 13 hours journey, to Holker, to stay with Evie and Victor. I was only able to stay four days as I had to go South for an Irish Industries Sale at Windsor, but T remained on for a Shoot. I stayed with Susie in London for one night and two at Englemere with the Roberts; sold woollies for two days and had tea with Mother at Windsor Castle, where she was then staying; spent the weekend at Bowood and then met T in London, where we stayed at Lansdowne House for a few days and did a Play every night.

On November 27th Dr Anderson and Sir B. Horsley had a consultation over T's leg, which had been giving him trouble again and they condemned him to three week's massage and electric treatment in a Home, to which he accordingly retired next day, while I returned to Curraghmore to look after the family.

While he was away, I went to a Shooting Party at Shanbally, given by the Pole Carews and Constance Butler, ending up with a day at Cahir Park – of which the shooting had been lent to them – and lunch and tea with the Rochforts, after which I went home.

Willie Perry came down for a hunt with me, but we had a miserable day. The Meet was at Rathgormac and the weather a real 'Rathgormac day' type; wet and cold. We had no sport and 6½ couple of Hounds were poisoned. It was not supposed to be malicious, but it was very depressing nevertheless and it was horrible to see the poor Hounds dying in agonies.

There was a sale of Disabled Soldiers' work in Waterford a few days later, for which I spent a night at the Imperial. Then came the usual series of charities at Xmas time; cloaks and jerseys given to the schoolchildren on the 18th (T gave me the red cloth for the cloaks, from Kilmacthomas Factory); distribution of club tickets, suits and flannel, to the people on the Estate on the 24th; work-house treat at Kilmacthomas (with D. Perry) on the 28th and distribution of flannels etc. in Portlaw on the 29th.

Meanwhile, T had come home; we had a short visit from Lady Gwendoline O'Shee and then our Xmas Party arrived: the Perrys, with Paddy, Mrs Wogan Brown, Major Askwith and Mr Humble. I think it was on this occasion that T and Willie devised an attack on Mr Humble on his way from Kilmeaden Station. Clark had to tell him that the Portlaw road was blocked by a landslide, so that he must come through the woods. There, T, Willie and Major Askwith, disguised in dirty clothes, bandama handkerchiefs, old felt hats and masks, suddenly burst out of the trees and held up the carriage, while Clark, with feigned horror and surprise, said, 'What is this, what is this'! Major Askwith held the horses while T and Willie each put a dirty face in at the window, then seized Mr Humble and bundled him into a sack. The plan was to tie him up to a tree where he was presently to be found and rescued, while they dashed back to the house in a trap which waited round the corner. But after the first moment of surprise, Mr Humble soon realized the joke and we always said that the sight of Willie's feet gave the show away completely. Anyhow, when Mr Humble murmured, 'Mind my hat William' they realized that the game was up and all came home arm-in-arm together, looking like unspeakable ruffians.

On December 23rd, we had the usual children's party for Katie's and Patsy's birthdays, combined with the Steward's Tea downstairs and the Xmas Tree for all together in the Lower Hall.

January 1904

One of our amusements that winter was coursing rabbits with my Italian greyhound puppies and their mother. She (Stella) was quite adept at the game and killed the rabbits in proper greyhound style; the pups, who were entered at 8 months old, were fairly good and it was very pretty to see them move, but they did not improve and soon grew tired of the sport.

The Adairs, Villiers Stuarts, Comr Forbes, Captain Pack Beresford and Major Bingham, the Ormondes and Constance stayed with us for a few days in January; Phyllis Hamilton was with us for over 3 weeks, the Dawnays and Crichtons for over a week and Col. J. Gough for a couple of days. I was hunting on an average 2 days a week and Phyllis rather oftener; she had brought with her a chestnut mare called Jane who was

Mr E. Guinness in Lord Iveagh's motor car at the front door at Curraghmore.

Mr Vere Ponsonby and his friend, Mr Lionel Rothschild, arriving at Curraghmore.

Curraghmore House, Portlaw, County Waterford.

Tyrone rode The Drake to victory in the Waterford Hunt heavyweight race in 1901 and 1902.

Tyrone's first pack of Hounds.

Tyrone with his Jack Russell.

the subject of much discussion. She had been bought from Willie Perry the year before and was alternately, according to Phyll, the biggest brute that ever was known, or the greatest marvel. On the bad days Willie came in for much abuse and then T and I invariably got annoyed after a bit. As a matter of fact, I believe Phyll did this chiefly to rise us!

Maud Morley married Mr Shelford on January 27th in Portlaw.

The Crichtons brought 2 dogs and assured us we should never know they were in the house. The first night, they both came dashing downstairs in hot pursuit of our Gyp, she yelping with rage, and they barking delightedly as they routed her; next morning our carpets and passages had been made so much use of that it was hard to think two dogs could have had such capacity!

Both Susie and Molly Crichton were expecting infants, so could neither hunt, nor go to the Hunt Ball, to which we all went on the 29th. We danced till 3am and slept at the Imperial and the next day the men and Phyllis hunted, the latter mounted by Mr Widger on a wild young grey horse. He amused us by writing the day before that his, 'old coachman' would take the horse to the Meet. One saw visions of a respectable old family servant, with cockaded hat etc., but the actual horse-copers ruffian, with a handkerchief round his neck, differed widely from the vision!

February 1904

On February 8th Blanchie, Katie and I went over to London, staying at Lansdowne House, for Kerry and Elsie's wedding, which took place on the 16th at Marylebone Church, Stratford House being lent for the reception afterwards. Blanchie (aged 5) and Katie (4) were bridesmaids and looked great ducks in their long muslin frocks with lace finches and caps. Blanchie was most self-possessed and Katie behaved very well. Her page (Pat Guthrie) took the greatest care of her and handed her downstairs at Stratford House in the most courtly manner.

While we were in London, Tony Anson was christened and the Teck-Albany wedding took place. On the 20th the little girls and I went to Badminton. The three children there were about the same age as B & K, so they had great fun together – also, a good many quarrels! Granny Beaufort came over from Stoke on purpose to see us and I photographed her with her five little grand-children and great-grandchildren.

We left on the 22nd; Constance Scott joined us en route and went over with us for a fortnight. She had once been to France, but never crossed the Irish Channel before and she was a very bad sailor and extremely nervous. I recommended xxx stout, which I always took at that time and, after some protest, Constance took it, but instead of getting straight into her bunk after she would wander about the cabin and, presently, when I begged her to hurry up, she answered in an aggrieved tone, 'But I want to wash my hands'! 'Well – wash them', said I. Then I saw her fumbling with the basin knob and, still more aggrieved, she murmured 'It says Pressh, but I pressh and noshing happensh'! Poor Constance, the stout not only went straight to her head, but she was sick the whole way over and that was from Milford, quite double the length of the present crossing. She was very much amused by all the old women driving ass carts and every time we met one she went into fits of laughter.

We found Prince Vuiceuz Auersperg (whom I had already met at luncheon at Lansdowne House) at Curraghmore and after he left came Reggie and Ben Herbert, Charlie and Aileen. The Huberts were with us for 10 days, during which time he had an attack of appendicitis, or something very like it; and she, having started a baby a few weeks, was walking very delicately! Aileen was with us for 3 weeks and Charlie for nearly as long and we had great fun hunting all together. Aileen contributed several sketches to my scrap book (Vol IX). The 'Delegate from America' was a stranger who appeared out hunting a few times and whom she sketched from descriptions only, but quite accurately. We wondered what sort of a Delegate he was, but it afterwards transpired that he was only delicate and home from America!

There was the sketch of the young cart-horse which, scared by our motor, leapt right over the bank by the side of the road and into the field; and another of our sad plight when the motor, having shied off a cow which wouldn't get out of the way, embedded its wheels in the boggy ground beside the road and utterly refused to stir out of it, while the men pushed and we stood miserably waiting in the rain.

Blanchie first tried the violin (the same I had begun on) when Aileen was there and she also made sketches of this, and the two little girls singing, which they did quite nicely then.

March 1904

I went to Dublin on March 17th for the first of the Yeomanry dinners, afterwards an annual event. A few days later, we went over to England for the Grand National; Aileen travelled with us as far as Holyhead and I well remember the difficulty we had in rousing her before landing (I think it must have been the stout again) and how, when I said, 'We are just getting into Holyhead', she merely murmured 'Holyhead; why Holyhead?' and slept again till I shook her.

T and I slept at Holyhead and went on early next day, lunching at Chester and arriving at Croxteth in the evening. On March 25th (my 27th birthday) the Grand National was run and won by Moifaa. There were 28 starters and 19 of them fell.

On the 28th (T having already gone to London) I started early, meaning to catch the afternoon train from Kingsbridge. I missed it by a few minutes and I well remember returning crestfallen to Powers Hotel, and the sympathy shown by Miss Power and all the staff, 'Isn't it too bad you've missed your train – Joseph! Her Ladyship missed her train, isn't it too bad'...and the same to James and Maria and the Buttons etc. etc.

Going by the evening train, I got an awful scare that my only companion in the carriage – an elderly bearded man – was going to drug me as he had a large bag and the carriage smelt strong of chloroform. After a few words of conversation I felt happier and though I kept an eye on him from behind my newspaper for some time, I finally concluded he was harmless (no doubt a doctor who had been at an operation) and shared my sandwiches with him.

April 1904

T returned three days later and the next fortnight was taken up with Point-to-Point meetings, and the last of the hunting. The Waterford Point-to-Point was on April 5th. T mistook the flags in his race and discovered his mistake too late. My Jack Tar, ridden by Mr Hanley, fell when he was winning easily. We stayed with the Perrys for the Tipperary Point-to-Point, near Killinan, in which T rode the Rogue, but was not placed. The Forbes, Perrys and Captain Kincaid Smith was with us for the 5th and there was, as usual, much walking of the course and discussing of the merits.

I remember a delightful run from Ballyvoyle on April 9th, when I rode the old Wanderer, who was then 18 or 19 years old, but carried me quite splendidly. I was following T – as always did then – and had hard work to keep him in sight after going up a long hill, but the Wanderer was a gallant little horse and was game up to the end of his life.

Mr George Malcomson resigned the Mastership at the end of that season. Mr Pollok was the next Master, but he was not appointed until some time later. I played at a concert in Carrick on the 12th and the next day we went out with 'the Bessborough Dogs', but had bad sport. T never cared to go out with them and would not treat them seriously, which rather distressed me as I felt sure they noticed his want of respect or interest. The Mander always declared that Bertie Ponsonby's mode of encouraging Hounds to go into covert was to shout 'Cabbages, fine cabbages', and certainly these methods were unusual and they never troubled to acquire any of the real science of hunting.

The last day that T hunted (in Tipperary – April 18th) I sat out till 7pm – hardly hunting weather. I remember a lovely walk through Portlaw Woods a few days later, when T and I dropped into Coolfinn via the hen house at the back!

On the 25th we motored up to Dublin, via Rathwade, but with our usual bad luck when going there we broke down about 2 miles this side of Bagenalstown, to which we had to walk, and then take an outside car on to Rathwade, where the Mander received us with brutal and unsympathetic laughter 1½ hours late for luncheon!

The year, the King and Queen came over for Punchestown week on a visit to Lord & Lady Dudley, and we were asked to stay at the Viceregal Lodge to meet them. They came straight from Kingstown to Naas on the 26th. At Naas the Procession was formed and we all drove in state to Punchestown. There was racing every day:- Punchestown, Phoenix Park and Leopardstown. The Dudleys had about 6 state carriages, all beautifully turned out and we processed everywhere. The King and Queen were splendidly received wherever they went and the visit went off very well. In the evenings there were dinners, a dance at the Royal Hospital and the Theatre.

Poor Lady Dudley was in bed all the time, as she had been threatened with a miscarriage and was not allowed to move, but she received everyone in her bedroom, where she lay in a pink-ribboned and be-muslined bed, beautifully coiffed, and wearing a low necked nightgown which was more like an evening gown.

The old Duke & Duchess of Devonshire were of the party at the Viceregal, and both T and I made great friends with the latter. T was charming to her and she took the greatest fancy to him, so they chatted away like old friends. Afterwards, T said to me 'I'll tell you what, that old Duchess is quite the nicest person in the party'. He always got on well with old ladies, for whom he had a specially gentle and courteous manner.

On the 30th, we left by motor, taking Edwina Roberts with us. It was a perfect day for motoring, but just as we were congratulating ourselves on not being in the train, the motor broke down! We were near Kilcullen at the time, so we went back there, hired a car, and drove to Crotanstown, from whence – after lunching with Mrs Greer – we made our way home by train. The crowds were awful, as hundreds of police were being drafted to Waterford for the King's visit and I can still see T walking up and down the platform looking for seats, with the sack containing all the wraps trailing behind him in the dust!

May and June 1904

*L*ord Dudley and his staff, and several other people, stayed with us for the King's visit and on May 2nd we all went in to Waterford to meet their Majesties. There was a great banquet at the City Hall, at which I found myself between the King and Lord Dudley. T, whose Yeomanry had furnished the Royal Escort, wore the S.I.Y. uniform, but he had to change after the Banquet, so as to receive their Majesties in ordinary clothes at the Agricultural Show. There was very little time for all this and, as he was driving up to the Show, he got held up by the crowd just as the Royal procession was coming along and suddenly realized that unless he took to his feet he had no chance of reaching the Showground in time. So he jumped down and ran for his life, till at last a Police Officer took pity on him and lent him his horse, on which he galloped up – top hat and all – and only just got through in time! The Show was not a brilliant affair and we felt rather ashamed of the poor exhibition of jumping.

After it was over, their Majesties went on to stay at Lismore and we came on also in the Royal train. They were only there 2 days and nothing of special interest occurred there, except a motor expedition over the mountains to Shanbally, in which I thoroughly disgraced myself. I had never been over any of this country before, though I had motored to Shanbally from the other side and was much looking forward to the drive in our little open car, with T and one or two others. At the last moment, however, I was told that I was to go with the King in his shut motor, a horrible thing like an omnibus and with solid tyres. This was bad enough, but after we had been a little way, I realized that I was put there as the local lady and expected to give information about the country we were passing through. It was too awful and I never had such a miserable drive. At last I recognized Shanbally and said 'Here we are', and then we went straight through the place and out at the other end; so, utterly flabbergasted, I ate my words and said it must be some other place, perhaps Cahir Park! Presently we arrived at a lodge and a beautiful rhododendron avenue and I said this must be the Ormondes' mountain lodge – for I had no idea that there was also a mountain lodge belonging to Shanbally. The King, of course, thought me an absolute idiot and I was unmercifully chaffed about the whole thing afterwards, but it really was a miserable afternoon. After admiring the rhododendrons we went back to Shanbally for tea and then back over the mountains via Cappoquin.

Their Majesties left on May 4th and that afternoon the Duchess drove me up to see Ballysaggartmore, which Claud and Clodagh had just bought. We returned next day. Edwina was still there and we had a very nice peaceful time after all the gaieties and pomp of the last 10 days. We generally rode before breakfast and took many long walks. There was a sudden cold spell for a few days and on May 8th and we actually had a severe hail storm and snow on the mountains.

The Perrys, Ansons and Mrs Bingham stayed with us for a few days; then, on the 16th, we went over to England, taking Blanchie and Katie with us, and Edwina also travelling with us as far as Bristol. From there T and I motored up to London – a distance of 120 miles – we averaged 20 miles an hour in our little car and thoroughly enjoyed the drive, stopping only for luncheon at Marlborough. We had taken Susie and Hugh's house, 34 Seymour Street, for 3 weeks, with servants and all complete, and we were very comfortable there and had quite a nice time in London, as usual spending a good many afternoons at Ranelagh and Hurlingham. We motored down to tea with the Marcus Beresfords at Bishopsgate and on to Englemere, where Lord Roberts and Aileen arrived after us, having just returned from visiting the Field of Waterloo. From there we motored to Farnborough, where Kerry and Elsie were then established; and later we took Blanchie to Deepdene to see Aunt Lily and little Billy and, incidentally, took Aunt Lily for her first motor drive, which (though it terrified her) led to her purchasing a motor soon after.

I remember a delightful ball at Devonshire House on Derby night at which we met all our old friends and contemporaries, and felt quite young again, and danced till 3am. When it was nearly all over, T and I were dancing together, and fairly letting ourselves go in the half-empty ballroom. We stopped for a minute near the old Duchess, who tapped me on the shoulder and said, 'Go on, go on dancing – I like to see you two dance'.

The next evening we dined with Captain E. Charteris – T's great friend – and afterwards went on to Lansdowne House to meet the King and Queen, who had, I think, been dining there.

Two days later, Edwina and I motored to Portsmouth (Alverstoke) over 80 miles, to stay with the Aubrey Smiths. He was then in command of the Training Ship *Iris*, and we went on board for Church and lunch next day, and afterwards visited the Docks ,and then sailed about in the harbour for the rest of the afternoon. Elsie came back with us on the 6th. We lunched with Elsie K at Farnborough and went to Hurlingham for a polo match on the way home.

On June 9th we left Seymour Street and moved Tyrone and Patsy to Lansdowne House; Blanchie and Katie had already been there for 10 days. Tyrone and Patsy had taken their place with us at Seymour Street. Mother always loved to have the children and was quite happy when she had them all with her, but T had a horror of 'sponging on the family' and also was rather afraid that the children would get spoiled by their fond Grandmother! However, Mother had her way this time and kept the children for some time. We ourselves went to stay with the Roberts at 47 Portland Place and were there for 10 days or more. Those dear people having insisted that we should treat their house as our own and come and go as we wished.

From there we went down to Hurlingham on Lord Shrewsbury's coach, and lunched with him before some big polo match; afterwards going on to Roehampton, where T played in a match. The following day we took the Hopes down to Coombe to pay an afternoon visit to the Charlie Beresfords. The party collected there was on the same lines as the one at Ham years before. Aunt Nina, freely painted and with eyebrows marked at impossible angles, was wandering in the wood with some foreign gentleman and did not appear for ages, while Uncle Charlie only turned up just as we were leaving. Kathleen seldom showed herself on these occasions and only came down when she realized we were there, so for some time we were left to our own devices with a lot of complete strangers, many of them foreigners, and we all registered a vow that wild horses wouldn't drag us down there again.

One night, Aileen, T and I went to see Réjane in *La Montansier*; other evenings, one amusement was a Ball at Buckingham Palace, and others the opera *Faust* and *Veronique*. One day Blanchie, Katie and Tyrone came to luncheon and another day I took them all to a children's party at Montagu House; while I very often took the two little girls to dancing lessons at Mrs Wordsworth's. They were all photographed by Speaight on June 20th and the next day Blanchie and Katie went with me to the Christening of Guendoln, Beatrix Wilkinson's eldest daughter, while Tyrone and Patsy were specially invited to her christening party in the afternoon. By this time, I had joined the children at Lansdowne House, as T had gone over to Curraghmore, en route to the Curragh.

On the 23rd I took the three elder children to a party at Buckingham Palace, at which little Tyrone caused some amusement. He had been very much worried some time because the Lifeguard's Sentry at Knightsbridge Barracks no longer wore his be-plumed helmet, and did not, he thought, look at all smart in a cap. Mother said he had better ask the King about it, so Tyrone – then aged three, and wearing a white tunic and panama hat – boldly addressed the King, 'Oh – King – why do your soldiers wear caps instead of helmets'? (only he said 'carps' and 'horlmets'). The King was much amused and was, I fear, quite unable to answer the question. On making his farewell bow, Tyrone was much bothered with his hat, so finally laid it on the grass before him and made obeisance over it, with both hands clasping his little tummy!

There was an enormous party at Lansdowne House the next evening, after a men's dinner, and that was the last of the gaieties there for me as I departed the day after – June 25th, leaving the children to go on to Eastbourne for change of air.

June and July 1904

I arrived at the Curragh at 10pm and went to stay with Lord & Lady Grenfell at the Headquarter Hut for 10 days and there on to Crotanstown for a week. I hardly knew the Grenfells before, but they were the kindest and friendliest of people and I soon felt as if I had known them for years. Mrs Wise was also invited there and we went on at the same time to the Greers. There the pleasure of our visit was somewhat marred by the present of Mrs Barclay, a sister of Lord Decies, whom I had always carefully avoided meeting and to whom Jean Wise had a strong aversion, which was evidently mutual, for Mrs Barclay never missed an opportunity of being aggressively rude to her. It was most unpleasant and we often wished ourselves back in the peaceful atmosphere of the Headquarter Hut.

I rode with Lord Grenfell or some of his staff nearly every morning while we were at the Curragh and we generally watched the Yeomanry at Drill or Field Day. They had improved a great deal since the last training and were really becoming quite a fine Regiment and, though T always lamented the shortness of the training and the want of compulsion in discipline, he was really very proud of them. They certainly looked very smart at the General Parade for Church and marched up in excellent order, and they were becoming much more efficient in the field and rode much better than they had.

In recognition of all this, they were allowed a sham fight against the 19th Hussars – who, I believe, were somewhat disgusted at having to take the field against mere Yeomen. There were the usual inspections and sports, with Sing Song after; General Morton's place had been taken by General Thorneycroft. The latter had a step-daughter who was most original and delighted in blurting out loud – and sometimes somewhat vulgar – remarks, which greatly distressed her gentle Mother. Once, when Captain Seymour (Lord Grenfell's A.D.C.) was dining there and was hesitating over his choice of wine after being offered all the contents of the cellar by the Butler – the charming young lady turned round to him and said, with the baddest of brogues, 'All Aleck's wine's muck'. She always called her stepfather Aleck, and they seemed to be the best of friends.

One day, T and I motored to Hollywood, taking with us Florita St. Aubyn, whose husband was Lord Grenfell's Secretary. We explored all the park and the woods, but as we penetrated into the latter we suddenly came on a lot of men, of the 'corner boy' type, armed with stout sticks, beating up the bushes and bracken, and yelling encouragement to their greyhounds and terriers, who were hunting hard. T was much annoyed and walked straight up to one or two of the men, asking their names and what business they had to be there. Of course, they did not know him and, as his only weapon was a light cane and some of them were unpleasant looking ruffians, Florita and I felt decidedly nervous. The men looked very surly and grudgingly gave names – but not their own – and then continued their hunting, quite unabashed; we were never able to identify them, but were told they probably came from Ballymore Eustace.

On July 12th, the training being over, we motored home and this time we carefully avoided Rathwade for fear of another breakdown!

While at the Curragh, we had been to see the Borrowes again, and now they came to stay with us, as Sir Kildare was playing in a cricket match in Waterford. Mr Pollok, the new Master, also paid us a visit.

We were only home for about 10 days and then started off on a motor trip, starting with a couple of days at Shanbally, where we met Lord Grenfell, and going from thence all the way to Recess in Galway, via Cahir, Thurles, Roscrea, Loughrea and Galway. It was a run of about 160 miles and we were pretty tired at the end of it and arrived fairly soaked as the rain had come down in torrents during the last 2 hours. Except for that, we thoroughly enjoyed it and, this being our first really long run, we felt we had done a big thing. The car was very small and I can't think how we got everything into it; a small box each, spare tyres and many tins of petrol, besides ourselves and the Chauffeur. The entrance was at the back, so there was no grid for boxes and whoever sat at the back (T and Honeysett took turns driving) was perched on boxes and bags and had no leg room at all. I shall never forget a nervous old lady who was on the road in front of us – a farmer's wife, in a decent black gown and mantle, driving an ass cart with long tail pieces at the back. In mortal terror at the approach of the motor, she hurled herself off the back of the cart – her gown got caught up on the tail shafts, well above her waist and, alas, she had no drawers! There was a wondrous vision of fat legs above the black stockings and her plight was so ridiculous that we sat there in the car, simply convulsed with laughter and when she had replaced her skirts we passed by, composing our faces to anxious concern for her welfare, but T's polite enquiry elicited no response but a scowl of furious rage and much outraged dignity.

At Recess, rooms had been arranged for us by old General Mostyn Beresford – 'the Snipe' – a great old ally of T's. During the 5 days that we were there they fished together all day and every day. Sometimes I joined them and sat in the boat listening to the Snipe's dissertations on fishing, interlaid with instruction in 'British-Israel Truth', for he firmly believed that we were descended from the ten lost tribes and was much distressed at our want of interest in the subject. He was a great old sportsman and had shot countless tigers in India in his youth. Since then, he had devoted most of his time to fishing and there was nothing he didn't know about it. He gave or left T all his fishing tackle and his collection of sporting books and T always said that he owed the whole of his knowledge of fishing entirely to the Snipe's teaching when he was a boy. Those two were perfectly happy together and, besides their common taste for fishing and sport in general, they both adored spring onions and garlic!! When they were lunching out, I always said I could wind them a mile away.

The Snipe was a woman hater and especially hated 'giggling females', and many were the warnings which T gave me on this subject. Mercifully, the Snipe was immediately prejudiced in my favour by the sight of the tiny box into which I had packed my few clothes and he was always most charming to me. On this occasion he tidied up his fishy sanctum in my honour and always made me sit in his own armchair after dinner.

Memoirs
Notebook Three

(Begun May 1914). Put aside owing to press of business during the War – but taken up again in March 1918.

July and August 1904

On July 30th 1904 T and I left Recess; I was very anxious to motor further North, but in those days there were many drawbacks to motoring, for there were not many petrol stations and still fewer places where one could get an electric battery renewed or re-charged and, as magneto ignition was only just being introduced, most cars were entirely dependent on their batteries. T was not ready to face all these difficulties in an unfrequented part of the country, so we decided to go South instead and work our way down to Co. Kerry. We stayed one night at Cruise's Hotel in Limerick, a horribly dirty and uncomfortable little hotel.

The roads all round there were atrociously bad and in the 97 miles we did that day we had the unpleasant experience of going through several thunderstorms. The next day we were more fortunate and did the 70 miles to Killarney fairly comfortably before luncheon. The day was drizzly and I remember that when we asked the German waiter what he thought of the prospects of the weather, he replied, 'Ah, the rain it is not much, it is only like a little perspiration'.

The next day we played the tourist and took a guide in the motor with us, round the lakes and Muckross etc. I remember that our chauffeur showed no interest whatever in the beauties of the place, but was quite thrilled over some skulls and other bones that were sticking up out of the ground in a part of the old Abbey!

On August 2nd we continued our journey and had a perfectly lovely drive round by Caragh Lake, where we stopped for luncheon – and on to Valentia, where we spent a night with the Fitzgeralds. Unfortunately, the next day was very wet and we had no view as we went along that lovely bit of coast road from Waterville to Kenmare, which I had been especially anxious to show T. We stayed three nights at Kenmare; T taking a day's fishing on the Sheen, and another at Glenmore. Then, the weather was so unsettled that T grew sick of the motoring and so we went home by train.

During the short time we were at home – only 8 days – and on a day when T had gone into Waterford, I had a visit from the Duchess of St. Albans, who brought over a large party to luncheon:- Clodagh, Sir Arthur Nicholson, Sir Alfred Austin and Reshid Bey. The Duchess nearly came to an untimely end driving over as the end of her boa slipped off the carriage and got caught in the wheel, which so rapidly tightened the boa round her neck that she was quite unable to speak and nearly suffocated. Fortunately, Clodagh noticed her dilemma and caught hold of the boa just in time to save her from strangulation!

Sir Arthur Nicholson was a most charming man and so interesting that I longed to get a chance of talking to him quietly, but the Poet Laureate was persuaded that he was the centre of attraction and expected everyone to listen all the while to his mawkish maunderings. His conceit was colossal and I believe that he also imagined that he had an irresistible attraction for the ladies! Reshid Bey, a young Turk, who at that moment seemed to have little to do beyond selling cigarettes in England, was a pleasant, easy going young man, who made himself quite at home and calmly stretched his length on the sofa after luncheon.

Sir Owen Slacke was with us for a few days and I rather think it was about this time that T decided to take over the management of his own financial affairs from him, though, as Trustee, Sir Owen still retained an almost unlimited control over all our investments. T had a sort of feeling that things weren't going quite right, but, unfortunately, he was not a very good business man and Sir Owen succeeded in putting him off the scent, both this time and on future occasions; and it was not until after T's death that it was discovered that Sir Owen and Mr Beauclerk (our Stockbroker) between them had defrauded us of thousands of pounds.

On August 15th we motored up to Glenbride – Commander Forbes joining us there. We were only there a week and the birds were scarce on most of the beats. T, impressed by the comfort of the shorts worn in the Tyrol the year before, now took to the same costume for Glenbride and gained such great freedom in walking that the poor Mander found it hard to keep up with him, as can be seen by his sketch in my book. While we were at Glenbride came the news that Patsy had got chickenpox at Eastbourne; two days later Blanchie got it, but the other two didn't develop it until 10 days afterwards. Luckily there were no complications, but it was of course a great worry to us.

Meanwhile, we had left Glenbride and gone to stay with the St. Aubyns at the Royal Hospital for the Dublin Horse Show. While we were there, the Grenfells gave a dinner and a dance at which we all enjoyed ourselves. One day we motored down to Kingstown, lunched on H.M.S. *Caesar*, Uncle Charlie's Flagship, and afterwards went all over her. Uncle Charlie was most kind to us and he certainly appeared to much greater advantage on his ship than surrounded with his 'Little Do's' friends at Coombe! All the officers and men were, I believe, quite devoted to him and he was said to look after his midshipmen with fatherly care.

On 27th I went down to Derreen, travelling with Louise Beaufort, who stayed there for about 10 days. The only other person there, outside the actual family, was poor Audrey Anson, whose husband – my cousin Henry – had died under such tragic circumstances 6 months before. Our hearts all ached for her, but her pluck was splendid and the memory of it helped me, even seven years after, to bear my sorrow.

T joined us a few days later and we stayed for some while at Derreen. There were several very large Japanese deer on Dourus – the point opposite Derreen – and as they did a good deal of damage, Father was anxious that they should be shot. T was delighted and went stalking at 4am several times, but the noise made by the heavy tread of Sheamus, the Keeper, usually frightened away every deer within miles. At last, however, T was successful in killing a very fine stag, whose horns were nearly a record and who was always spoken of as 'The General' on account of his noble proportions. The Leeds were on their yacht in Sneem Harbour and one evening Mother, Charlie and I went over and dined with them on board, while Leeds came over to fish at Glenmore another day.

September and October 1904

On September 6th I went off to Cork for an Irish Industries Sale, returning 2 days later with Uncle Freddy Hamilton, whom I met at Mallow. The sale lasted till 10pm each evening and it was weary work, but all the sellers were very kindly looked after and entertained by Mr Power, of whiskey fame, who gave us luncheons and dinners, provided smelling salts and eau de cologne for the very weary, and finally saw us all off, providing each with a bunch of violets and a bundle of newspapers!

I remember a big man at that sale, and whom we had begun to eye with some suspicion. At last he came and turned over my gloves and said they were very nice, but that he wanted to have a good look round before he decided on anything. Presently he returned and, with a strong Irish American accent, said 'May I enquire whom I am addressing'. I gave my name, whereupon he at once said 'Well, then I guess I'll just purchase a pair of gloves from you'. After much trying on, he selected a pair and as he went off with them he said 'Well. I guess there'll be many a cold day in winter when I'll be thinking of you'.

After I got back to Derreen there was a school treat, at which T, as usual, was very good at organizing the races and steeplechases etc. One day, he and I, in the absence of all the others, went off to explore Coomenguirah, the pocket in the mountains above Glenmore. I remember, when we got to the solitary farmhouse up at the top, how charming T was to the old couple living there and with what good grace he submitted to the customary drinking of new milk, while he chatted away with the old lady, as far as her limited knowledge of English would go. He left Derreen on September 14th, going to Limerick on Yeomanry business en route to Curran, where he was going to do some stalking and fishing with the Hamiltons.

I left five days later, taking Uncle Freddy with me to Curraghmore for a few days. On the way we had breakfast with Kerry and Elsie at the Falls, and also spent an hour at Mallow looking for the Spa (which Uncle F would call the Spaw) which, when found, turned out to be a most unattractive looking well in the middle of a small house, whose owners apparently used the water for all purposes of cooking, in spite of the very strong properties it was said to possess.

The children, having at last got over the chickenpox, came home on the 20th and T returned 4 days later, but he was not with us for long as he went off to Styria again on the 29th. Before he left, Mr Pollok came to stay with us and we went out cub hunting at 6am two mornings running. We also had a flying visit from Mother and

Charlie, who were motoring through from Derreen. T was away for over a fortnight; he had a very good time in Styria and the following extracts from a letter received from him tell their own tale.

'I have had splendid sport here. I got a nice stag on Sunday evening!! (tell it not in Gath) and yesterday morning I was called at 3am and started at 3.30am in the dark, went up for 2¾ hours – very steep, and got a very fair stag at 6.15, just after daylight. He fell dead about 50 yards from where I shot him, hit through the lungs. I had barely shot him when we heard another roar just above. I went and saw him and could have had a splendid shot at him, but decided to let him go, as he was just about the same as the one I had just shot. We then went on further and came across a fine buck chamois and stalked him for nearly two hours, when he finally got our wind and went. I lay up then for 3 hours until 3 o'clock and had lunch and some sleep, and then went on again. We could hear several stags roaring in the distance and I decided not to shoot until I saw a really nice one. Eventually I successfully stalked him and shot him clean through the heart at 100 yds; an old stag with a very fair head. I could easily have shot five stags in the day if I had liked to make a slaughter, but am not so bloodthirsty as all that; and I eventually got back here at 7.15pm, pretty well tired out, but having had a most enjoyable day'.

After his return, T was persuaded to write an account of this day's shooting for the *Country Gentleman*.

As I have already mentioned, Lady Gwendoline O'Shee, Clodagh Anson, Magdalen Herbert and Miss Martin stayed with me while T was away and on October 15th he returned.

Charlie had left for India – to re-join his regiment – on the 14th. 10 days later Kerry and Elsie came and stayed with us on their way to England.

November 1904

On November 1st the Opening Meet was held in Waterford and T, of course, went to it, but I was to get no hunting that winter for I was what Mrs Brand called 'carrying'! For the same reason I did not accompany T when he went on a visit to the Londesboroughs at Blankney, but I went with him the following week to Rossmore and afterward to Abbey Leix. In those pre-thermos days, I always took a little tea basket with me and brewed tea in the train, in spite of T's protests at the nuisance of it. On this journey, a man who was also bound for Rossmore, and whom T knew slightly, happened to be in the same carriage with us, so of course I offered him a cup of my tea. Luckily for him, the cup was very small for the brew was a horrible failure and, having turned away to look out of the window, I happened to turn my head back just in time to see our friend hastily pouring his share under the seat!

Amongst the party at Rossmore were Mary Abercorn, Lord & Lady Annesley, Sir Archibald and Lady Edmonstone etc. Lady Edmonstone's laugh was a constant source of amusement to us, for its range depended entirely on the extent to which she was amused and at its top pitch a hooting owl wasn't in it with her. Lord Rossmore was, as usual, most amusing and somewhat 'risqué' in his stories, for at that time he had not 'taken religion', which caused him afterwards to reform all his wicked ways for a time, and to give up after dinner stories entirely. After a three day's shoot, we departed South and, in passing through Dublin, we paid a visit to Lady Grenfell and the newly arrived little daughter, after which we went on to Abbey Leix for a couple of days and then home.

November and December 1904

The great domestic event that autumn was the starting of a schoolroom, Blanchie being now six years old and Katie nearly five. T, on one of his trips to London, had interviewed a governess called Miss Scott, who accordingly arrived on November 22nd and the schoolroom was established in the little room on the West side, which is now the 'second schoolroom'. It was at this time that little Katie asked 'Can God see everything'?, and on being told 'Yes', she said: 'Then I'm sure he must be very surprised to see us doing lessons'. The little girls took fairly kindly to their work, though Katie was at times very tearful over it. Blanchie made rapid progress and was very soon able to read and write.

Another household excitement was the arrival of the new crimson pile carpet for the front stairs and first floor landing. There was rather an ugly blue and red brussels there before, which was quite worn out and the acquisition of the present carpet was a great delight.

Phyllis stayed with us for nearly a month in November and December and hunted a good deal with T; he, however, had to go over to London to have his Rider's Muscle treated again, as it was most painful and troublesome. While he was away, Phyll and I went to Ballysaggart for a couple of days to stay with Clodagh, who was alone with her children, Claud having gone out to his ranch in Texas.

On December 1st, I opened a Y.W.C.A. sale in Waterford, at which, after the usual singing of hymns, an old clergyman prayed earnestly that all present might be imbued with the spirit of generosity, and ended by calling a blessing on 'this thy handmaiden, who has opened our Bazaar'!

Phyllis had an interesting experience of the blood-charm one day that she was hunting. She had cut her horse very badly and got separated from T and everyone else, so she made her way to a farm to ask if they had a bandage of any sort. The farmer's wife said they had nothing suitable there, but that if she would go up the road to old Mackey's house, he would be able to 'do something' for her. The old man, who was a retired blacksmith, came out at once, but instead of producing a bandage, he asked Phyllis her name and for the use of her handkerchief, which was quite a small cambric one. This he tied very loosely round the cut, then he went behind the horse; and Phyllis, wondering what he was doing, suddenly turned round and discovered him on his knees in the road, his hat off, and his arms extended in prayer. Not till then did she think of the blood-charm, of which she had some prior knowledge. The incantation ended, Mackey got up and told her to go on her way and only to stop for a minute when she had gone a short distance. After that, he said, the bleeding will stop and you'll have no further trouble with it. It happened exactly as he had said and yet the cut was a very deep one and had been spurting blood till he touched it.

Not very long after, I met a man ('Skibbereen' of the S.I.Y.) who 'had the blood-charm', and had himself used it successfully and he passed it on to me, one of the conditions being that it must always pass from man to woman, or from woman to man, or the charm will be broken. I have never had a chance of using it, nor do I know whether I should have the necessary faith, for I do not believe that the power can be given to all alike. Undoubtedly, however, these and other charms are well known in Ireland and are still used fairly extensively by some of the poor people. T, though a sceptic in many things, firmly believed in the blood-charm after Phyllis's experience. Shortly after this, he took a toss, and hurt his shoulder, which disabled him for a week. Phyllis left and we had a short visit from Captain Jennings, the new Adjutant of the S.I.Y., a young man who, unlike his otter hunting brother, was mostly good looks and 'blather'.

Christmas approached with its usual sequence of charities. We had 340 children for the school treat and I had a new recipe for a Xmas pudding, made of dates, which we gave to all the people at the Almshouses and Sallyhene Cottages that year. The Industry had a tea party and many of the workers who had joined the Industry Saving Club, drew out quite tidy little sums for their Xmas shopping. The flannels and clothes were distributed as usual and we had a children's tea party for the double birthday and the Stewards' tea on New Year's Eve.

The Greers and their two boys stayed with us for Xmas and I remember some long walks with Captain Greer, in a vain effort to see something of the stag hunting in the woods and fox hunting from Guilcagh, in which the others were taking part.

On Christmas Day, Little Tyrone came to Church for the first time; Blanchie and Katie being by then regular attendants. Blanchie always sang the hymns and chants, long before she could read, and picked up the tunes wonderfully quickly, but when she happened to know the words, great was her joy, and she sang most lustily. Her favourite hymn was 'Pleasant are thy Courts'. She had rather a curious pronunciation and in the second verse she always sang 'Happy Bords that sing and fly', which delighted T. Behind us in Church sat Miss Curtis, who, in the Benedictus, always made us jump by the violent emphasis she laid on 'them that hate us', and whose 'Amens' filled the Church with their sonorous sound. The position of the Pulpit and Organ were at that time reversed and we sat on the right of the Aisle. The moving of the organ to its present position was a great improvement, as, on the left side, it stood out into the Church and looked all wrong.

Writing of Blanchie's quaint pronunciation reminds me of a charming phrase of hers when someone asked her the cause of a little scar on her leg. She was then, I suppose, about three years old and never could manage her Cs and Ks, and her reply was 'I tut it on Tatie's Tart'. Another incident of those earlier days occurred in my Sitting Room when she bumped her head against a table and, observing that I was busy writing, she turned to the footman and, blinking back her tears, she presented the injured part to him, saying 'Henry, shall we tiss it'? But this was years before the time of which I am now writing, when Blanchie and Katie, though actually only 6 and 5 years old, were looked upon as quite old and responsible persons, and even Tyrone was promoted – on his 4th birthday – to the wearing of a Covert Coat and Cap, with a knitted waistcoat and collar and tie like a man's, and a little pair of brown leather gaiters, which he was immensely proud of and called 'my lellar daiters'. Patsy, roguish and twinkling with wickedness, was a great duck; friendly with all, but especially with men!

Until schoolroom work claimed them, the children always used to come down to the Dining Room while we were at breakfast. T was very strict and would not allow them to worry visitors, nor to 'play to the gallery' and, as a rule, having plenty of toys to play with in their corner, they were very good. But when Patsy started crawling she disregarded all these conventions and when any man she took a fancy to went across to help himself to bacon, Patsy – on all fours – started in hot pursuit and presently looked up triumphantly at him from the region of his feet. By this time, however, she was 2 years old and able to pursue on foot!

We had a flying visit from the Aubrey Smiths just before the New Year and the Greers stayed with us till January 4th.

January and February 1905

T started 1905 with rather a bad attack of influenza, which kept him in bed for several days; he was still subject to this and also to occasional attacks of malaria, which, though they generally passed off very quickly, had a most depressing effect on him.

The Russo-Japanese War was in full swing then and on January 2nd Port Arthur surrendered.

Mother came to us for a few days and after her the Hopes; and on the 21st T went off to hunt in Tipperary, en route to a shooting party at Eaton. While he was away, I went to stay with Kerry and Elsie at Sheen Falls – near Kenmare – for a few days and on the 28th we were both home again. Various people came and went during the next fortnight. The Ansons and their two children, Major Askwith, Comr & Mrs Forbes, Col. Riley, Mr Tommy Ponsonby and Kerry and Elsie.

In the middle of all this, we had great worries over our horses. A horrible disease called 'Epizootic Lymphangitis' had been brought into Ireland by some of the Army horses that year – or rather in 1904 – and there had been some cases not far from us. Evidently they must have infected some stable where T had put up his hunters, for on February 7th two of his best hunters, 'Richard' and 'Trustee', showed signs of it. They were immediately isolated and submitted to very severe treatment, both external and internal, but to no avail, and they had to be destroyed a week or ten days later. Everything that had touched them was burned and the whole place disinfected, but we were in terror that there would be further cases and all our horses were quarantined. After a time, we got permission to bring out harness horses as the width of the yard was between them and the hunters. For the rest of the season, T had to hunt in Tipperary, where he fortunately had left one or two hunters in Willie Perry's charge.

A month later, my little horse, Jack Tar, developed suspicious symptoms, so he was immediately isolated and kept under careful observation. T had, shortly before, received a letter from an old Anglo-Indian Gentleman begging him to try his special homeopathic cure for the 'Epizootic' and, as it was very simple, consisting merely of a white powder which had to be placed on the horse's tongue and was moreover (according to the old Gentleman) infallible, T decided to give it a trial. First, however, the head off one of the Jack Tar's spots was sent up to the Veterinary Specialist in Dublin, who, having examined it, wired back 'Epizootic Lymphangitis undoubted'; and the horse also had the peculiar look about his eyes and the full veins, which went with the disease. He was removed to the kennels which were then empty and treated according to old man Brown's directions, all symptoms gradually disappeared and in a short time he was perfectly well again. Then those miserable vets, unwilling ever to give credit to what they could not understand, merely said that it could not have been Epizootic Lymphangitis at all!

On February 16th, while Kerry and Elsie were with us, we went up to Coumshingaun Lake; the next day, the Ansons, Elinor De la Poer, Captain Conolly and the Knight of Glin came to stay and all went into Waterford for the Hunt Ball. I was still fairly respectable in appearance and, when at dinner, I told Captain Conolly I hoped he was prepared to dance hard the whole evening, he gallantly replies 'Yes – if I may dance with you'! Nevertheless, I stayed at home!

The party dispersed in the next few days and later on came Alex Beauclerk for a few days, and then Edwina Roberts paid us a fairly long visit.

March 1905

On March 25th we had our Point- to-Point and a party for it – Perrys, Mrs Brown, Mr Head, Mr Brook, Mr T. Ponsonby, Mr Holroyd Smith and Mr Ikey Bell, and Edwina, who was still with us. I remember, one night, hearing voices in T's room and T coming through to mine (leaving all the doors open) to say that Ikey Bell was feeling very bad and had I a pill that I could give him? I protested ignorance of the gentleman's inside, but after some parley with T, who demanded something strong (the doors still open!), I gave him a box of canon balls, one of which had reduced several of my friends to a state of collapse. What was my horror when T presently told me that Ikey had taken two. Nest morning, my patient was looking greenish-yellow and wore a pained and aggrieved air all through breakfast. I felt quite anxious about him, but when I enquired of T after, he said 'Ikey says those pills of yours are no earthly use'! Moral: never prescribe for an unknown inside!

On the 28th, at the Army Point-to-Point at Knocklong there was a special race for the North & South Irish Yeomanry. T rode in it, but owing to the quarantine could not run any of his best horses and he did no good. The North won, much to our disappointment and somehow we were never able to defeat them in that race.

T brought back Lord Shaftesbury with him and I put my foot in it badly by chaffingly asking T whether he had been last in the race, whereupon Lord Shaftesbury had to acknowledge that he had occupied that position. The Doynes were also with us at that time.

April and May 1905

On April 1st came the news that my dear old Granny – aged 92 & 8 months – had died of pneumonia at Coates. This was a great sorrow to all of us, for there never was an old lady more generally and genuinely beloved by all who knew her. Always bright and cheery, thoughtful and sympathetic, she took the warmest interest in all of us and our children, although we – her descendants – numbered close on 200 at the time of her death.

Barely seven weeks later, T's paternal Grandmother died and one couldn't help contrasting the two for, though Christina, Lady Waterford, had five splendid sons, her descendants numbered but fourteen and for several years we had seen very little of her, owing to her bad health and failing mind. She died on May 19th and on the 23rd she was buried in the big family burial place at Clonegam. Uncle Charlie and Uncle Marcus came over for the funeral; also Jack Leslie. I shall never forget that day; the Uncles were really devoted to their Mother and T said they quite broke down at the funeral – Uncle Charlie especially weeping bitterly, but nothing could stop their chaffing and joking and even at luncheon they made everyone laugh, while at dinner that same evening they kept us all in fits of laughter.

All this happened just a week before Billy was born. It was rather curious that both Tyrone and he should arrive a few days after a family funeral at Curraghmore!

Before Granny Waterford died, there had been various diversions to which T had, perforce, to go without me. The Tipperary Point-to-Point, in which he was 3rd in the Heavy Weight on the Rogue; the last days hunting in Tipperary; Punchestown – for which he stayed with the Iveaghs, while Mrs Villiers Stuart kept me company; and a party at Gurteen for a Clonmel dance. Then we had Buldoo, Mr Langrishe, Mr Lambert & Mr Humble to stay a few days – during which time, of course, Hounds and horses were never mentioned – and later on came Susie and the Forbes and Buldoo again. Mrs Forbes was in the same condition as myself, only not so advanced, and was much annoyed at having another child when her youngest was already 11 years old.

Much chaff passed between T and the Mander and it was in answer to some ribald letter of Ts that the Mander sent the card illustrating 'the Pot called the Kettle Black', which is in my book.

Little Will Forbes was not born until October 26th and, though for some time he was always referred to as 'the unnecessary infant', he very soon established his dominion over the whole family.

I remember one evening when, hearing there were fox cubs in the 'White Rabbit Burrow', T and I went out to watch for them and lay on the ground behind a fallen branch for about an hour before they appeared, when we were rewarded by seeing six or seven of them, evidently 2 litters. They played about together only a few yards from us and the sight was well worth the cramp and the midges we had suffered from during the long wait.

T played polo in Waterford a good deal that summer, and I have hazy recollections of some row which occurred on the ground, in consequence of which T wanted to horsewhip Mr P Kenneally and do something equally awful to Mr Barron, at which Buldoo Bryan grew much alarmed and the Mander had to use all his arts to calm T down. Luckily, the whole thing blew over and was soon forgotten. On the whole, it was a very peaceful time. I sat out a great deal and went for long walks with T almost up to the last, and as time went on he would never leave me for long, several times motoring up to Dublin at cockcrow so as to be back at night.

On May 28th Major Bryan brought his sister-in-law – Mrs Bellew – to lunch with us; the next day T was obliged to go up to Dublin on Yeomanry business, and of course that decided the infant to start arriving at 2am! However, all was well, for T, warned by wire, hurried back as fast as the motor would bring him and got home at 4.30pm on the 30th and William didn't arrive until 8.35pm that night. The Diary describes him as a 'fine fat child 8½ lbs, dark hair, very light blue eyes', and his length was 20 inches. The day before, T had wired me from Dublin 'Togo has sunk 15 Russian ships, captured six and 3,000 prisoners'. There was great excitement over this and for some time afterwards Billy was known as Togo; and so, funnily enough, was the Forbes baby when he arrived.

Billy caused us a great deal of anxiety during the first few weeks of his life. I think there was an escape of gas (though it had been tested) in my dressing room; anyhow, whatever the cause was, the little fellow was always ailing, could keep nothing down and cried most pitifully; though, with little fists doubled up, he seemed to try hard not to cry. We tried him on humanized milk, malted milk, cream and whey, and I don't know what else, but for the first four weeks he lost weight steadily, till, at 4 weeks, he weighed 1lb 1oz, less than when he was born. Then an ass was procured for him (Nat's mother) and from that moment he improved and soon put on weight rapidly. How often I longed to be able to nurse, so as to save the child from all these miseries, but evidently providence had not meant that I should and I could only be thankful that little Bill was spared to us, for I heard afterwards that, once or twice, he was very nearly gone and one time, at about 8 weeks, when Nurse Monk came back to him after a moment's absence, and found him quite grey and cold, she thought he was dead and had a terrible fright. All this was hidden from me and Nurse Monk always came smiling into my room and saying that he was better, but I knew he was much worse than they said and the first time Mrs Brand was allowed into my room alone, she gave the whole show away by saying, 'Oh – poor darling child, he was very near gone the other day', and then plainly showing that she thought it would be a marvel if 'the dear child' pulled through! It was a terribly anxious time and the poor little fellow's weary wailing made one's heart ache. The other children were very pleased with him – when they were allowed to see him – and I think Tyrone was especially delighted with him. One day, he was sitting beside me on my bed and, feeling very old with the new baby brother, he patted my cheek in a fatherly way and said 'Oh, you funny little thing, and you call yourself Mother'!

Mother arrived when Billy was a week old and stayed for eight days, so she was with us during the most anxious time and was a great help. T had to go up to Dublin several times while I was laid up and also to London for the wedding of Princess Margaret of Connaught. During his absence that time we moved Billy into his room and cut off the gas in my dressing room; and undoubtedly the child did better after this.

June 1905

Major Bingham and three of his brother officers of the 3rd D.G. stayed a couple of nights for a polo match in Waterford. Mr Pollok also stayed. There was some excitement over a new motor car (our 2nd) – which arrived on June 8th and T took Mother on a drive to Fethard in it.

I remember a very unpleasant time with a rotten wisdom tooth, which was causing trouble and which I decided to let Dr Walker pull out. He duly cocained the gum, but as the tooth broke away every time he touched it, he finally had to dig it out and I thought it would never stop bleeding after.

On June 22nd I went downstairs, having seen my poor skinny little baby in his bath. Lady Duncannon came to tea and was so kind about our anxieties; in fact, it was she who strongly advocated ass's milk and she ever after took a special interest in Billy and called him her boy.

The Perrys, Comr Forbes, Mr Filgate, Mlle Berton and Uncle Freddy Hamilton, came to stay with us that week for 2 or 3 days, except Mlle Berton, who stayed on alone with me after T and the others had left.

On the 26th I was churched and Billy was christened in Portlaw; his Godparents were Susie, Capt. Edmond Charteris, General Mostyn

King Edward VII and Queen Alexandra driving through Waterford, May 1904.

King Edward VII and Queen Alexandra in Waterford escorted by the Southern Irish Yeomanry.

Beatrix at the YWCA Sale in Waterford, December 1904.

Garden Party at Curraghmore, September 1906.

Beatrix with her children.

Crossing the Clodagh river above the Waterford Hound Kennels.

The Opening Meet in Waterford, 18th October 1907.

Beresford (the Snipe) and Commander Forbes, the latter being the only one present. He was called after him, but more especially after dear Uncle Bill. A curious thing happened at Billy's baptism; he was never properly 'received into the Church'. Mr Flemyng's handling of babies always made me nervous and Billy was so fragile that I suppose I unconsciously held him more closely and protectively than I should have otherwise – anyhow, Mr Flemyng, knowing his delicacy, thought I did not want to hand him over, so he baptized him in my arms!

July and August 1905

T and the Mander went off that afternoon, T for the Curragh, where I joined him on July 4th, having weighed and photographed my baby, and left him really on the mend. T met me at Kildare in the new motor and drove me to the Headquarter Hut, where I was to stay again with the Grenfells. The Northern Yeomanry were finishing their training at the Curragh and Lady Shaftesbury was also staying with the Grenfells and I shall always remember her padding along the passage to my room some time after we had gone to bed, because she had forgotten to ask how my baby was and she knew we had been so anxious about him. We were practically strangers at the time and I was much touched and thought her a dear kind woman.

The next day we lunched at the S.I.Y. Camp and T came over to tea. On the 6th the Grenfells gave a garden party and on the 7th they had a man's dinner party, so we dined peacefully with Florita St. Aubyn in her little hut and afterwards watched one of those gorse fires which are a constant source of anxiety at the Curragh.

On the 10th the 'Barn doors' (N.I.Y.) left and also the Shaftesburys and the next day we had our sports – at which I gave the prizes –

dinner in Camp and singsong after. On the 13th I drove out early to see Lord Grenfell and General Rimington inspect the S.I.Y. and two days later the training ended and T and I motored home, stopping for tea at Rathwade en route.

That was very peaceful time at the Curragh. The weather fine and hot and we used to sit out in the garden of the Headquarter Hut all day long. The Grenfells little girl 'Nina' was a dear fat baby and Barbara St. Aubyn, a little older, was a most attractive child and much of our time was spent with these two little girls.

Not being fit enough to ride, I didn't see so much of the Yeomanry that year, but T and some of the officers came down occasionally. T did not like leaving camp too often and sometimes rather grumbled at being expected to come down to the Headquarter Hut. I begged him not to come, as he had this feeling, but he did not like to refuse the Commander in Chief.

There had been a good many changes in the Yeomanry since the first training; several officers had left, Major Burns Lindow now commanded the Dublin Squadron (a new one) his place as Adjutant having been taken by Capt. Jennings. Mr Phelps had been promoted from the Ranks and other new officers were Mr Gethin, Capt. Tremayne, Major Williams, Sir Richard Levinge, Messrs Goulding, O'Grady (Athlone Pursuivant) Ball and Sir James Cotter, a Ward in Chancery who was always getting into trouble. Mr Goulding was a smart young man, much admired by the ladies, and at the Sports he was unfortunately overheard saying to one of them – with a conscious smirk – 'Do you really want my photograph in uniform'? He never heard the end of this and whenever he approached Skibbereen, or some other joker would strike an attitude and begin talking about photographs.

On July 15th we were home again and found little Bill much improved, though he had had to give up the asses milk. The monthly nurse stayed 7 weeks and then we had a hospital nurse for him, as Mrs Brand was taking the other children to the sea, which would not suit him. He weighed 8lb 14oz at 7 weeks and after that his improvement was very steady; Nurse Horsefall, who stayed 6 weeks with him, carried him to the top of Mother Brown on the Sheep Walk, and even the Tower, every day and he soon grew fat and sunburned and a really bonny boy. When she left he weighed 11lb 8, and measured 24 inches and he had got safely though his vaccination and other troubles.

On July 17th the children went to Ardmore for change of air; T and I motored over to see them in, taking Blanchie, Katie and Tyrone with us, and returning home in the evening. It happened to be the Patron Saint's Day, on which, the tide being low, a large stone on the seahorse was left high and dry. This stone is hollowed out underneath sufficiently to allow a person of average size to crawl through and great merit can be acquired by doing this on St. Declan's Day. From our window we had a splendid view of the spot and it was most amusing to see the people going through – three times each being the amount necessary to obtain full benefits – while some of them stuck and some, being too fat or too stiff to attempt the feat at all, were content to creep thrice round the outside of the stone, rubbing against it all the way.

The Perrys came to stay with us soon after, and one day we motored to the mountains and took our luncheon up to Coumshingaun Lake. The luncheon was mostly packed in a large Pannier hamper and T and Willie agreed to take turns carrying it up. I well remember the wiles by which each tried to arrange matters so that the other should carry it up the steepest part and the swearing that went on over the weight of that clumsy old basket, the way being steep, and the day exceeding hot.

Later on in the month, we motored over to Ardmore to see the children and spent the day there. We dabbled in the sea with the family who were all very happy. Patsy, in her seaside attire of knickers and jersey, looking a great duck and just like a little boy. From there we went on to Ballysaggartmore, where we stayed three nights with the Ansons. T hoped to get some salmon fishing, but unfortunately the water was very low and, though the river was simply fully of fish, there was no chance of getting one by fair means. Therefore, when fishing by the Weir one day, T was tempted to do some poaching and, aided and abetted by Claud, he made some contrivance with a bit of lead, by means of which he very shortly had hooked a fish. Unfortunately, just as he was about to land it, one of the Devonshire Watchers appeared on the opposite bank, keenly interested in the catching of a fish on such an unpropitious day. T dared not risk his scrutiny of the fish and tackle, so gave a mighty jerk to the line and then, 'Oh – dash it – he has broken me', but there was a look in the eye of the watcher which denoted strong suspicion!

When we left Ballysaggart, Clodagh pressed some delicious ripe peaches on us to eat by the way. We placed them between us, meaning to eat them when we had gone some little way, but, alas for those peaches! A chicken ran across our path and T bounded up to see if we had killed it, then he sat down – on the peaches! They were beautifully ripe and their luscious juice penetrated through overcoat, jacket, breeches, pants, till all were stained and glued together and poor T himself sticky to the skin! Oh, how he swore at those peaches and at Clodagh for giving them to us and at me for putting them there and at the chicken for getting in the way and at Honeysett for driving over it; and when we arrived at Durrow, where we were stopping to lunch with the Kennedys, he looked quite shy of his appearance and had to hastily explain matters and have all his clothes cleaned!

The day after we got home we settled all about the electric lighting of the house, which was to be done while we were away, for we had great plans for the following winter, which we had decided to spend in East Africa on a big game hunting expedition.

T had, some little time before, received a petition from all the farmers and gentry in the neighbourhood, begging him to take over the Mastership of the Hounds the following year; this he had consented to do, so, considering that we should in the future be much more tied down in the winters, he thought it would be a good moment to choose for a shooting expedition, while we were still perfectly free. He had thought of a trip to E. Africa ever since he returned from Central Africa. One of his reasons for selecting that part of the World being that the climate was perfectly healthy and that I could quite well go there with him. As time went on, he grew rather nervous about taking me for fear I should get ill or something, and sometimes he would say that he thought I had better 'stay at home with the babies' and let him go alone. But I think he really wanted me to go and I was very keen about it and made light of all his objections.

It was finally settled that I should go. Father and Mother were very doubtful about the wisdom of the expedition and Father, especially, was averse to my going, but with their usual tact and goodness they said very little and refrained from any interference. Imagine my annoyance, then, when I found that Lady Fitzgerald – the Knight of Kerry's wife – had told T that Father was terribly nervous and distressed at my going and thought it a great mistake. This was in September and T then again said I had better stay behind and I had the greatest difficulty in reassuring him. In fact, this foolish remark of Lady Fitzgerald's quite got on his mind and made him nervous about me all through the trip!

But to return to my tale: I went over to spend a week with Evie, at Holker, in August; I went and returned by the most direct route, viz North Wall to Keysham, and had two awful crossings on a horrid little tub of a boat which came in hours late each time. When I got back to Dublin and tried to do some shopping, the world rose up to meet me in such a fashion that I was afraid people would think I was drunk. At the Royal Hotel my friend Miss Power recommended brandy and when I protested, and said 'What would Lord Waterford think if I came home drunk', the good Lady reassured me and said, 'Ah now, never fear that I'd send you back tight to his Lordship'!

I joined T at Glenbride that afternoon and the next day being the 12th August, we went out shooting together. Later on came Mr Adair, Claud Anson, the Knight of Glin, Mr Somerville and Sir R Levinge to stay and Major Williams motored Mr Gethin and Col. Moore up for the driving, but the birds were scarce and wild, and results were very poor.

Meanwhile, Blanchie, Katie and Tyrone had gone to Derreen and there we joined them on the 26th after a few days at home; while Patsy and Mrs Brand returned to Curraghmore and little Bill at last was received into the Nursery.

The three elder children were nearly 4 weeks at Derreen, where they had a very happy time prawning, digging, climbing and learning to row. Unfortunately, Blanchie's eye was bad most of the time and spoiled a great deal of her fun; and with this she generally had an internal upset for the sea never agreed with her. Little Tyrone was the happiest of the three for, like T, he loved the sea and thrived there and made friends with all the boatmen, who loved to neglect their work in order to play with him. I remember one day when T and I took him out sailing and T was much annoyed with me because, when the little fellow started yarning, I gave him a biscuit to nibble and he was promptly sick! The children had several successful days' fishing, one day getting 45 mackerel and a pollock, and another day 65 mackerel and 3 pollock.

Charlie Cavendish was born while we were at Derreen (on August 29th); a most welcome addition to the family. Next day, we heard that peace between Russia and Japan was assured.

September and October 1905

On September 1st Mother, T and I motored over to Killarney to see the Kenmares and Lady Dudley, who was staying with them and 2 days later they returned the visit. T was invited to shoot stags at Killarney, and got three, one of them quite a fine one, the head of which hangs at Curraghmore.

The children left on September 11th and T and I went to the Falls for one night, joining our little family next day, and the diary notes that Bill weighed 12lb 8oz and was 'looking lovely'.

We were at home less than 3 weeks, during which we had visits from the Marcus Beresfords, Comr Forbes, Mother and the Kennedys and did a certain amount of cub hunting. Then we went up to Dublin and stayed at the Royal Hospital for a couple of nights, the party including Miss Scott, in charge of Blanchie, who came up to have her eye examined by Dr Maxwell, and incidentally came in for little Nina's first birthday.

On October 2nd T and I went over to England and spent a fortnight in London – at Claridges Hotel – getting our outfit for E. Africa, both clothes and camp outfit and stores. Lady Delamere happened to be in London at the time and was most kind and helpful over clothes etc., and also promised to write to her husband in order that he might make things easy for us in E. Africa. We also met the Cyril Wards and discovered that they had just made up their minds to go out there, so we decided to join forces if possible.

T had a nasty influenza cold, with a touch of malaria, while we were in London and, though he was only laid up for 2 days, it left him rather shaky and affected his nerves most strangely and he didn't get over this for quite a long time. We went down to Minehead one day to try our rifles at the Ranges there. T gave me a beautiful little

Mannlicher-Schönauer on the same lines as the one he had used in Styria, and himself had a Mannlicher, a 303-500 and a Paradox.

On October 9th we went down to stay with T's cousins, the Londesboroughs, for a shoot. We missed our train at King's Cross by 3 minutes and on arriving late in the evening were received with shouts of laughter, as T had done exactly the same on his last visit. Londesborough made himself quite agreeable and kept fairly calm over the shooting, though we were told that at times, if he wasn't hitting well, he would get into a terrible state and use the most profane language. On one of these occasions it was said that he had laid down his gun in a ditch, taken the 2nd gun from the loader, and laid it beside the other, and then, kneeling down, had said in a loud voice, 'Oh Lord – you know that shooting is the only thing in the world that I care about and yet you won't let me hit a single bird – D... you! D... you! D... you!', and he was the mildest of men as a rule.

After spending a Sunday at Bowood, we returned to Curraghmore and spent 2 or 3 weeks there, setting our house in order before departing on our trip. Major Bryan paid us several visits during that time and the Perrys came for 2 nights. We made all the final plans for the electric light. Then we paid farewell visits and, at last, said a sad goodbye to the children and went off to London. We were three days at Claridges and I remember a comical visit from Aunt Nina, who, to my surprise, actually came to see us there. She said she knew we were going away somewhere, but when I tried to explain she always said, 'Where's that?' and professed never to have heard of E. Africa, Uganda, or the Red Sea, or Aden; till I gave it up in despair and realized that she evidently preferred to remain in ignorance.

November 1905

On November 7th we left England; Father and Mother coming to the station to see us off. As T kept a detailed diary of the whole of our trip, I will not write much about it now, for the whole of the diary was typed out and put in the big album with photographs etc. We went first to Egypt for about four weeks and had quite a pleasant time there, for although it was rather early to go there, and the weather was hot, we had the advantage of arriving before the rush of tourists and were able to do our sight-seeing very peacefully.

We found some old acquaintances of T's – the Todd Hopkinsons – on board the boat, and through them got to know Mr Crawley, who was very kind to us in Cairo. We stayed there for five days and then trained up to Assouan, stopping at Luxor on the way for two days. After spending four days at Assouan we returned by boat – one of Cook's Tourist Steamers, and as there were then hardly any tourists coming down the river, we had the boat almost to ourselves and thoroughly enjoyed the peace and quiet of it and the wonderful beauties of the Nile.

At Assouan we had the good fortune to see the ruins of Philae in all their completeness, for the water was not yet up and, except for the high water mark from the last season, there was nothing to mar the beauty of those wonderful ruins.

At Assouan, Golding my maid, got ill from some tinned food she had eaten at Luxor and I was obliged to leave her behind when we started down the Nile. She was to join us by train, but grew so much worse afterwards that she was unable to move for many weeks. She was, in any case, to have gone home from Egypt, as I did not want her in E. Africa, but it was a great worry leaving her behind, ill and amongst strangers.

We were not long enough in Egypt to fully appreciate its charms and I think we both felt impatient to get started on the more serious part of our trip, and only looked upon those few weeks in Egypt as a sort of padding to fill in time, and we were not altogether sorry when the moment arrived for us to catch our Mombasa-bound boat at Suez. T's servant, Goodchild, came on with us, and on the *Koerber* we were joined by Dr Storrs, who was to do the trip with us, provided with a case containing all the necessary drugs and paraphernalia in case of accidents or sickness. There we also found the Cyril Wards, Lord Warwick and Mr Alwyn Greville and Col.Patterson and Mr Moreton Frewen. We formed ourselves into a table and, owing to the desperate thirst which assailed us all, and the multitude of Geisshübler bottles which collected on the table – we each took it in turn to be the Mattoni-wallah, or purveyor of mineral water for the day. All, except ourselves, were going out to look at timber forests, with a view to planting rubber. Mr Frewen was the originator of the idea and Col. Patterson was acting bear-leader to Lord Warwick and his brother. He knew the country well, having worked on the Uganda Railway for years, but he was generally so busy flirting with a pretty girl on board, having left Mrs P in England, that we saw little of him between meals and did not regret it! On arrival at Mombasa he hastened off to give the girl and her sister a ride on a trolley and never gave a thought to Lord Warwick's luggage, the most important part of which went on to Beria in consequence.

We had imagined that we should be able to get ponies in E. Africa, but on arriving at Aden we heard that they were very scarce and that it might be quite impossible to get any. T and Mr Ward gathered together all the ponies they could find in Aden, mostly miserable little rats out of the cabs and had them all put through their paces, finally selecting three – a nice little grey arab with a great many 'ifs' and two rats – one very old and the other very young! Then arose the question of first choice, as T was to have two ponies, and Mr Ward only one, and of course both wanted the arab! Finally, they agreed that the matter should be decided by a 'family game' of Bridge, at which they were both pretty good, but Irene and I hopeless novices. Never have I felt as anxious over a game and Irene was as bad. We were both in terror of playing the wrong card and kept on looking nervously at our respective husbands, who much enjoyed our agonies. We were game all and then it was my hand to play, or, rather, I think T left it to me to make trumps and, trembling with anxiety and excitement, I made 'no trumps', on which we won the rubber!

Needless to say, T chose the arab and then took the young rat and we had the ancient one; our two did us very well, the groggy arab was a charming hack and usually was my mount (we called him 'No Trumps') and the Doctor rode the ancient rat, which turned out to be a capital pony, hardly a racehorse, but thoroughly hardy and well-seasoned. The young rat died at Mombasa, too weak to stand the modulation there, so ill-luck certainly pursued the Wards.

We crossed 'the Line' on the 13th December and the next day we reached Mombasa, where we landed and spent a couple of days in collecting some of our outfit before proceeding to Nairobi. The journey up was a wonderful experience. We shared a special train with Lord Warwick and others and were therefore able to stop whenever we liked and, as lion had lately been seen on the railing line, the men were advised to have their rifles handy. The Engine Driver promised to stop if he saw a lion! In this we were disappointed, but there was hardly any other beast that we didn't see – in fact, Colonel Patterson declared that he actually did see three lions in the dim distance. Another person saw a rhino and on every side we saw hartebeest, gazelles, zebra and ostriches; for we were passing through the Reserves and the animals there, having been unmolested for so long, take the train quite calmly and fed quite close up to the line.

We spent 5 days in Nairobi – staying at the Norfolk Hotel and then (December 20th) rode off to our first camp – the Wards, T and I and Dr Storrs. Two days later we were joined by Mr Percival – the Game Ranger – who stayed with us for 6 days and was a great addition to our party as he knew every bit of the country and likely spots in which to find lion etc.

We were out for 11 days that time, shifting camp at intervals and we had the most wonderful luck with the game and came back with 4 lions, besides rhino, hartebeest, gazelles etc. Our camp was most comfortable and we had plenty of good food. Altogether it was a very happy time, though it was nearly spoiled by an accident to T's 2nd Gun Bearer on the first day out. This man, crawling behind T during a stalk, somehow let off the gun he carried and severely wounded his own leg. Luckily we had the Doctor with us and were also near enough to Nairobi to send the man into hospital there the next day. The accident upset T most dreadfully. He always imagined himself to be very unlucky and instead of being thankful that he didn't receive the shot, he made up his mind that our trip was doomed to disaster and that he ought not to have brought me. I went out stalking with him next day and I had my first shot at a hartebeest and was fortunate in securing it, T himself getting another. This cheered him up very much and the world ceased to look so black.

Then came the excitement of the lion hunts and T was in his element. Here I must confess to a slight inaccuracy in my diary, made with intent! In the first lion hunt Mr Ward was not very lucky, or he was so excited that his shooting was somewhat wild. In consequence of this, T shot 2 lions before he had hit any and, though he did get one later in the day, he was rather sick about it and inclined to take it to heart. The next day, when the party found a big cub in a reed bed, T and Mr Ward both fired at it, but Mr Percival said it was undoubtedly T's shot that scored. T, however, made Mr Percival say it was Mr Ward's and I had to keep up this fiction in my diary. The plot was most successful, as Mr Ward returned in great glee and was quite happy after that. I would not have mentioned this, had not the show been given away by Mr Percival in an Article entitled, 'The Finest Sport in the World' (in describing this hunt) he simply states the 'Lord Waterford promptly shot him', and entirely ignores Mr Ward's attempt.

There was always a good deal of jealousy between T and Mr Ward and, as they both possessed pretty violent tempers, I was in perpetual dread of a flare-up. T was a really keen sportsman; he had acquired a great deal of experience in Central Africa, and had also studied the subject of big game shooting in all the best books. Besides this, with his gift for picking up languages, he was soon able to understand and make himself understood by the Shikaris and therefore got on with them far better than did Mr Ward. The latter cared little for the science of the game and several times spoiled a combined stalk by his blunders, much to T's annoyance. However, they mercifully did not fall out seriously and when, later on, we went our different ways, we all parted the best of friends. All the same, I would recommend anyone who goes on a shooting trip not to combine forces with another party unless they are quite certain of being really kindred spirits.

When we first planned our shooting, T said that he intended to do his serious hunting in the early morning and to take me out in the evening, but as time went on he became more and more engrossed in the chase and I felt that it irked him a good deal to have to take me out, particularly if he was tired after a long stalk in the morning. I always felt I was there on sufferance and, as I hated to be a nuisance, I soon gave up asking him to take me, unless he suggested it himself. At the same time, he was always so nervous of my getting into trouble that I could never go far from camp without him and I had the most strict orders never to go near a reed bed, or high grass, which might conceal a lion. Mr Ward was far less alive to the danger of these places and T used to get perfectly furious when he heard of Irene calmly walking through them. His care of me was most touching and at night, when I visited a certain little grass shelter behind our tents (and away from the light of the bonfire) before returning to bed, he always took a lantern and a gun and waited outside for me! His anxiety on this score was not unreasonable, as lions came very near our tents several times and after some mysterious beast – probably a lion – had entangled itself in our tent ropes and broken the pole in extricating itself. We thought it was time to have a second fire behind the tents to keep such visitors away.

January 1906

After our first trip on the Athi, and a couple of days spent in Nairobi, we went off again to another part of the Plain and stayed out for 25 days. Mr de Crespigny, A.D.C. to Col. Sadleir, who had been 2 years in the Country without seeing a lion, got 3 days leave to come with us and actually got his lion! On this occasion, T again showed great unselfishness over the lions, as he not only – in agreement with Mr Ward – left the first lion to Mr de Crespigny, but he also made Mr Ward take first shot at the next one, in spite of its being very doubtful whether they'd ever come up with the third member of the party. Luckily they did; however, and there were great rejoicings in camp when news came that each 'Bwana' had got his lion. Apropos of Mr de Crespigny – a charming but somewhat crazy person – he told us a delightful story of how a Bishop, lately arrived at Nairobi, came to call on him. Mr de Crespigny was unfortunately out, but two young lion cubs, which he had reared, were lying in the veranda and showed great interest in His Reverence. The poor man hastily left his card and walked with all the dignity he could muster to the garden gate, which he carefully closed behind him. The cubs, however, wanted to see more of the visitor and, after following him down the path, they lightly leapt the gate – and the last thing that was seen was a pair of gaitered legs flying through a cloud of dust and the playful cubs still pursuing. They were nearly full-grown and had to be shut up soon after, so small blame to the poor Bishop if he did feel alarmed.

It was no uncommon thing for lions to come quite close to houses on the outskirts of the town and when we were there, there was great talk of a lame lioness which had been seen by several people near the Club. The only person who had a chance of shooting her was a native soldier on guard. She came quite close to him, but he did not consider it right to fire without orders!

But to return to our camp – my diary gives a full account of the doings during the next few weeks, so I will only say that the Wards left us on January 17th and that we had a very big adventure on the 26th when T narrowly escaped being mauled by a wounded lion which attacked the Gun Bearers on each side of him and actually covered his shoulder with saliva, blood and hairs! It was a nerve shaking business and, though T remained wonderfully calm as far as concern for the danger to himself, he once more became dreadfully nervous about me. We were on our way back to Nairobi at the time and he informed me that he intended to give up the rest of the trip and, after some sight-seeing, to take me home. I was dead against this plan as I knew how he would regret it afterwards and that I should always feel he'd given up on my account. We argued the point at great length, but I had a trump card and when I suggested that people might think it was funk that drove him home, he very soon stopped talking about it and began instead to plan another trip to the North of Nairobi.

The nicest camp we had during that trip was the one near Donyo Sabuk; it was good shooting ground and we stayed there 10 days, the Wards leaving us on the 2nd day. By this time I had become quite accustomed to camp life and though the mornings without T were rather long, I managed to find plenty to do. T usually went off between 5 & 6am, and often wasn't back till 3.30pm. I used to get horribly anxious about him sometimes and was always much relieved when he was safe in camp again. After he had washed and eaten, I used to produce my diary and write up the day's events from what he told me. He never bothered to keep a diary himself (Col. Lawley did this in Central Africa) so mine was the official record and I was very careful to note all details of the stalks correctly, though it was occasionally very difficult to get the information from him for he abhorred regularity and for choice would never do today what might be left to tomorrow.

We had brought a small library of standard books – Surtees, Dickens, Thackeray etc. with us and I had wool and needles with which to knit comforts for some of our men. There was also some mending to be done, but our wardrobes were very simple and on this 2nd trip I had reduced mine to a minimum and given up the wearing of any linen. Vest and drawers, 'Rational Stays', stockings, Burberry breeches, skirt (very short) and coat, a flannel shirt, field boots and soft felt hat (except when a topee was necessary) – this was all one required in the day time, with an overcoat to wear after sundown. The men usually changed into their pyjamas after the hunting was over and dined in these and an overcoat, with soft 'mosquito boots' or shoes, but I found this costume was too encouraging to the ticks and that it was best to keep them out by remaining in breeches and long boots.

One evening, when T was resting in pyjama kit, some ostriches appeared close to the camp and he forthwith proceeded to stalk them. Pyjamas are not well suited to stalking and he returned before long, very sore and much scratched, while the ostriches trotted off in the opposite direction.

Another evening, when I was out a bit later than usual with Dr Storrs, T came out to look for us, attended by a small crowd of natives. He looked so comical in pyjamas, Jasper jacket, felt hat and rubber boots, that I roared with laughter, but soon found it was no laughing matter as he was furious with me for staying out late and I was in sore disgrace for the rest of the evening. There was practically no twilight there and the sun set so quickly that it was very easy to get overtaken by the dark, especially if one was intent on a stalk as I had been that evening. T and I were caught like that on two other occasions and, as we were then some distance from camp, it was really most unpleasant and I was frankly terrified (December 28th and February 10th in diary).

The first time was on the Athi and I well remember that ride home in the dim light and all the queer shapes that appeared on every side, and how T suddenly peered to the right and then said, in a hoarse and very pre-emptive whisper, 'Come up on my left'. He never said another word till we reached the camp (after crossing a horrid patch of long grass) and then he told me he had heard something grumbling and grunting quite close to us and he thought it was a lion.

The other time was with Lord Delamere and, as he had had an injury to the spine and could never ride faster than a gentle jog, one had the unpleasant certainty of not being able to get away if a lion did appear; and when a low shape was seen in the grass quite close to W. I thought our last hour had come, but luckily for us it was only an ant bear, or some beast of that kind.

There was always great excitement when a Porter arrived with letters and papers from home and I was always anxious for news of the children and eagerly looked for letters from them, or from others telling me about them. They spent most of the time at Bowood where I knew they were in good hands, but sometimes I felt terribly lonesome without them.

February 1906

On January 28th we were back in Nairobi and on February 1st we were off again up the line, intending to make a short trip to Uganda, while our camp moved by road to Entebbe, where we were to meet them later. But news reached T of a large herd of elephants in the neighbourhood of Njoro – where the Delameres lived – so he decided to give up the lake trip, but decreed that I should continue the journey with Dr Storrs and Goodchild (T's Servant). Accordingly, at 10pm on a dark night he left the train and, as we puffed out of the station (Nyoro), I could see two little lights flickering in the dark, as he and Lord Delamere walked off together towards the house where Mr Clutterbuck – Lord Delamere's Agent – lived, and I felt quite forlorn!

We were away less than a week and I thoroughly enjoyed the trip, though I longed for T to be sharing it with me. Uganda had quite a different charm from S. Africa; there was a wonderful warmth and depth of colour about Entebbe and, but for the dread of the Tsetse Fly, there would have been nothing to mar one's enjoyment of all the beauty. But it was awful to think of the havoc caused by this insect – whole islands swept of inhabitants and the deaths from sleeping sickness averaging over 1,000 per annum round the lake.

I found an old acquaintance in Mrs Wilson, wife of the Deputy Commissioner, and was most hospitably received. The H.D.C., Captain Cole, taught me several of the customs of the Country and years afterwards, when we met at St. Moritz, and immediately started grunting out the Waganda salutation, our friends thought we had gone quite mad.

On the way back from Entebbe our boat called at Jinja and from there I brought away the grey parrot 'Kasuku', which has been at Curraghmore ever since. I had a curious experience in the train on the return journey. I was sharing the carriage with an English lady from Mulhoroni – where there had been a Nandi scare – the night was very hot and we had left several of the windows on her side of the carriage open, without drawing up the wooden shutters. The Lady wore a good deal of jewellery and hung her watch up beside her before she settled down for the night. I was just going off to sleep when something disturbed me and, opening my eyes, I thought I saw a shadow at one of the windows, but it immediately disappeared. Again, I tried to settle down, but twice more I had the impression of a shadowy form at the window and, unable to stand this any longer, I woke my companion and made her put away her watch while I pulled up all the shutters. Evidently one of the natives had climbed out of the window further down the train and crept along the footboard on thieving intent.

At 2am next morning we arrived at Njoro and what was my delight to find T waiting for me at the station with Lord Delamere's mule-cart. We had a mile to go to the Agent's house; the lantern kept on going out and T was not in a happy mood, but 2am is a trying time to wait at a station and he had had no luck with the elephants, and felt he might just as well have gone across Victoria Nyanza with me.

Next morning, or rather later on the same morning, we pursued our way to Njoro, five miles further away. T had put up our sleeping tents outside the 'Boma', or enclosure, there and we shared the Delamere big grass hut for our meals. The Clutterbucks had quite a nice bungalow, comfortably furnished, but the Delameres lived in great discomfort, Lord D being perfectly happy in a grass hut and not taking any trouble about building a house, though the foundations *had* been laid. Lady Delamere, in desperation, had built herself a 2 roomed bungalow outside the Boma and in this she had a tiny Bedroom and Sitting Room very prettily furnished. But Lord D still used his little grass hut inside the Boma – a smelly place when the cattle were all in – and Lady D had to walk quite a long way from her cottage to the Dining Room grass hut. She had been in England that winter and only arrived home the evening after I got there. She had brought quite a lot of smart clothes with her (for Nairobi Race Week etc.) and it seemed so queer to see silks and velvets being unpacked in those surroundings.

The Hindlips, who lived 9 miles away – on the other side of the railway, lived much more comfortably and there was quite a homely look about their place. Lord Delamere lived very simply and as long as he had gallons of weak tea, he was perfectly happy and saw no necessity to get in any stores other than rice, flour and tea, so that the tinned fruits and other things we had brought with us were a real luxury there, and quite a treat for Florence Delamere. She has brought back a gramophone as a surprise for Lord D and he had ordered another as a surprise for her! There was seldom a moment when one of these instruments wasn't discoursing sweet (?) music and there was something utterly incongruous in the hearing of the latest music hall song in that lonely spot on the edge of the wild. I generally went to bed early and lay in my tent listening to 'In my Little Corner Cosy', or 'I like you in Velvet' – in Maurice Farkoa's best style. They had a tame hartebeest which had a nasty way of waiting behind a shed and butting out at you as you passed, and one day he held up Florence as she was going to the dining hut, stepping daintily through the mud in a velvet tea gown – till someone came to the rescue and drove him off. I think F was very glad to have us there, as she was often very lonely and, though she was devoted to her husband, it must have been a most trying life. Our tents were just behind her cottage and we always had a fire lit at night, as we were on the edge of the jungle and there were all sorts of wild beasts about.

We also had our 'Askari' Sentry on guard as usual, for the Nandis, who were then in rebellion, might have paid us a visit any time. Lord Delamere was quite unmoved by all these dangers, and never took any steps to protect his wife from them. She was full of pluck, but her nerves were sorely tried and I can't help thinking that the strain of that life may have had a good deal to do with her death a few years later.

March 1906

The day before we left Njoro, T hit the fresh spoor of the elephants he had been seeking for so long and after following them up for some time, he succeeded in getting 2 of them. This was all that was wanted to make our trip a complete success and I *was* pleased when he rode in, beaming with delight to tell us the news. Next day we were off and on February 26th we left Nairobi for England.

While out in B.E.A. we met several interesting people; there was Mr Ewart S. Grogan, author of *From the Cape to Cairo*, who was the first man to undertake this perilous journey and who, with his brother, was well known for his prowess at Big Game shooting; Mr Jackson, the Sub Commissioner, who afterwards filled important Governorships; Mr MacMillan, an American who had built a sort of ranch in the middle of the Athi and lived there with his intrepid wife, and a Mr Bullpit. Mr Hill, who managed the Government Farm at Naivasha and there conducted experiments of great value to the Country, and Col.Patterson, author of *The Man-Eaters of Tsavo* – an absolutely true record of the early days of British enterprise in B.E. Africa. Then there was Mr Tonks, with whom we stayed at Mombasa, on our way home; a most lugubrious Lawyer, but the personification of kindness.

Among our fellow passengers on the homeward voyage were Lord Carlisle and one of his younger sons; the latter was a hopeless creature, addicted to drink and had got in so much bad scrapes that his poor old Father had come all the way to Nairobi to bring him home. He disappeared at Mombasa and was only retrieved just in time to catch the boat, having been at the old game again, and for several days we saw nothing of him. Grogan junior was also on board and Mr Charles Craven, an enormously tall man who had been a great boxer, and might have done good things, but for the same failing as Mr Howard. He was charming when sober, but frightfully rowdy at other times and he nearly came in for a duel on this trip. He and several other kindred spirits – amongst them a fat Marseillais whom we nicknamed the 'Kiboko' (rhino) used to foregather in one of their cabins after dinner and drink till all hours, making a great noise of it.

At Port Said a French couple came on board; the man small and timorous, the lady stout and determined. They unfortunately were given a cabin next to Mr Craven's and, after being kept awake half the night, the lady urged her husband to go in next door and tell the men to stop making such a noise. Monsieur was, however, much too frightened, so Madame rose in her wrath, walked into the next cabin in her night attire and shrilly complained of the goings-on. Mr Craven, stretched full length on his bunk, and very drunk, merely said in his worst French 'Dites-lui – si elle ne sort pas, je casserai la gueule à lui'. After this awful insult, of course Monsieur had to challenge him to a duel, but his relief was so intense when Mr Craven apologized humbly next day that he seized him by the hand and wrung it warmly. I heard all this from Mme Logerais, a very nice doctor's wife, with whom I made friends.

M. de Bricusse, the Author, was also on board and Lord Carlisle made an excellent sketch of his wife for me. The boat *Iraouaddy* belonged to the Messageries Maritimes and there were very few English people on board. T, who always got on well with foreigners, soon joined a little bridge playing circle and spent most of his time with them in a small deck-cabin. He was very good to me when we came in for bad weather and I succumbed to sea sickness and I was so touched at all his little attentions.

At Port Said I received some rather disquieting letters from my Mother, to whom our Governess had behaved very rudely and disagreeably, even setting Blanchie against her, and I foresaw there was trouble ahead.

On St. Patrick's Day we landed at Marseilles and on March 18th we were once more back in London after an absence of nearly 4½ months. It was a great joy to get back to the children. They were all much grown and those few months had made such a difference in them. At first they were rather shy with us, but we soon got over that. Blanchie and Katie seemed very grown up, but the most altered of all was Billy, whom we had left small and rather puny and who was now quite plump and such a darling.

Relations between Mother and Miss Scott (the children's Governess) were very strained. I was inclined to take the latter part at first, but subsequent events confirmed all Mother's complaints of her and I found that she had acquired a most strange and unnatural influence over the children, but it was a long time before I realized this and it was only 2 years later that we parted with her.

We stayed at Lansdowne House when first we came back. Our original plan had been to go straight over to Curraghmore, but while we were away the electric light had been put in and, like all such jobs, had taken longer than was expected, so that the house was not yet ready for us.

W (I shall henceforward describe him thus, to distinguish him from little Tyrone), went over on the 25th for about a fortnight as he had a good deal of business to transact over there. Meanwhile, I had quite a gay time at Lansdowne House, where Father and Mother entertained a good deal at that time and there were constant lunch and dinner parties. I came back very thin and brown (or yellow?) from B.E. Africa. We came in for very cold weather and I found the east winds most trying and felt rather seedy for some time. The E. African climate, which is most stimulating while you are there, produces this reaction in most people and Irene Ward, who arrived home with her husband about a fortnight after us, was very unwell for several months after her return.

April and May 1906

Early in April, the children and I moved to No. 5 Seymour Street, which we had taken for 6 weeks from Col. Wyndham-Quin. It was a very nice house, but badly needed doing up. There was also a faulty sink near the childrens' rooms, which must have been the cause of their constant feverish attacks and which worried me very much. At one moment, the children all developed queer coughs of a whooping cough nature and for nearly 3 weeks we were more or less in quarantine for this. In the end, we all moved to Lansdowne House again, though only for a few days, before going to Ireland. After W returned from Curraghmore we saw a good deal of the Cyril Wards and there was much comparing of notes and photographs between us. We spent a few days at Badminton and later on W went to the Iveaghs for Punchestown, but I was too seedy to accompany him.

W was to be back in London for his birthday on April 28th and, as there was to be a great wrestling match that night at Olympia between the redoubtable Hackenschmidt and Madrali the Turk, I bought 6 tickets for the show and arranged a little dinner party for W. What was my dismay when he wired to say he could not get back for another week! There was I, left to cope alone with this most unusual performance. However, it seemed a pity to waste the tickets, so I collected my party and we witnessed the match, which was a most disappointing one as Madrali was finished in the second round and the whole show was over in a few minutes.

It was that Spring that we bought the lease of 51 Upper Brook Street. We had long ago promised to buy a house in London and when we saw this one – still very much in the rough after being practically re-built – it seemed the very thing for us.

In the middle of May we left for Curraghmore. The day I arrived there (May 14th) came the news of Granny Beaufort's death, so W stayed in England until after her funeral. She was the most wonderful person and held herself so beautifully that she never looked old, in spite of her many troubles. Her manner was rather stern and abrupt and therefore somewhat alarming, but there was no limit to her kindness and she was very much beloved.

There was much to see and do at Curraghmore when we got back there and great was our delight at being home again. Also, the newly installed Electric Light was a great joy.

W and I attacked the rooks with great energy that spring, getting 70 to 80 one afternoon; the next day we were at it again and afterwards came on to the Kennels (where W spent most of his spare time) to look at the Hounds. In stepping across a newly cemented gutter there, I slipped up and came down with a crash on the base of my spine. It hurt horribly, but I said nothing – nobody having seen me fall – and walked as best I could to where W was standing gazing at a hound. Hardly had I got hold of his arm when I fainted. There was a great commotion and I remember W and Hayes (the Huntsman) both struggling to undo my tie – which was a sort of stock – and making it considerably tighter before they finally succeeded. I went from one faint into another and poor W was dreadfully alarmed; however, after a while I was very sick and then got better and was soon taken home and put to bed, where I remained for a week, as the Doctor feared the after-effects of the concussion, which was pretty severe.

The next event recorded in the diary is Bill's birthday, May 30th, when he weighed 23½ lbs and measured 29 inches. On the next day W and I motored to Fethard for the Christening of Arthur John Perry, to whom I was Godmother.

June 1906

On June 5th W and I motored to the Curragh for the annual Training of the S.I. Yeomanry, taking Mr Somerville and Mr Gethin with us. W, of course, was in camp, while I stayed with the Greers at Crotanstown. Jean Wise was also there and Miss 'Fox' McNeill, a lady of independent habits, who was as cute as a fox, knew all there was to know about horses, played tennis extremely well, lived on 2½d a year and was withal of a somewhat masterful disposition, but a real 'good sort'. She and I crept out after dinner once or twice, walked across the Curragh and sat near the S.I.Y. camp, listening to the band, unbeknownst to any of the officers.

The camp was only about ¾ mile away and one evening, when the Greers had brought their gramophone into the garden and had put on a very good 'Melba' record, it was actually heard in camp and the men were wondering where this beautiful voice came from.

I rode a good deal with Mr Allan Lendrum, a young cousin of Mary Greer's, and watched the Yeomanry at their drills and manoeuvres. General Baden Powell stayed at Crotanstown one night. Urged by Mary Greer, he drew some extraordinarily clever little sketches, two of them being of men in the Yeomanry – which he had been inspecting. I was hoping to secure these for my book and what was my disgust when he tore the whole lot up before anyone could stop him.

General Rimington commanded the Cavalry in Ireland that year; he always showed great interest in the Yeomanry and often followed them about when manoeuvring, besides the formal inspection.

One Sunday morning, I photographed the S.I.Y. as they marched away after Church Parade and was lucky in getting some quite good panoramas of them (Book XI), including a nice photograph of W.

Blanchie, whose eyes were troublesome then, had to go and see Dr Maxwell, the Dublin Oculist, and Mrs Greer kindly invited her to join me at Crotanstown first. She was then 7½ and just old enough to thoroughly enjoy such a treat and to delight in seeing her Father's Regiment and the camp and all. She was rather upset by the journey and was overcome by sickness at the Wingfields, where we had tea, but was quite all right next day. We went to hear the Band play midday and stayed to luncheon in camp; in the afternoon there was a Gymkhana at the Polo Ground. Next day we walked about watching the S.I.Y. on the Curragh and later went to the Yeomanry Sports, at which I gave the prizes. It was a great experience for little Blanchie.

On June 21st, after going up to Dublin, we returned home, where W joined us a few days later. The only other incident I remember that month was a Prizegiving at Bishop Foy's school, followed by luncheon at the O'Haras (Bishop).

July 1906

W was very strong on exercise just then and one day in July he announced his intention of walking into Waterford, which he did in 3 hours and 7 minutes. On July 20th we had a large tennis party, about 50 people, and 2 months later we gave a garden party, at which there were about 180 people. We had the Yeomanry Band down for the occasion. Lady Bessborough's brother, Mr Montague Guest, took some very good panoramic photographs that day.

On July 21st the Fishguard and Rosslare line was opened and W went to Rosslare for the ceremony, which was performed by Lord Aberdeen – the Lord Lieutenant. W thought him very much wanting in dignity on this occasion and told me that when one of the local officials discovered that he had left his hat at the other end of the platform, Lord Aberdeen was most anxious to run and fetch it for him.

We had a good many people staying with us that summer: Perrys, Somervilles, Doynes, Kennedys, Durham Matthews, Forbes, Wicklows etc. etc., and several Masters of Hounds at different times.

Also we had Miss Gwennie O'Shee to paint 'Wanderer' and Miss Florence Fraser to paint two of W's hunters. Unfortunately they arrived within a few days of each other. Gwennie O'Shee did all her painting in the open, as she maintained it was impossible to get the proper effects otherwise. Miss Flo Fraser painted anywhere and everywhere and fairly enraged Gwennie when she said she could always manage by 'allowing for this' and 'allowing for that', and that she didn't think it worthwhile to take the horses out. One certainly has to allow for a good deal when looking at her pictures!

I now come to an incident which, though apparently trivial in itself, cast a shadow over my life for quite a long time.

Ever since W had decided to take the Hounds, he had thought of little else. All his spare moments were spent at the kennels and he was simply longing for the beginning of the hunting season. So impatient was he that he decided to start cub hunting on July 25th and, accordingly, he was out at cock-crow and killed 6 cubs that morning. His Valet – Goodchild – who was out on foot, told my Maid when he came in to breakfast that the cubs were very small and that it seemed a shame to kill them, but W was so keen that his Hounds should have blood, and so delighted with the way in which they hunted, that he came in quite jubilant. I can see him now, as he came into the Lower Hall with Commander Forbes behind him and I going to the top of the stairs to welcome him. But my welcome was not wholehearted enough, for I was thinking of the very young cubs and I knew he had started cubbing much too early; so when he triumphantly informed me that he had killed 6 cubs, I – fool that I was – said I had heard they were nothing but babies and he afterwards declared that I had sneered at him before all the servants. Goodness knows, I never meant to do this and I honestly thought I had said it chaffingly, but of course I ought never to have said it at all, for to him it meant utter want of sympathy and lack of understanding of his ambitions and he felt that I had failed him at one of the biggest moments of his life. He brooded over my unfortunate remark till he magnified it a hundredfold and for days he would hardly speak to me. I tried to have it out with him several times, but it was no good and I shall never forget the utter misery of those days.

We were all busy with a bazaar for the Martin Hospital. The house was full of people and one had to go on as if nothing had happened, in spite of the horrible estrangement between us. I was quite glad when W went off to the Carlow Puppy Show with Commander Forbes, but when he came back 2 days later things were very little better, though Commander Forbes had been doing all he could to set things right. At last W forgave me, but I don't think he ever quite forgot that morning and he was always persuaded that I took no interest in his Hounds. I must candidly admit that I did not want to stand gazing at them for hours on end and that I thought it a pity he should become so engrossed in them that he really neglected a good deal of his other business, but I was immensely proud of them and much interested in the young entry and in all his schemes for breeding etc. Many was the hour I spent with him in the evening working out pedigrees to the 5th or 6th generation.

The breeding constantly occupied his thoughts and one occasion he had been sitting absolutely silent all through dinner, with an expression as if all the cares of State were on his shoulders, when suddenly he straightened himself and thumped the table vigorously, and with a beaming smile, he exclaimed 'I've got it, yes, I've got it'! 'What?' said I excitedly – 'Yes' he said, 'I'll send Gaylass to the Warwickshire – and then followed the family history of the said Gaylass and her future husband with all the points in favour of such a match. He had evidently been working this out for the last hour and probably during much of the evening before that. He only cub hunted once again in July and then did no more of it for several weeks; nor did he ever start so early in the season again.

Paddy Perry spent some time with us that summer. He was only about a month older than Tyrone, but much more self-possessed, full of pluck and with an imagination which never failed him when he was anxious to impress people. Tyrone, who was then rather fat and limp, and decidedly unenterprising, got more and more depressed when Paddy boasted of his exploits and, at last, when I went up to hear his prayers one evening, he threw his arms round my neck and, bursting into floods of tears, he said 'Mother, Paddy can't really swim, can he?'

August 1906

In August, Patsy and Bill went to Duncannon and I took the three elder children to Glenbride where Mary Doyne and her Robin met us and a week later came W, Mr Doyne and Commander Forbes. How we all got into the old house – which had not then been added to – I can't think, but the Mander was the only person who had a room to himself. It was on this occasion that he did the sketch entitled 'Bobby caracoles' after seeing Mary and me very nearly pitched off the fat pony on which we were both riding astride.

W only spent a week with us and then went off to Scotland to stay at Blair Atholl till 31st, so Mary and I were soon left alone with the four children again. Robin Doyne, being the oldest boy present, though some months younger than Blanchie, was inclined to assume the leadership of the small party and always insisted on being 'the General' when they played at soldiers. This somewhat annoyed the others, but they were excellent friends on the whole. Robin proposed to Blanchie soon after he arrived, but changed his mind later and decided to marry Katie. One morning, when I was dressing, I heard a great commotion in the passage and presently Robin appeared with Katie leaning on his arm. She was tastefully draped in bath towels and had a wreath in her hair and a bouquet (I think of heather) in her hand, while Tyrone, as bridesmaid, carried her train. The kitchen maid – who took the clergyman part – awaited the party at the end of the passage. Blanchie, meanwhile, with rage in her heart and a fierce frown on her brow, had sought refuge in my room, so as not to see the hateful sight, though she assured me she didn't care in the least and that she hated Robin. I'm afraid the others rather enjoyed her discomfiture as she was somewhat dictatorial in those days and they wanted to pay her out, but I'm thankful to say that this was but a passing phase. Robin soon after tired of his wife and informed her that she was dead and buried; a fickle youth indeed!

We always – except on long expeditions – took a dish of pudding out for the children when we lunched out. Each had a bowl and spoon and looked charming sitting there in the heather – till the bowl upset over the child and neighbours.

One day we took them all to the top of Mullaghcleavaun (2783 ft high). We started at one o'clock and didn't get home till 8.30pm and it was a weary little party indeed on the return journey and we nearly lost our way. Another day, Tyrone fell into a stream and had to be wrung out, while Bone – who always accompanied us on these expeditions – poured whiskey in his boots to prevent him from catching cold. It was a very hot summer and we had a glorious time and were out from morning till night.

September 1906

By September 3rd we were all back at Curraghmore, or rather W and I went to Bessborough for a couple of days for the Iverk Show etc. It was the first time we had stayed there together and we quite enjoyed it as they made us so welcome and it was a most pleasant party. The Bessboroughs were a most united family and I loved to see Lady Bessborough with her three boys, especially with Myles, whom she adored.

W started cub hunting again on September 8th and continued it regularly after that. Susie and her boys came to stay, also Aileen and Edwina, for a short time and Susie and I performed at a Concert at Mount Congreve.

W and I then went to Derreen and it was this time that he shot the big Japanese Deer, commonly called 'the General', which had defied all attempts till then. It weighed 12 stone and had a fine head, which is now in the Dining Room at Derreen. Phyllis and Uncle Freddy Hamilton were there. It was a good year for deep sea fishing and I remember one day when we went out at 4pm and stayed out till nearly 11pm after conger, of which we caught 21, besides 80 or

Beatrix at the schoolchildren's and workers' Coronation Treat distributing buns and tea at Curraghmore, 30th June 1911.

Industry Knitters (ABOVE) *and Best Knitters* (BELOW) *at Curraghmore. Beatrix Waterford's Knitting Industry provided employment for many girls and women both in Curraghmore and Portlaw.*

Red Cross War Hospital Depot Workers, Curraghmore 1915.

Beatrix helped in the training of nurses at Curraghmore.
BACK ROW L TO R: *A. Flynn, Mrs Annesley, Beatrix, Mrs Walker, E. Thompson, Miss Bowesman, Mrs Eaton, C. Ryan, B. Power, V. Villiers Stewart*
FRONT ROW L TO R: *D. Ruttle, Hugh, E. Flemyng, M. Curran, Miss Wallace, Mrs Gethin, B. Crane, N. Collie, G. Malcomson.*

Lady Susan Dawnay in her Red Cross War Hospital Depot at Ascot.

90 other fish. W put in a couple of days at Killarney, where he killed a nice stag and we were home again by the 25th.

A great sorrow fell over the Yard 3 days later when Bone's little girl, Mary, who was the same age as Patsy, died of cerebral meningitis after about 4 weeks' illness. Poor Bone, who adored the child, was absolutely broken-hearted and nothing would comfort him.

Father and Mother paid us a visit on their way back from Derreen and when Father left for London W went with him to have his leg treated, as he had strained the 'Tailor's Muscle' very badly and could not ride with any comfort. This muscle was a perpetual worry to him and spoiled much of his pleasure in hunting as he had no grip and it often hurt him abominably. Mr Percival – our E. African friend – was staying with us at the time and stayed on with Mother and me. Such an odd little party and Mother found great difficulty in following all his stories of people in E. Africa and their doings.

October 1906

On October 6th Mother and I went over to England by the new Rosslare line, for the first time, and motored from Bath to Bowood, going on to London 2 days later. I spent the next two weeks in visiting at Lansdowne House, Camberley (with Susie) and Englemere, and in furnishing our new London house, 51 Upper Brook Street, into which I moved – camping fashion – on October 22nd. Susie stayed with me and Aileen and Edwina suddenly proposed themselves to stay the night and do a play with us. Hastily, we ordered in beds and draped the windows with brown holland, as the blinds were not yet up. Food was procured and also a ½ bottle of port from the stores. Bin No. 20, vaguely chosen as sounding respectable. It was a nauseous drink, but we made the best of it and the house warming dinner was a most cheery affair. Then we went to see du Maurier in *Raffles* and were spell-bound with excitement. On our return, pyjamas (all mine) were laid out for the guests, as the house felt cold and rather damp and I was afraid they would all get rheumatics. Presently, we all met in pyjamas and pig-tails – the queerest party imaginable, and partook of Bangers & Biscuits before going to bed.

Next morning – whether from too much excitement or Bin No. 20 – I know not – Aileen was laid low with a splitting headache and when Evie – beautifully dressed and groomed – came to see her she found her lying under a miscellaneous collection of rugs and fur coats, with her head swathed in wet towels and the bed surrounded by screens to keep off the light from the uncurtained windows.

The following week I had to go to Liverpool (staying with the Hall-Walkers at Gateacre) to sell Curraghmore Industry Woollies at the Irish Industries Sale and, though we did extremely well and made over £100 at our Stall, I was rather sad over it as it caused me to miss our first Opening Meet in Waterford.

November and December 1906

I was home on November 3rd and started hunting with W soon after that. I hadn't hunted for 2½ years and it was a great joy going out again and seeing W hunt the Hounds. I soon gave up following him, however, as I saw I should only be dreadfully in the way under present conditions and, on the whole, it is best to keep out of sight of the Master as much as possible. As a matter of fact, he did not always hunt the Hounds at that time and was by way of taking turns at it with Haynes, but his mind was entirely taken up with watching the Hounds at their work and he generally helped to whip-in if he wasn't hunting them.

Later in that month he and several of the children got influenza – which with Blanchie was followed by tonsillitis and a good deal of throat and gland trouble – he wasn't able to hunt for a week and I went out by myself one day at Dunhill and tried to tell him all about it afterwards, but I was never any good at describing a hunt as I have no bump of locality and a hopelessly bad memory!

January and February 1907

Some time after this, on a day when we met at Gardenmorris, I amused myself by counting the jumps in two runs. One of them was fairly fast, lasting 55 minutes and in this we had the same number of jumps, i.e. 1 per minute on an average! The other was a slow hunt of 3½ hours, with many checks, the total number of jumps was something over 100. There was a wonderful fox in Carrigmore then. His history may be read in my Scrapbook No. XII, in an article by Maintop (Commander Forbes) in the *Country Gentleman*, October 1907, and he was already well known before the date of which I write. Mr Pollok had hunted him 5 or 6 times in 1905, the longest run then being 3 hrs and 5 minutes, when they covered over twenty miles of country. On January 19th W hunted him for 2 hours and on January 19th for 3 hours and 20 minutes. On the latter occasion again covering over 20 miles; and he only just saved his brush both times owing to darkness coming on. Then, on February 26th 1907, when W was unfortunately laid up with a bad leg, he gave us the record run of 4¾ hours, which, as ridden, measure 26 miles. I was riding Brian, who remained game to the last and was one of the only horses that saw the hunt through, for Haynes had changed on to his 2nd horse and most of the field had gone home exhausted. I was frightfully proud at being able to give a good account of myself to W, but very sad that he hasn't been there too. The old fox became too cute for us after that and used to slip away long before Hounds entered the covert, but early in the following season – October 29th 1907 – he met his end after a good hunt of 1 hr and 40 minutes.

But to return to the winter of 1906-7, we had a very amusing party that Xmas, when the Ansons, Perrys, Rimingtons, Captain J.G. Beresford, the Knight of Glin, and Mr Humble stayed with us. There was a fair amount of snow and we tobogganed several days. Mr Humble was, as usual, the butt and we very nearly killed him between us, as I first of all nearly ran him into a tree and then W said he would take him down the steep pitch below 'Mother Brown', and at the last moment gave him a strong shove off and let him go by himself, having previously told him on no account to look round. Down the hill went 'Uncle Charlie', gaily shouting tally ho as he passed the convulsed audience and making no attempt at steering as he imagined W to be behind him all the time. He headed straight for the ditch and we held our breath as he came near it, but luckily he rolled off just in the nick of time.

General Rimington's wife, who was Irish, but had been caught in S. Africa, caused us much amusement. She was one of the most frankly vulgar women I have ever met and I was told that I only saw her in her most refined and chastened moods! The first night they stayed with us, just as the ladies were going to bed, she demanded a whiskey and soda and kept us all hanging about for ages while she drank it. 'Mike' evidently reproved her for this for she took none the following night, but she asked Dollie Perry to come and undo her gown and when the door was shut, she said 'I'll tell you what, now, I think I'll have a whiskey and soda. You know, in these real good houses, they wouldn't like ye to have a whiskey and soda in the Drawing Room, so I always carry some about in me bag', whereupon she produced a large flask and a bottle of Perrier, which was half empty and quite flat and proceeded to mix herself a good strong drink in the tooth glass!

The bed in the Queen's Room was rather small for two and the mattress at that time badly needed renewing. 'Mike' was very long and thin; Mrs Mike was of generous proportions, and she told me that they hadn't sleep very well the first night, the bed being small and Mike's knees so bony, but after that she added, 'We got the hang of the bed all right'.

When we were at the Curragh the summer before, she had made W (who hated cats) buy a Persian kitten off her for a guinea and she said 'You may be sure I made the most of that afterwards for it isn't every day a real live Marquess comes along, and everybody wanted to buy a kitten after he'd taken one!. This same lady, when visiting me at 51 Upper Brook Street some time later, gazed round the Library appraisingly, declared her approval of it and then delighted me by saying, 'It must be very nice for you to have a ventre-à-terre in London'!!

W's youngest Beresford Uncle 'Delaval' died in America that winter; he seldom came to England and we had not succeeded in meeting him the last time he came over, so I had never seen him. He was buried at Clonegam on January 18th 1907. He had a 'coloured' Housekeeper called 'Flora Wolff' and there was some anxiety lest he might have married her, in which case she might presently appear at Curraghmore with rows of little part-coloured children. I believe she really was very fond of him and looked after him well, and when one of his friends went to his place to settle things up, she said she intended to come and weep on his grave at Curraghmore. Luckily we were spared this trial and the lady did not assert herself further.

During that winter we had dancing classes for the children, held alternately at Curraghmore, Rocketts Castle and Mount Bolton. There were about a dozen in the class and a very nice teacher called Miss Graham used to come down from Dublin once a week. At Xmas, I made a sort of little bazaar at which my children could buy presents for everyone, as they had no chance of shopping. They brought their little purses solemnly bought the things from me, after much deliberation. I'm afraid they found the shop prices very high when they grew too old to make their purchases at home.

'Goal Ball' was in full swing that winter and I played a great deal, but nothing would ever induce W to join in the game, though I felt sure he would have enjoyed it had he ever given it a trial.

Mr Willie Malcomson died in January 1907. His wife did not long survive him for she died at Madeira, where she had gone for change of air; and only a few months later, their only daughter, Susie, died in England.

Amongst our guests that winter were the de la Poer girls, Lady Bessborough and Gweneth, the Harold Brasseys, Kennedys, Kerry and Elsie, Aileen, Major Buldoo Bryan, Mr Nicholas Lambert and the Durham Matthews.

An entry in my diary of, 'tea with Mrs Lowndes', reminds me of a dinner party when this lady – wife of the D.I. was our guest. After dinner, seeing her sitting in an armchair with no-one talking to her, I went across the room and sat on the arm. She begged me to take the chair, but I, quite happy where I was, refused, and when she pressed me again, I said 'Oh no – thank you, I love an arm'. Whereupon she looked at me most archly and said, 'Oh, you do, do yer'!!

I spent a few days at Shelton with the Wicklows and went with them to a place called Kilmacurragh, where an old man called Mr Acton had a most wonderful garden, full of tropical shrubs from all parts of the world. He was a recluse and hated seeing people. I only had a passing glimpse of a wild looking old man, with straggly hair and one prodigiously long tooth, which stuck out like a tusk. Some time before his sister had died. He ordered a very light coffin for her and rejected one after another because they weren't thin enough; when he finally got what he wanted he wheeled the coffin to the garden on a barrow and buried the lady there beside his favourite horse.

W and I went backwards and forwards to London a good deal that winter; his leg was a constant worry to him and after he strained the muscle very badly on February 25th he was not able to ride at all for ever so long and could only watch the hunting from a motor, which was most trying for him.

March and April 1907

In March we went to stay with the Durham Matthews at Curragh Chase – Aileen with us – for the Yeomanry Point-to-Point Races at Kilmallock. The S.I.Y. won the event that year. From there we went on to London, where I had still a good deal to do in furnishing our new house, and W came there for the first time. A few days later – after the Annual St. Patrick's Day Irish Industries Sale – we went to Croxteth for the Grand National and, as usual, had a very pleasant time there. The Grand National was won by Eremon, Newey riding, and the amazing thing was that the latter had ridden most of the course with only one stirrup!

We were home on March 23rd and were joined there by Commander Forbes, who had been specially invited to see the new Hounds which W had just bought from the 'Four Burrow'. A few days later we had a visit from Lord Grenfell – then Commander-in-Chief in Ireland – and his wife, with Mr Bridgeman, A.D.C., and my book shows (Vol. XII) some very excellent photographs taken by Alice Grenfell.

The hunting season ended on March 30th and then followed the usual Point-to-Point Races in Waterford, Kilkenny and Tipperary. W, of course, could not ride that year, but his mare 'Gibson Girl' (which Clark always would call Gibson's Girl) won the Waterford Heavy Weight race, with Mr Kenneally riding her. Also a match against Mr Boyse's 'Loftus'.

After that came the Hunt Ball and then W went off to Punchestown, where his horse A.D.C. came in 2nd for the Gold Cup. The following week we had a visit from Count Schönborn, who had come over to buy hunters for himself and family, and after he and other visitors had left we went – taking in Tipperary Point-to-Point en route – to stay with the Donoughmores at Knocklofty.

W went on to England, but I stayed for the Tipperary Hunt Ball, a lively entertainment as usual, at which we danced steadily from 9.30pm to 4.30am. It was six o'clock by the time we got to bed and a few hours afterwards I was motoring home so as to be back in time for our Puppy Show. With me went Mrs Church, 1st cousin to Willie Perry, with whom she was not on speaking terms, owing to some foolish joke of Willie's, which she had taken as an insult. Various other causes for quarrelling had arisen since, and I spent most of the time during that motor drive in arguing with the lady and trying to persuade her to drop all this nonsense, but without much success. As if this wasn't enough, I had afterwards to keep a watchful eye on her and her Mother – Mrs Bookey – in order that they shouldn't bump into Mr Humble, with whom they were also not on speaking terms, owing to an abortive engagement between Mr Humble and 'Miss Bookey' many years previously. People who nurse their past in this way are really most trying!

The Puppy Show was a great success: W had returned from his flying visit to London. Six Masters of Hounds came to stay and all the Puppy Walkers were lavishly entertained and seemed well pleased with the Show. There were some splendid puppies, conspicuous among them being 'Dancer' and 'Diligent', whose photographs appear in my book.

Among the Masters staying with us was Mr Nicholas Lambert, a great character, who hunted the Kilkenny Hounds, and was commonly called 'Dirty Lambert', in order to distinguish him from his cousin, 'Liar Lambert'! He really didn't look particularly dirty, but always had a greasy lock of hair falling over his forehead and was very untidy. He began by calling W 'Lord Waterford' – then 'Waterford', then 'Tye' and, finally, when well mellowed by champagne it was 'Toye, me dear boy', accompanied by a slap on the back.

May and June 1907

A week later I was in London and by May 2nd W and all the children had joined me there and we were all settled at 51 Upper Brook Street. W did not stay long, however, as he went off with Commander Forbes on May 7th to take the Waters at Aix-les-Bains, doing a motor tour through Touraine etc. On the way there Commander Forbes wrote an account of this tour in the *Country Gentleman*, entitled 'On the Roads of France', which will be found in the scrap book, Vol. XII. There was a very warm friendship between these two, in spite of the great disparity of age and I always looked on the Commander as W's best and truest friend, owing to the confidence between them and the Mander's excellent influence and frank speaking.

W was away for 4 weeks, during which time I indulged in German Measles and after 12 days quarantine went to stay with the Hopes at New Lodge (Forest Row) for change of air. W and I had lately been invited to join the 'Sea to Sea Club' and I remember going to rather a deadly dinner given by them, taking Susie as my guest.

W was back on June 5th and that same night we went to a Ball at Devonshire House, where we danced till 3am, and I remember that, as people gradually melted away in the small hours, W and I were left dancing together, with only 2 or 3 other couples. W always danced with great energy and a long swinging stride and in the nearly empty room he fairly let himself go, till, exhausted and breathless, we stopped near the old Duchess. She looked affectionately at us and then, tapping me on the arm with her fan, she said, 'Go on dancing, I like to see you', and on we went again till the music stopped.

Three days later, W went to Newbridge for the Yeomanry Training and was away for nearly 3 weeks. During this time I went out a good deal to dinners, dances etc., and also went to Court, at which I presented John Hope's wife – Betty.

The Digbys gave a dance for Margery – then about 19 – and I helped them by taking a large dinner party on to it. That summer I got up some dancing lessons for grown-ups in order to learn reversing, which was considered very vulgar in my youth, but was then becoming most fashionable.

One Sunday Kerry, Elsie, Clodagh and I motored to Coombe to see the Charlie Beresfords; there was no sign of them when we arrived, but various other stray guests were scattered about the house and garden and we all made ourselves more or less at home, till our hostess returned from a walk in the woods with one of her long-haired friends. We didn't see much of her and Uncle Charlie only turned up just as we were leaving and we came to the conclusion that we might just as well have remained at home. Kathleen, who could not get on with her Mother, established herself in a Dairy some little distance from the house. It was a queer place; the Dairy itself was her Sitting Room and there were one or two tiny bedrooms off it, but her one idea was to be independent of her Mother and to see as little of her as possible, as she knew her presence always irked her Mother dreadfully.

Some time after this, Kathleen stayed with me in London and I took her to a very stately Ball at the Benckendorffs (Russian Embassy). She was in a queer mood that night; first of all she hid behind me and wouldn't dance at all, then she either snubbed her partners, or else talked at the top of her voice, attracting everyone's attention. Finally, she planted herself in a most conspicuous position in front of several Royalties and made such loud remarks that I blushed for shame and vowed I would never take her out again.

I spent some days at Englemere for Ascot Races, at which there was great excitement over the disappearance of the Gold Cup, which was actually stolen from the place in the Stand where it was on view – no clue being found. After the races came the Garden Party at Windsor – a very fine sight – and then I returned to London where W joined me a few days later.

July 1907

The next month was fairly crowded with gaieties. I remember a concert given by Mr Ralli at which we heard the new Tenor, McCormack, for the first time; a visit to the Crichtons and Jerry Wards at Ditton, when we were somewhat embarrassed by meeting Baron de Forest with his second wife (née Ethel Gerard), whom he had married after forcing the

Menier wife to divorce him. A beautiful Ball at Grosvenor House and Rivallon de la Poer's wedding at Brompton Oratory.

Then there was a visit to the Royal Academy with W, who always caused me great anxiety on such occasions, as his favourite trick was to draw my attention to some picture and then, while I gazed at it, to slip off and disappear into one of the other rooms. After that, he would generally contrive to stalk me while I hunted everywhere for him, a most foolish proceeding! After being subjected to this game two or three times, however, I insisted on taking his arm and clung to him firmly until we left the building.

We sold Ford that summer, to Lord Joicey, and as we had reserved certain pictures and furniture out of the sale, I had to go to Ford to make the selection. I took an expert from Christie's with me and spent a whole day going through the rooms very carefully with him and marking the things that were to come away. Amongst these were the three Reynolds pictures, now in the Yellow Drawing Room and many other Delaval portraits, besides some valuable bits of furniture, consoles, cabinets, mirrors etc., some of which were sent to London and the rest to Curraghmore.

This reminds me of an incident which happened many months later – in fact over a year – when all the pictures had been done up and sent to Curraghmore. W was very conservative and hated changes and whenever I asked him to help me to re-arrange the pictures in order to make room for the new ones, he merely answered that they would do very nicely as they were, that he did not intend to alter any and that the new ones could be put up anywhere. Now, 'anywhere' didn't exist, as the walls were all covered and it was necessary to weed out some of the very moderate pictures then hanging in the Drawing Rooms in order to accommodate the far more valuable ones from Ford. At last, in desperation, when W was away for some weeks, I decided to risk the consequences and proceeded to pull down and re-hang in every room except W's own. It was a big job, but I determined to get it done before he returned and to have everything in order so that he might perhaps not notice the changes at once. I had often effected changes in this way, for when he was engrossed with his hounds, or anything of that sort, he noticed very little around him. Then, when the change dawned on him, I was able to say quite truthfully, 'It has been like that for ages'! But the scheme didn't work this time. Often, when Bone was helping me with the hanging, he would murmur, 'Well, I only hope we shan't have to put everything back again'; and the large wall mirrors between the windows in the Blue Drawing Room were a special anxiety.

Everything was finished and W returned. He crossed by Rosslare and motored from Waterford and, as bad luck would have it, his train was so early that he arrived home about 6.30am and, not liking to disturb me so early, he took a stroll round the rooms!! One after another my enormities flashed upon him and when he came up to my room he informed me that everything would have to be put back exactly as it was before. 'My word, I knew it', said Bone, when I repeated this order to him, and for some days I really thought we might have to restore things to their original positions, but I think W was really rather pleased with some of the changes and the subject was gradually dropped and the alterations tacitly accepted.

The visit to Ford was rather heart-rending in some ways for the old people there were so terribly hurt at our selling the place, and when I went round to say goodbye to some of them, they looked so reproachful, and one of them said, 'Oh, Lady Waterford, Lady Waterford, how could you do it?' They could not understand that Curraghmore must come first, as our real home, for to them Ford was the home of the 'family' and seemed much the most important. It was certainly far better for us to have only the one place, as it was most expensive to keep up both and the annual move cost an awful lot. Also, now W had the hounds he could not be away from Curraghmore for so long. The place had been let for some time to the Mossops, with whom I stayed while up there. It was all looking very lovely in that bright July weather and I felt quite sad when I drove away for the last time.

Later in that month, W and I went to Englemere and from there made a round of private schools at Farnborough, Eversley and Wokingham, with a view to entering Tyrone for one of them, but later on W saw West Downs and like that better than any of them and we never regretted the choice. We also went one Sunday to Wellington and attended Chapel there; afterwards going round the College with Dr Pollok, the Head. I was rather keen on sending Tyrone there, but W was not favourably impressed by the appearance of the boys and we neither of us cared much for Dr Pollok, in spite of his great reputation, so Tyrone was finally put down for Winchester.

The children had been with us in London all this time and had had their little diversions, including a children's party at Buckingham Palace, to which I took the four elder ones, and several visits to the zoo. Blanchie no longer wished to kiss the porcupine, as she was so anxious to do on her first visit, but they all loved going there. I remember one occasion on which Victor and I took 8 of our children together and had great work in keeping an eye on them all. Mrs Charlton painted a miniature of Katie that summer – not at all a successful venture – and W insisted on my sitting to Saniton, who shone at Silver-point sketches, but did not succeed in catching much of a likeness to me.

One day we dressed Billy – aged 2 – in a blue serge suit of Tyrone's, much to his delight, and the photograph of him – looking exactly like my Mother – can be seen in my book.

In the 3rd week of July, the children left London and W and I went to Bowood for the Royal Visit, of which photographs will be seen in the scrap books. On the way down, W was hunting the bookstall for something to read and I advised him to get Elinor Glyn's *Three Weeks*, which I had heard everyone discussing, but had not read myself. He read a few chapters in the train and on arrival at Bowood put the book down on the centre table in the ante room to the Library, just where anyone passing was bound to see it. My Father found it there presently and wanted to know who had left such a horrible book about, whereupon W, Adam-like, said it was his and 'Bertie had recommended it' to him. The offending volume was only removed just in time before the Royalties arrived.

There was a notable gathering at Bowood for the Royal Visit, including Lord and Lady Salisbury, Lord and Lady Crewe, Lord and Lady Ilchester, Count and Countess Benckendorff, M. de Soveral (commonly called 'the Blue Monkey'), Mr Balfour, John Revelstoke, Evie and Victor, Kerry and Elsie. Princess Victoria came with the King and Queen and all made themselves most agreeable. Gottlieb's Band discoursed sweet music in the evenings and one night they played with Dr Alcock at the Organ.

The visit was a very short one – only 2 days – and when the King and Queen drove off, I took some panorama photographs of the Cortège, and the King very kindly remained standing while I did one of them.

On July 23rd W and I motored to Swindon and crossed to Ireland via Fishguard, but we did not remain long at home, as W had to make another flying visit to England and I joined the children at Duncannon for a few days.

August 1907

W came straight there from Rosslare on August 3rd and after a happy morning spent in making sand castles with the children we made for home in the motor.

A visit to Gurteen – the Clonmel Horse & Hound Show (at which our 'unentered ladies' took a 2nd prize) – a Concert and Bazaar at Tramore (self playing) and then Dollie Perry and I went down to Duncannon in Peare's motor boat, lunched with the children and motored on to Bannow – Mr Boyse's place. Old Mrs Boyse was a very quaint person and had a way of standing in the middle of the room, 'C'estomac bien avance', and two fingers poised on her cheek, sometimes she could remain like this, quite silent and oblivious of time, till Dollie forcibly removed her. The house was fairly close to the sea, where there was a long stretch of the most glorious strand.

I paid another visit to the children on the way home, where Yseult de la Poer and Col.Lysaght joined us for the Tramore Races. Cub hunting had now begun and occasionally we also went out with the hounds at exercise. We kept French hours that summer, with Déjeuner at 11.30am. This fitted in very well with cub hunting as we were going out at 5am then. We had our African Shamiana Tent pitched on the lawn and usually had tea out there; and very often I used to take out my ring-tailed lemur, 'Mokolo', and let him play round the tent. He had a disconcerting way of suddenly jumping on one's shoulder and when this happened to our Rector, Mr Flemying, he gazed nervously at Mokie and remarked that he had never before seen one of these little animals so close!

Another day, when the Duchess of St. Albans came over, he followed her about, always preparing to spring up, while she, looking first over one shoulder and then over the other, tried to keep him off with her parasol and had a most miserable time! He was sometimes very difficult to catch and I have seen the Butler and two Footmen all stalking him round the Portugal laurels and trying to put their feet on the string which hung from his belt, while he always eluded them at the last moment and often left them sprawling! One day he got into the kitchen and jumped on to the range; his poor little feet were terribly burned and he was very sick for some days. Later on I got a wife for him and they had lovely twins the first year, but after that the babies always came prematurely and died after a few days. They all went to Dublin Zoo in the end, except Mokolo, who died 5 or 6 years later.

I remember a Gardenmorris tennis party, to which W walked most of the way and an awful Bazaar at Stradbally, during which Grace Malcomson and I played and sang at a Concert, poising ourselves on an upturned packing case which wobbled horribly.

Later in the month I motored up to stay with the Ernest Guinnesses at Glenmaroon for the Dublin Horse Show. W joined me there after another dash to London for the Evicted Tenants Bill and we motored home on the 30th, doing the journey in 4¼ hours.

September 1907

In September little Tyrone and I spent 12 days at Derreen, W being there for a week, and I remember a lovely day when Elsie and I took Tyrone on a donkey up Glanrastel Valley and, owing to various contretemps, didn't get back till 8 o'clock, when we were met by Father and W in a search party and caused much agitation!

Mr Great Aunt Georgie (Marquise de Lavalette) died in July of that year and Mother's brother-in-law, Lord Winterton, died on September 5th, so that Mother had to leave Derreen two days after I got there to go to her sister; which was of course a great disappointment to me.

I motored home, stopping at Ballysaggartmore en route to see Clodagh and bring on Susie, whose children also came to stay with us. Later came Evie, with Maud and Blanchie, so we had a fine houseful of children (9) besides other visitors. Amongst these were Leonie Leslie (married to Jack Leslie, W's cousin) and her son, Norman, a delightful boy; and I remember a dark morning when we went cubbing in Portlaw Woods at 4.45am, Norman Leslie and Maud Cavendish with us, and their keen enjoyment of it. Then there was the usual Iverk Show at Bessborough and one night we dined there and danced afterwards till midnight, and I remember Norman and his Mother dancing together and how proud she was of him. Poor thing, she lost him quite early in the war.

October 1907

Later came Maud Ryder and then my brother Charlie, and on October 3rd he and I went over to London together, as he was going off to India on the 10th and I wanted to see all I could of him. He and I were very devoted to each other and it was a great joy to me to spend that week with him. Then I saw him off at Victoria Station and went back feeling very sad.

Two days later I was back at Curraghmore, just in time for Blanchie's birthday, on which auspicious occasion Patsy went to Church for the first time. On the 16th, W and I celebrated our Copper Wedding Day (10 years) and felt quite ancient! Some days later, Blanchie went for her first ride with W, much to her delight.

On October 28th we had the Opening Meet in Waterford (of which there is a photograph in the Scrap Book XII, but the day was wet and sport bad. The next day (when I was not out) saw the death of the famous Carrigmore fox, whose history I have given before. Two days later W hurt his foot out hunting and was unable to hunt for a week. It was at this time that old Johnny Ryan, for many years Stud

Groom at Curraghmore, died, and both W and Major Bryan went to his funeral. Johnny Ryan was the only person with Henry, Lord Waterford, when he broke his neck hunting in Kilkenny. He had ridden many races for him and was then acting as 2nd Horseman. He was a dear old man, of a stamp seldom seen nowadays.

November and December 1907

On November 11th, the Agreement for the sale of Ford to Lord Joicey was at last signed. A few days later I went over to Manchester, stopping a night in Dublin on the way, to have the children's (B & K) eyes examined by Dr Maxwell. Mary Doyne came up for some slight operation the same day and I went to meet her at Westland Row. Dear Miss Power – of the Royal Hotel – insisted on sending the Bultons to escort me to the station and he carried on a running conversation all the way there as we walked. I found Mr Doyne looking as if the world was coming to an end so, after leaving Mary at the Portobello House, I carried him off to dine with me and tried to cheer him up.

I stayed with the Brackleys at Worsley Old Hall for the Irish Industries Sale in Manchester. We did extremely well there, making about £85 at the 'Curraghmore Industry' stall. On the way home, I stayed at Knocklofty to practise for and play at a Concert in Clonmel; quite an ambitious affair, at which I played in a Septette, as well as a solo.

On December 17th Elinor de la Poer was married to her Humphrey Weld, from Gurteen, and Patsy was train bearer, her partner being little Suirdale. Patsy looked the greatest duck in a long white velvet frock and was much interested in the proceedings in Church and the tricks and quick changes of the R.C. Bishop, which she described graphically afterwards.

The year closed with the usual Xmas festivities, including a School Tea in the Riding School. We had the Ansons, Kennedys and Mr T Ponsonby with us for Xmas and at the New Year the Donoughmores, Perrys, de la Poers and Mr Elliot. Captain Connolly, Mr Humble, Mr Seigne, Bertie Ponsonby etc. etc. Ermyngarde de la Poer was then engaged to Mr Elliot and there was much chaff against her and her 'Fweddy'. They were married the following June and we all went to Gurteen for the wedding, at which Patsy was bridesmaid with the Rogers's girl.

January and February 1908

In the Visitors' Book for the New Year there is a picture of a large beetle and thereby hangs a tale. Amongst the 'Xmas Surprises' I had bought some most life-like India rubber beetles and, in order to cheer up Mr Humble, we put one of these in his napkin at dinner, not knowing that he had the utmost horror of such insects. When it dropped out, he leapt up and refused to be comforted till we removed the beast, but during this time another was put into his soup and, being 'Cockie Leekie' that night, the beetle and the prunes were almost indistinguishable, so that we only just prevented him from putting it in his mouth. This new discovery agitated him to such an extent that we could hardly get him to sit down again and he was much too frightened of beetles to touch the thing, so never discovered it wasn't real.

There was a 'Ladies Dance' on January 3rd and the Hunt Ball on 22nd, both in Waterford, and we were kept up till late hours. Kerry and Elsie were with us for the latter.

We played much Goal Ball that winter and had great fun, but W still refused to have anything to do with it and never could be induced to play.

The hounds showed great sport that season and I can remember many a good day, but these are all shown in detail in W's hunting diary. There was one day when 9 of us went out during the New Year party. I remember a specially good day at the Tipperary end of the County (January 18th) when we had a good hour and a half from Ballydine, the first 20 minutes of which was at racing pace and then 22 minutes fast from Cregg. Brian was a bit lame after the first hunt, so W let me ride his 2nd horse Skittles – a great favourite of mine. W also gave me an occasional mount on two other hunters of his – Rockmount and Gibson Girl, but I found the latter a bit big.

Towards the end of January Billy Lambton came to stay with us and during his visit W was asked to take the hounds to Co. Tip for an 'Invitation Meet' at Farranaleen near Fethard. We stayed with the Perrys in Fethard the night before and drove to the Meet with them. It was a bad scenting day and the luck was against us, for we drew covert after covert blank and the Field were most unruly and tiresome. At last we found, and got away from Ballyluskey and had a very fast, '13 minutes without a check, 3 mile point, over 4 we ran'. W's diary continues, '200 people out and desperate bull-riding: Millet distinguished himself by being 17 yds ahead of the leading hound at one time until wire luckily stopped him. Hounds hunted beautifully together, with rare music and drive: everything else blank'. He had previously noted that we, 'caught him by a farm on the Killenaule Mardyke Road'. Of the Ballydine day he notes the 'tremendous pace to Kilcash – more than half the field choked there...killed in open at Ballinure...best day of the season'. I was lucky in being well up in both these hunts, which was of the kind that will always stand out in one's memory.

We reckoned that we rode 30 miles on the Farranaleen day and we came home the same evening – a fairly long day.

They are also connected in my mind with a certain Captain Phillips, whom someone named 'the local Hero' and who was a perpetual thorn in W's flesh. He was as keen as mustard and always cheery and good tempered, but he had an unfortunate knack of getting in the way of hounds and all W's sarcasm and abuse failed to cure him, nor did he ever seem a bit abashed. He generally lost his hat and failed to retrieve it; and I remember him in the Ballydine hunt – tearing down the steepest slope of Curraghdobbin Hill, wild-eyed and hatless, while W yelled at him to 'hold on there'. At Farranaleen, W looked round in despair at the huge and wild field, then said 'Anyhow, thank goodness we shan't have that fellow Phillips over riding hounds today', Phillips having told him that he would be away and unable to come. In the middle of the run, however, a disreputable figure in mufti appeared, all smiles and riding desperately, and there was our friend, who, on his way back to Waterford, had got out at Thurles or somewhere, helped himself to somebody's 2nd horse and caught us up just before we found. I adjured him not to disgrace us and he really showed some self-control that day.

In February Aileen Roberts came to stay with us and hunted with us for nearly a month; and during part of that time we also had the Forbes, Lord Lovat and Peggy Fraser staying with us. Patsy, who was then 5 years old, was always very friendly with men. She always called Peggy 'Miss Fraser', in spite of being asked by her to say 'Peggy', but Lord Lovat became 'Simon' very soon and Patsy was not in the least shy with him.

On February 1st the King and Crown Prince of Portugal were assassinated, which caused no small stir.

On February 2nd Susie's 3rd boy (Ronnie) was born – a fine big fellow.

March 1908

On March 8th I went over to England with Aileen. I ought not really to have been hunting for the last 2 months as there was a babe coming. By that time I thought it as well to go away – far from temptation – particularly as I had business to do in London. The Drawing Room at 51 Upper Brook Street had just been decorated and now had to be arranged; and there was the usual Irish Industries 'St Patrick's' sale, which took place at Londonderry House that year.

W came over for a week, during which time we went to the Palace to see the famous new dancer Maud Allan, who danced as a child of nature – very scantily clothed. She was marvellously graceful and it was really a joy to watch her, provided one wasn't too close. She was the first to introduce this particular style of dancing and all London was talking of her at that time. Another, and very different memory, is of going to St. George's with W to hear our old friend Mr Neligan – now Bishop of Auckland – preach.

W went back to see the Hunting Season out – it ended on March 30th and he notes in his diary that hounds had 'Hunted 83 days, and accounted for 87 foxes after the Opening Meet; found 156 foxes, and had 42 first-class days' sport'.

There was another Yeomanry Point-to-Point that month; the South Irish Horse won it, but it was afterwards given against them by a point in favour of the North, to our intense disgust and chagrin!

The old Duke of Devonshire died on March 24th and Victor then succeeded to the Title and all the many estates and houses, at the same time giving up Holker, where he and Evie had always been so happy.

After my Uncle Winterton's death, Aunt Georgie came to live in London. She was more or less of an invalid, as she suffered from acute arthritis and could hardly walk at all. We used often to go and see her and her house became quite a family meeting place, as all the relations liked to go and see her. My Mother went constantly – in fact, nearly every day. Aunt Georgie was her favourite sister and they were quite devoted to each other.

W bought a new motor about this time, a Gladiator, with a limousine body, and I found this very useful in London. One of my first drives in it was to Southall to see my beloved old Nurse 'Daidai' (Mrs Vale); Dollie Hamilton – who was then staying with me – accompanying me.

April to August 1908

On April 3rd, Beatrix Wilkinson's 2nd child (Muriel Phyllis) was born and I went to see her soon after. The child was rather a queer looking little creature and had a most peculiar cry, 'like a puppy', someone said, but it was not until some weeks later that it was discovered there was something wrong with her and it gave me an awful shock when Claud Anson informed me that 'Beatrix's baby was handicapped', and I was quite nervous lest this abrupt disclosure might affect my baby, but mercifully it did not. Muriel was afterwards pronounced to have Down's Syndrome – and with treatment and training she improved wonderfully as time went on.

The three elder children joined me in London and I remember a children's party with a conjuror at Buckingham Palace and a very nice children's party at Lansdowne House.

On April 6th Charlie returned from India and on the 17th W came over and we both went down to Deepdene for Easter, the children joining us there next day. We were there four or five days and then returned to London, via Englemere, where we lunched.

The following week – W having meanwhile gone over for Punchestown – the children and I spent several days at Englemere and saw the Dawnay family move into Milcote, a little house they had taken, quite close to Englemere; and one day Susie and I motored over to Bishopsgate to pay a visit to Uncle Marcus and Aunt Kitty.

A few days later, I left for Ireland, joined W at Farmleigh – the Iveagh place in the Phoenix Park – and went on home with him in the afternoon. The children arrived the following day with their new Governess, Miss Millar, and Father and Mother paid us a flying visit on their way back from Derreen.

My new Maid, Alice Smyth, arrived about the same time, succeeding a somewhat sour person called Golding, who had been with me about eight years and had of late been a sore trial to me.

W was away a good deal during that summer, for three weeks (May 15th to June 7th) at Aix-les-Bains for 18 days (June 9th – 27th) with the S.I. Yeomanry, for about a week in July with Commander Forbes, visiting Peterborough Hound Show and making a tour of English Kennels.

In August he and Claud Anson went for a fortnight to Glenbride and, besides these absences, he was often away for a few days. During all that time my friends were very good to me and as I had decided to remain at home quietly all that summer and autumn. Relays of them came to stay with me. Edwina Roberts was with me from May 18th to July 3rd and at different times there came also Norah Churchill, Mrs Kennedy, Jean Wise, Mary Doyne, Helen Forbes and Mrs Durham Matthews. The three latter and Edwina were with me at the same time. Unfortunately Mrs D.M. got rather on the nerves of the others; her point of view seemed always different from theirs and it was not a happy combination. I remember one day in the Blue Drawing Room, when we were all looking at the large picture in the Carved Adams frame and Mrs D.M. exclaimed, 'It's awfully pretty isn't it, just like a drop-scene'!; and I could almost hear the groans of the others. She was a charming little person really, and very bright and attractive, but perhaps rather superficial and frivolous.

Miss Martin used to come up with her box whenever other visitors failed. She always said she liked to be with me when there was an infant coming as then she didn't feel that her slow walking impeded me. She was the best of friends and companions on all occasions. I always loved to have her with me.

It was a very fine summer and we spent most of the time out of doors. The Shamiana was pitched on the lawn and I used to do much of my writing out there. Tea was generally brought out and sometimes even dinner. Occasionally Edwina and I took our tea out on one of the hills. One day we went, a party of ten to Coumshingaun Lake and another party of 11 (with Doynes) to Serouty. A Group taken on the latter occasion is in Book XI.

We kept French hours all the summer. In June all the children were photographed by Croker, with very successful results. In the middle of July, Patsy and Billy went off to Glenbride with their Nanny, Miss Brand. Soon after that came Lord Conyngham and his otter hounds. They did not show very good sport and only killed 1 otter in 4 days, but it was a pleasant outing and the children enjoyed it hugely. They were given the otter's pads, which they joyfully put into their pockets, with the buns provided for their midday lunch!

Mr Caldecott came with Lord Conyngham and I remember a nephew and niece of Miss Martin's (Gerald and Helen) who came out every day. Kathleen Beresford was with us and was well to the fore; also the Kennedys.

I was a good deal occupied with the Portlaw Laundry that year, having taken it over from Eva Malcomson in the Autumn of 1907. It was formerly in two small houses in William or George Street, where it had no room to expand, so I took a lease of the large house on the Square, moved the existing Plant and fitted the place up according to our needs, at a cost of £200. The Laundry was originally started by Susie, but had gone through a good many vicissitudes since and needed to have some capital spent on it. There were other troubles yet to come, as we suffered under a very queer tempered Manageress at first and then with a dishonest Laundry Maid, who rifled the cash box and robbed us of £16, but in time it became a most thriving concern and provided an excellent training for the Portlaw girls and we gradually received washing from further and further afield from Co. Tipperary, Kilkenny, Wexford and even from Co. Wicklow. The 'Industry' was also doing good work and provided employment for many women and girls in Portlaw and Curraghmore. Nina Ryan – daughter of old Johnny Ryan, the Stud Groom – was my right-hand in both these concerns.

Besides the Ford pictures, which I have already written about, the arrangement of which took up so much of my time that summer, there were a lot of books from Ford and Miss Martin and I tried to arrange these also, but soon found this to be beyond our powers and it wasn't until some time after W's death that all the books were properly arranged and catalogued with a card-index.

Two new ponies came for the children that summer (Fanny and Toffee) and now all three were able to ride together and I remember W taking them all out for the first time one day in July.

Father, Mother and Norah Churchill – on their way to Derreen – paid us a short visit and, during this, we entertained some Italian Officers who had come over to Ireland to buy horses: Maggiore Fadini Mazzini and Capitano Pape. Mazzini had lately got married and his wife accompanied the party by special permission of the Military Authorities. Fadini kept her in great order, however, and she always had to be up at cock-crow and ready to start off at a moment's notice. A bambino was already expected and, though it was very early days, the Officers used to make perfectly candid allusions to it and nobody seemed in the least abashed. 'Je dis à Madame que son petit sera un Paddy – et encore un Ivrogne,' said one, apropos of meeting some very drunken people! My own condition was obvious, but it rather took my breath away when Pape, on leaving, made a low bow and wished me luck with my baby! Capitano Pape took a great fancy to Norah and, with his little straw hat at a rakish angle, made eyes at her most boldly, much to our amusement. We took them round the stables and the kennels and they were greatly interested in all they saw. One of them took many photographs, which are in my book with the cards and autographs of the party.

On August 1st the elder children went to Glenbride with Miss Millar and remained there until after the baby's arrival. Evie and her three elder children came for a few days en route to Derreen.

We did very well at Clonmel Show that year, winning the Championship and 1st in unentered dogs, and 1st for unentered ladies. W, who motored over with Kathleen, came back in great spirits.

The Curraghmore Cricket Club was then going pretty strong under Bone's Captaincy. I remember a match v Kilmacthomas, and there were also sports which we all attended.

One hot day in August, the Duchess of St. Albans bought over Lady Margaret Charteris and Lord Ormonde, and a few days later Lord Obby appeared with some very strange friends of his Mother's. The Lady was a distant cousin of hers, who had lately married a most uncanny creature. He had travelled all over the world and lived for many years with the Eskimos, till his behaviour to the ladies caused such scandal that he had to fly for his life. Later on, he was warned off the race course at San Francisco! He was very tall – quite a fine specimen – with rather shaggy hair and beard. He had an impediment in his speech and every time he wanted to speak, he began by stretching himself and emitting a vast sort of yawn! I was alone with Miss Martin at the time and the man made such an impression on me that I told her I shouldn't be surprised if my baby were born yawning! At tea, the wife told me that her husband liked to have his tea in the slop basin. I thought she was joking and paid no attention, but he wouldn't touch it in a cup, so it had to go in the slop basin (in spite of the crack!) and he tossed it off at one gulp. Another peculiarity was that he played upon a golden flute at all hours of the night and took about with him a nervous little lady who played his accompaniments and whom he nearly ate up if she made a mistake!

September 1908

We returned from Glenbride and Dublin Horse Show on August 29th and cub hunting started on September 4th. On the 11th W went over to Dromana for the funeral of Major Villiers Stuart, who had been in the S.I. Yeomanry. The following week we had a visit from Captain Dick Molyneux – an old brother officer of the Blues – and I remember how he nearly put his foot through the Laurence picture of the 2nd Marquess, when stepping back to admire the effect of some others we were hanging!

On September 21st came the thrilling news of Charlie's engagement to Violet Elliot. He had first met her in India, as a 'flapper', and had promptly fallen in love with her. She was very much younger than him, but the difference in age never came between them and I was overjoyed to hear of their engagement. It took place at Derreen and a few days later they arrived at Curraghmore by motor as he wanted to introduce Vi to me himself. She won my heart at once, and W's too, and it was delightful to see Charlie's happiness. They were only with us two days and, as they had to go back to India soon after, I did not see them again until after they were married.

I remember one lovely morning that September, when W was cub hunting, and suddenly there came a burst of music quite near the house. I dashed out of bed and got to the window just in time to see hounds go racing by round the corner of the house, over the flower beds and down the steps; it was a lovely sight.

On September 30th came Father and Mother and the very next day, at 3.30pm, Hugh was born and the diary (Mr Rochfort was also at Curraghmore when Hugh was born) records his weight as 8lb 4oz, and his height 22 inches. He was quite a satisfactory babe, though he caused the Doctor and me a good deal of trouble in arriving, as he had turned a somersault at the last moment and was in a very difficult position. Dr Walker, however, managed splendidly and I also had a very good Nurse from the London Hospital – 'Nurse James'. She was excellent with the baby; got him out at 10 days and had him out a great deal. He had a bit of a setback after being circumcised, as he fought against the chloroform (only 23 days old, and yet so stubborn!) and had to be given more, which upset him considerably, but after recovering from this he made excellent progress. A photograph of him in his bassinette (Book XI) gives quite a good idea of his funny little face.

October and November 1908

Patsy and Bill had returned from Glenbride on September 8th; the other children returned on October 6th and were wildly excited over the arrival of the small brother. Mother left the same day (Father had left on the 1st) and on October 4th W went off to Styria to shoot chamois etc. with the Schönborns. He returned in time for the 11th anniversary of our wedding day and a few days later I was down and we kept Blanchie's birthday (10th), which had been deferred till I could join the tea party.

On October 27th W had his Opening Meet in Waterford and on November 2nd Katie rode to the Meet – at Guilcagh – for the first time. Later in the month W took all 3 out for a hunt in the Demesne, which was a great joy. It was about then that W made a small school for jumping horses at the Pheasantry. There used to be a 'Pound' in the pleasure grounds (near the path to Pheasantry), but this was most unsightly and the new place was much better. However, it was not very much used.

On November 4th we had a visit from Lady Charles Beresford with Captain Franklin and Mr Maclane. They had landed at Dunmore East from the Admiral's Yacht and had motored over to see us. Aunt Nina was a wondrous sight; dressed in a long trailing black satin skirt and pink blouse, and a pink velvet opera cloak, topped by a little shiny black straw hat such as French cabmen wear, and enveloped in a thick veil. She showed no interest in the baby and said she disliked them all; then proceeded to abuse her own daughter, Kathleen, and complained bitterly because she didn't get married – although every time K had been engaged she and Uncle C had interfered and prevented a match!

On November 27th I went up to Dublin to try on habits and other clothes and then on to London, where Susie and Hugh Dawnay stayed with me for 10 days. At the end of that time, Hugh left for

Somaliland, where he had a staff job with General Johnny Gough, his great friend. Susie stayed on with me and Aileen and Edwina joined us for a few days. I remember going with them all to see Barrie's delightful play, *What Every Woman Knows*, besides several other plays.

December 1908

On December 10th I left for Ireland, stopping a night at Glenmaroon (with the Ernest Guinnesses) on the way and, while there, I went to see Mrs Flemyng at Elpis. This was not long after the beginning her illness, which ended fatally some months later.

I was home on the 12th and the following week came Susie and her 3 boys to stay for Xmas. The party included Mr Chris Kennedy, Mr Ikey Bell and Father, who had been left alone owing to Mother having gone to India for Charlie's wedding. He was very lonely without Mother, but it was a great delight to have him with us and he was so good to all the children and gave lovely presents to every one of them.

The usual Xmas festivities followed in due succession; School Treat in the Riding School, distribution of cloaks and jerseys to school children, giving out Xmas Club tickets and clothes on the Estate, presents at the Almshouses and 'Xmas Charities' to the Portlaw people. Then, after Xmas, the Steward's Tea and our own children's tea party, followed by a Xmas Tree in the Lower Hall for all the children and gifts for all the servants and stewards; and, finally, on December 31st the treat for the workers at the Laundry and Industry – tea, gramophone etc. Father and Mr Bell only stayed a few days, but the Dawnays and Kennedys stayed on and later came the Doynes and Robin, the Perrys and the Elliotts.

Evening Standard Article about Beatrix's Husband's Death December 1911

An Irish Mystery: Peer's tragic death
Ill-fated House of Beresford (From our own correspondent)
London December 8th December 1911

Early last Saturday morning the dead body of Henry de la Poer Beresford, 6th Marquis of Waterford was found in the River Clodagh, near his residence at Curraghmore and at an inquest later in the day a death by drowning was announced. The evidence threw little light on the mystery surrounding his decease.

The story of the all-night search for the Marquis was related by his agent, Captain Gethin, who was later informed of the finding of the body. This witness had assisted in taking the body out of the water. There was a footprint almost touching the water's edge a little way from the direct path, which was, however, indistinct. To get to where the body was found, the Marquis had to cross a stile ten feet high. He was making improvements at this place, and was much interested in the work that was going on, and was anxious to have it finished before another flood came. The place would have been dark at the time Lord Waterford went there. The banks of the river where the tragedy occurred are very steep. There were no marks of violence on the body.

The untimely death of the sixth holder of the title brings to mind a singularly tragic family history. A strange legend about the family has always fond credence among the peasantry of Munster. The story goes that in the dark days of the penal period a young Catholic peasant was dragged in chains into the courtyard at Curraghmore by order of the then head of the clan. He was ordered to be flogged and put to death.

He was flogged in the presence of his widowed mother, who was on her knees to the Beresfords and begged for mercy. The mercy was refused and the boy was put to death. Thereupon the mother, in the agony of her grief, uttered an awful prophesy that not one of the heads of the Beresford clan would die in his bed. Be that as it may, the nobleman who was found in the Clodagh last

Saturday, is the fourth successive Marquis of Waterford to die a violent death.

The 3rd Marquis of Waterford was hunting with the Waterford hounds in County Kilkenny, and jumped his horse over a fence on the public road, the Marquis being picked up dead. His neck was broken.

The 4th Lord Waterford, who had been a Protestant clergyman in his early days, spent most of his time wandering about the beautiful grounds of his demesne. One day he was missing and after some days he was found in a little shooting box in a remote part of Curraghmore. The mystery of his death was never properly cleared up, but it was stated to have been caused by poisoning consequent upon eating diseased shellfish.

The 5th Marquis of Waterford, father of the late holder of the title, perished by his own hand in 1895. In the Land War in the early 'eighties the County Waterford peasants objected to certain landlords hunting with Lord Waterford's hounds. They did not object to Lord Waterford himself who was reputed to be a good sportsman and a fair landlord, but Lord Waterford, who was a strong-minded man and a Unionist, sternly refused to submit to popular agitation, broke up his great hunting establishment in the county and went away to England. One day when out hunting in England, he rode for a gate, which was held open by a small branch of a tree. A sheep, frightened by the horse, dashed through the gate before him, knocking away the branch, the gate being liberated began to close. As Lord Waterford galloped through, his foot was caught by the railing and he had to be lifted from the saddle, a cripple for life. His spine had been so badly injured that for years he did not get off his back. At last his life of pain became unbearable to him and one day he crawled to the gunroom at Curraghmore and taking a gun from its rack loaded it and blew out his brains. Among other members of the family who had died violent deaths were Lord Delaval Beresford, who was killed in a railway accident in El Paso, Texas four years ago, and Captain C C de la Poer Beresford who lost his life in Aldershot last year while gallantly attempting to stop a runaway horse.

Ireland at War
Beatrix and her son Tyrone get mixed up in the fighting.

Our drive to the Kilkenny Races was uneventful, save when, running up the steep slope of Creggan Bridge, we discovered at its summit no bridge but a gaping chasm where torn masonry stood out above the stream that rippled far below. Jamming on his brakes Paddy stopped in time. The delay caused was but that of ten or fifteen minutes while we wandered through lanes in our efforts to rediscover the main road. We arrived in Freshford in time for the first race, and spent a wonderful day clambering through very muddy ditches in company with a joyous and friendly crowd. Sometimes in rained, and a cold wind blew along the uplands; but in Ireland we adapt ourselves all too easily to circumstances the most uncomfortable, and no mud could damp the cheering.

We set out for home between four and five. The rain had ceased, and it was such an evening as can only be found in Ireland after rain. All green things lifted their drenched heads from the earth. The furse was as a golden veil drawn over valley and hill. The air smelt of furse and wet clay. For an hour we mounted the Walsh hills. Furse blossoms paled in shadow; but beyond, the sky had opened in glory of deep gold. We reached the edge of the Suir Valley. The near hills across were of a sudden black, startlingly near and meaningful. Far off, yet seeming to stoop and overhang them, slept the deep blue line of the Comeraghs. A solitary cliff, standing out where the sky paled, was a portal to an unknown land.

We had come but lately from the etched beauty of England. But colour here possessed not surface only, but depth, significance. Ireland became a living thing folding all tired wayfarers to her strange heart.

We descended into the valley, rounding the Creggan Bridge by the same devious route of ruts and boreens. At the railway crossing at Carrick we were stopped by sentries and had our permits examined. The town lay below us, with its twisted streets and its foreign looking towers, sleepy in the evening light. Descending we passed the burnt-out ruins of the Court House and the Police Barracks and 'The Park' with its ambitious avenue of cypresses and its ill-kept grass. In a narrow street, carts were blocking the way while their drivers engaged in pleasant conversation. Young boys and children with muddy faces were playing and shouting. A wire entanglement stretched half-way across the road, and near it strolled some half-dozen Free Staters[1] with rifles slung across their backs. A dog lay asleep in the mud. It rose as we approached and strolled amiably towards our front wheel. One of the Free Staters ran out and kicked it. It leaped aside squealing.

We stopped at a garage, and Paddy, who was our coachman's son, descended to buy petrol. As we sat waiting in the car, we heard several short cracking notes, each succeeded by a hollow sound, as by an echo. 'Hallo' said somebody, 'is there a battle going on?' Preposterous idea! The crowd, the Free Staters, strolled leisurely as before. Perhaps some boys were playing hurley down the street. Or 'perhaps' said one of us, 'somebody's beating carpets'.

Tyrone had thought the noise too faint for rifle fire, but as we drove towards the bridge it increased. Paddy explained that the Irregulars were sniping Free State troops from the surrounding hills. It was apparently their habit to do so every evening.

We came out upon the bridge. The cracks grew loud and rapid. We heard the hiss of a bullet as it passed close to the hood, and after that the long bridge seemed endless. At the further side an arch was missing, but the gap had been spanned by a narrow wooden structure. 'Paddy,' I said faintly, 'hadn't we better go a little faster?' We bumped in a flash across the woodwork. We had not been crawling so slowly after all!

We had reached the shelter of houses upon the further shore, and were climbing up the street. 'Aren't we fools to go further?' said someone. But Paddy, who had driven through the War unscathed, refused to be perturbed. He had been told in Carrick that we would be safe once we had crossed the bridge.

We turned into a road which ran straight at the hill above. We were greeted – or so it seemed – by a hail of bullets. Some children, playing in the mud, jumped aside as one struck the road near them. There was a crack as if the car was hit, and Paddy ducked his head over the wheel. I said: 'Look here, this isn't good enough,' and Paddy, very cool though he must have been hit at the

---

[1] 'Free Staters' was a term used to describe those in Ireland who supported the Anglo-Irish Treaty of 1921 that led to the creation of the Irish Free State in 1922. The 'Irregulars' or Republicans were anti-Treaty.

time, drew the car in close to a cottage and pulled up. I opened the door, and Billy and I both fumbled desperately at the curtain above, keeping our heads down. They were still firing hard at the car. Tyrone told us not to get rattled, and, leaning over from the front seat, helped us to undo it. Then we bolted like rabbits into the cottage.

We found Paddy with his head down dripping blood. He was tugging at his over-coat in a vain effort to loosen it at the throat, so I pulled it off for him and we made him sit down by the fire. He remained there with his head in his hands, the blood dripping till it made a little pool in the uneven mud of the floor. It was so dark in the cottage that we could scarcely see, but I held a candle above him while the 'lady of the house' washed out the wound with some water which she brought in a little tin mug. A deep furrow seemed to run right across his head, but it soon ceased to bleed. We bound a handkerchief about it and tried to reassure him and ourselves. Outside, the firing still continued. But we felt gloriously safe between the damp walls of the cottage, with its huge open fire and tiny windows.

A small crowd was now collecting, strolling in and out from the street as if all were quiet outside. Awed exclamations of: 'Is it hurted he is?' – 'Well! Isn't it a fright?' – fell from their lips. They were like children gaping with wonder at some new vagary of the powers that rule. 'Indeed,' they said, 'It isn't that they intended firing at you at all. There is a concert given at the Christian brothers today, and they had orders to stop all amusements in the town. They thought it's Free Staters you were, coming out for to take them.' One imagined the fury of English citizens, had anyone dared to snipe their town, their quick contriving of some method of defence, their angered rising as one man. Impossible, one felt, to stir anger in these too forgiving ones. Let Carrick be fired at for another two years, they would still stroll on, always good-natured, apologizing for the firers, adapting themselves to this as to the mud upon the race-course, as they had adapted to all the trifling inconveniences since the beginning of time. They were very kind to us, retrieving hats that had fallen in the road, bringing in wraps and tea-baskets from the car, while two of them set out across the town to fetch a doctor. Our host – a little bent cobbler in spectacles – fumbled in obscure shelves for a pot of ointment which, he said, would prevent the wound from festering. We refused him as gently as we might. We could see his kind dirty hands applying it last to some sick calf. As to his lady she firmly brushed him and his idea into the background. And: 'Mind your feet now on this ould floor' – she had turned to me. I had realized that I had kicked off my wet shoes in the car, and was walking shoeless upon the muddy flags. Her manner suggested that it was the most natural thing in the world to travel in stockings. In a moment somebody had fetched the shoes, and scraping off the caked mud, she dried them by the fire. Billy suggested that we should all feel better if we ate something, and pressed sandwiches upon us. We would none of us own that our teeth were chattering.

The evening drew in, and we began to grow anxious as to how we should get home. Everyone reassured us. 'Anny time now you can dhrive on and there's none will touch you. What way would they harm you at all, and they knowing who you are?' 'But how,' we enquired, 'could they possibly have found out?' Only since has it occurred to us that some of them were perhaps standing in the doorway. 'Indeed, you're all right now,' added our hostess, with comforting finality and a supreme disregard for consequences. 'Sure, is'nt the firing all over for the night. They'll fire no more today.' Her remark was greeted by a loud: 'Ping! Ping!' from outside. But we took it in the way it was meant.

The boys returned from Doctor A's. He had refused to come out. He was, it appeared, one of the leading Republicans in the town. They brought, however, a small dressing and bandages, and Mrs G., after searching her brains as to how a true V.A.D. ought to put on a bandage, fixed it as instructed by the assembled company! All murmured their disgust at Dr A. They related how, once before, when a Free Stater lay wounded on the bridge, he had left him untended. The man had died afterwards.

Paddy seemed to grow worse. 'I'm all right,' he maintained doggedly but, on watching him, we saw him rock to and fro in his chair. The crowd, tenderly solicitous, were sure that he ought to see a doctor. At length, as the firing subsided, Tyrone and another set out for the town, taking him with them.

They were gone for over an hour. The firing had ceased, leaving a warm, still dusk and a murmur of voices up and down the road. We were holding, it seemed, a small reception in our cottage. Some men who sat inside the open chimney – blackened beam so low that it almost touched their heads – rose to give us their seats as we came in from the cool of the doorway. Events of such deep significance as had occurred during the past hour ought, it was felt, to be discussed with due solemnity.

The Free State heroes of Carrick were brought up for judgement. Our jury thought nothing of them. 'Sure they're no good at all. Didn't one of them dhrop his rifle wid the fright he got one time, and he hearing a shot from the hills?' O Shade of the *Morning Post*! Here is a gloomy picture for you. But Ireland is possessed of many and lively imaginations, and one must always allow for the sympathies of the speaker. The little cobbler declared that men were no good that fought only for money. They must have some principle, he said. He began a learned disquisition on the War of Independence in America. In shadow – out of the leaping firelight – some three or four fowls sat meditating upon the edge of a table. Now and then one flew up or dropped to the floor with a thud and scuffle of wings. Whereupon one of the party jumped almost to the ceiling!

There came a tap on the door, and a little old schoolmaster entered. He was returning up the hill with his wife, after doing some small commissions in the town. He carried a tin can of milk. He leant across a short counter which stood out into the room beside the doorway, its bitten oak stacked with an amazing collection of boots and little tins and mysterious paper packages, and requested a box of matches. Our hostess bade bad him come in behind the counter, introducing him deferentially to the company as Mr X. She was a homely woman, abundantly shapeless, with a black grease-stained apron and wispy grey hair. But she announced each incoming guest in the manner of a hostess at some world-moving reception. The little man came in, enquired after Paddy's wound with lowered voice and eyes, and, as the emissary between great nations at War, expressed his regret for an unfortunate mistake.

A woman entered. She must have been a tinker, for she was dressed in grey rags, and her hair fell in grey matted ringlets about her face. She peered among the guests for the boy who had been hurt. 'God save him, the poor creature,' she crooned, in her wild sing-song voice. 'Indeed, he blessed himself this morning. It is he blessed himself this morning.' She fell back and was lost in the crowd. A handicapped person stood by the fireside, gazing foolishly at all around. Some children crowded in at the doorway, laughing at him.

Time passed. We drifted out into the darkness, empty of danger now yet heavy still with meaning, as if great perils had lurked and dallied there. The company descended upon the car. Someone produced a candle, and we searched the inside for bullets. The rest stood about it in a little dark mass, the candle's gleam lighting the hood from within, a beacon to all lurking danger, daring the night to prove friendly. A bullet was discovered. We returned triumphantly into the house. The children still followed, laughing at the handicapped boy, and taunting him with cries. The bullet was examined by the lamplight, all pressing about the proud discovery. Deep theories were advanced with regard to elevations and ricochets. The 'lady of the house' enquired if she might show it to 'himself', who had retired, it seemed, to an inner room. She hobbled off through the door, holding it within her cupped hands. All waited in silence for the verdict. Presently she returned. 'Himself says,' she announced, with deep solemnity, 'that if it is through his head it had gone, nothing could have saved him.' All listened as to an oracle.

Paddy returned at last, up the hill. He had been first to the Republican doctor, who had left a message saying he was not at home. Another doctor was found to be (genuinely) away. A third, however, had washed out his wound and bandaged it. A quarter of an inch of bone had separated him from death.

He had been told not to drive the car any more, and we were still six miles from home. But, coming out into the night, we heard the chink of a bridle. A shadow in the dimness, an inside car, was awaiting us. Between the shafts a trace-clipt colt stood sleepily, a rug thrown over its flanks, the warmth of its rough coat scenting the dusk. At the animal's drooped head, a form already familiar was offering to take us home. We accepted. Everyone helped to push the motor up-hill into a shed. But on mounting we found that there was no room for the boy who had brought the colt. Paddy, still undefeated, wanted to walk! 'Would you trust us with the trap?' we cried to the unseen givers, and voices declared we were welcome; but the colt's master feared we might not manage the little horse. He started to lead it up the hill. The night was full of friendly presences wishing us 'safe home'.

Leaving the town behind us, we climbed slowly up the long hill. In the lonely spaces above, the boy left us, handing us the reins and turning homewards. We tried to press money into his hands, but he brushed it aside as unnecessary. The colt, when left alone with us, developed a remarkable tendency to stop instead of going forward when touched by the whip. He also, at the smallest provocation, swung round and backed into the ditch. We had no lights. I drove, trying to keep my eyes on the elusive white wraith of the road; Tyrone, who had sprained his ankle not long before, ran at the colt's head for a great part of the way. We circled two trees which Republicans had felled to check the movements of Free Staters. A rain-coated man appeared out of the darkness and struck matches to help us. He seemed vague as to the lie of the land, saying he was a stranger in those parts. We did not pry into his business. He had been very civil about the matches.

In the vaulted shadows of trees the colt stopped altogether. He had heard the sound of a waterfall. Nothing would move him. We all turned out of the trap, and pulled. Paddy was gallant, though his head must have been aching dreadfully. One of the party was very touched by a message he sent from his bed the next day, apologizing for treading rather heavily on her toe. The colt moved at last. We were at our own lodge-gates, and could borrow a lantern. Holding it out over the trap's side, we descended the last hill at a wonderful speed and arrived with a flourish in the Court Yard. It is rumoured that next morning, when the colt was returned to his owner, it took six men to get him out of the yard!

Paddy recovered, though slowly. The Republicans sent messages by devious ways, full of regret for having fired on him, but warning him not to drive up from Carrick in the evening, as they could not see clearly when the sun was low behind the hill. He also learned that, watching from the heights, they had seen Free Staters run out when the dog slipped under our wheel, and had imagined they were boarding the car.

A few days later we rode down to Carrick (in the morning when hostilities had not begun) to discover the owner of the trap, and see if he might be persuaded to accept the price of its hire. He was a baker who lived close to the bridge. He would take nothing from us, saying that our father had been his great friend long ago. 'I would do more than that,' he said, 'for the love of the late Lord.' We discovered our cottage among a sleepy row that blinked into the sunlight, their uneven walls washed in varying shades of rose or saffron or slate grey. A curly-headed boy with a blacksmith's apron, and a very big open smile, waved at us from one of the doorways. He was the colt's master. We met the 'lady of the house' trudging up from the town, a shawl thrown over her head. She apologized for not knowing who we were the previous night. But if were strangers to her she was very kind to us.

In Ireland nothing happens as it ought to, and the results of this affair are not such as are chronicled in histories. To say that Billy has asked that very wise man – the cobbler – to resole a pair of his boots, and we have ordered a balm-brack from the baker, may seem irrelevant. Yet so do great events leave their traces behind them!

Derreen

Beatrix Waterford and her mother, Lady Lansdowne visit Derreen after it was burned and looted.

"It was nothing personal, Lady, it was nothing personal – but just part of the programme."

A little sitting-room in the Kenmare Hotel, an aged Priest clasping my Mother's hand as he repeated those words with pathetic earnestness, my Mother apologizing for withdrawing her hand in order – ostensibly – to blow her nose (down which something suspiciously like a tear was starting on its course), the Priest's prompt seizure of the other hand, which then received its due share of petting and stroking – this scene is one which will endure in my memory, and like many others, will bring back the tear and the smile ever associated with Ireland – though I think heartache and laughter would more nearly describe those emotions!

My mother had come to Ireland the week before, and after a few days rest at Curraghmore, we had set out on the expedition which had only lately become possible – to visit the beloved place in Kerry, and to see the havoc wrought there by fire and loot, and to form our own ideas of the possibilities of the future. The railroad to Mallow being yet mainly out of action owing to the still ruinous condition of two of the principal bridges, we motored the first seventy-five miles. The road (showing a very fair surface on the whole) passed over three or four bridges which had been only temporarily repaired and here and there a ruined Police Barracks stood out dejectedly; otherwise there was no sign of the troublous history of the past years. Indeed my Mother, who had not passed through that country for about ten years, commented on the improved appearance of the cottages and farms, and the more prosperous look of the inhabitants. The sun shone brightly. But there were sufficient clouds to dapple the mountains with deep purple shadows, making them full of mystery; while the shimmering showed those long dark streaks which suggest a track leading far away to the unknown.

Leaving the Comeraghs and Dungarvan Bay behind us, we came to the Blackwater, and followed it – sometimes close to the banks – sometimes far above it – for the rest of our drive. Lismore Castle appeared on our left – at first sight as beautiful as ever, but on closer inspection showing many broken windows, filled up with sand bags and deal boards. The Free State troops were still in possession, and we heard sad tales of the damage done both by them and their predecessors, the Republicans, though no doubt the presence of the 'Staters' had prevented more fatal disaster, and had been of great benefit to the law-abiding people living in the neighbourhood.

Our train was not due to leave Mallow Station until 3.30, and it was fully an hour before that time that we drove up to the queer little Station which was doing duty for all the trains starting from that side of the Blackwater. The unfortunate travellers from the East and North, on arriving at the main Mallow Station, were hurried out of the train, and themselves and their belongings bundled into motor cars, vans, and lorries of all descriptions – of which a perfect fleet awaited each train – driven several miles round through the town, over the Blackwater, and up to the afore-mentioned Mallow South Station, which was no more than a siding flanked by a few sheds of corrugated iron, where the travellers jostled each other, fell over the luggage, and struggled to get on to the high footboards of the train. We made a pile of our luggage on the platform, and perched ourselves upon it. The Killarney train came in, and spilt a motley crowd on to the already crowded platform. We thought this must be our train; but no, it was making a semi-circular journey to Cork, and we must wait till the train from there took its place. 'Mind yourself, now' – I had gone forward to make these investigations – 'Mind yourself – ye'll be killed surely' shouted an excited official, as a huge motor lorry – followed by a covered van with mails – came lumbering up on to the platform. The crowd compressed themselves into a yet smaller space, the motor engine throbbed, the drivers and porters all yelled and gesticulated, till at last they had the cars in the right position, and started hurling their contents into the Cork luggage van. It was strenuous work for the porters, and one brawny fellow, on whom the others piled all the heaviest stuff, protested occasionally 'Easy now, you'll split the back of me – 'tis the devil's weight – ye'll have me killed'. Another, who had brought our luggage up, (and found a bond of sympathy with my Mother through the prawn net she had insisted on bringing) treated the whole affair as a huge joke, and turned on us a twinkling blue eye over a long-toothed grin whenever anything particularly tickled his fancy. The last thing on the lorry was a crate containing two large sheep: the bottom was held on by two or three rusty nails, and as even these were coming out, the moving of it was an intricate affair. The van wouldn't hold it, so it was dumped beside us, and we spent the rest of our time in trying to prevent two little ragged children from poking the sheep's eye out with a bit of wood.

At last the Killarney train had started for Cork, and our train had made its leisurely appearance: we were hoisted up into it, our grinning porter had the prawn net in the rack with a last twinkle of appreciation, and we were off on the second stage of our journey, in company with a most polite old gentleman (who produced newspapers and Railway Guides) and a chubby-cheeked Free State Officer, with a Gunners' badge on his tunic collar. Free Staters travelled on each train, and guarded every station: it was very recently that lines had been torn up, signal stations destroyed, and other means taken to interrupt communications. There seemed to be a happy understanding between the Staters and the officials; for at one small station we waited nearly quarter of an hour while the soldiers ran across the field to an adjacent 'Public' and having quenched their thirst returned at a more leisurely pace. They also had many friends at the stations, where pretty girls waited to meet them as they passed through.

The familiar stations succeeded each other: Lombardstown, Banteer, Millstreet, Rathmore; and each lap brought us nearer to the beloved Kerry mountains, shimmering with their glacial markings, and the little silver streams tossing joyously down the rocky slopes.

We left the Killarney express at Headfort junction, and remembered the days when a cumbersome pair-horse landau took us the rest of the way home: twenty miles to Kenmare, and nearly as many more to Derreen, a long and weary drive – but then there was home at the end of it, and now – nothing but a ruin!

'Loo Bridge' – the station and its appurtenances seem to have been entirely wrecked here: 'Morley's Bridge' evidently not considered worthy of so much attention; 'Kilgarvan' from whence, despite its bad reputation, one remembered that thousands of Sphagnum dressings went to our Hospitals during the Great War; and then we glimpsed the Kenmare River, with our own beloved mountains in the background, and a few minutes more brought us to the end of our first day's journey.

The ubiquitous 'Tin Lizzie' which was to take us to Derreen the next day, met us there, and having made sure that the prawn net was not forgotten, we drove up to the Hotel, which we found very comfortable accommodation, and an obliging Manageress (Miss Ryan) who had taken the place of the Germans who used to run this and other Railway Hotels. We had not been there for half an hour, when Father S. was announced; he could not bear that we should go to Derreen thinking that there was any antagonism there against the family, so had to come at once to see my Mother to try and explain the situation as he understood it. Who shall blame him if he glossed over a few unpleasant facts, and did his best to temper the wind to the shorn lamb?

He told us of the widespread plot to get rid of every landlord, so that the land might be free for all, how those who destroyed the house were incited and even paid to do it, how the crowd afterwards went mad, and completely lost their heads; and ever and anon came the earnest must understand refrain 'you must understand that it was nothing personal to Lord and Lady Lansdowne; no, it was nothing personal', with redoubled strokings and pattings of my Mother's hand.

Then he related how he and the C.C. had told the people of the wickedness of these doings, and for three months had fulminated against them from the pulpit, even refusing Absolution to anyone who kept stolen goods in their houses, and urging them to return the loot – and this many of them had done, as we should see when we visited the places where furniture and other things had been dumped; and besides this Father S. had opened an account in the Kenmare Bank, to which had been paid various sums for the wine drunk by the raiders, etc. And he told us of the difficulties in getting to his duties during these troubled times, when bridged were destroyed and roads blocked – 'but in any case, I would have no "Stations" in those places where there was stolen property; no, I would not; nor would I give Absolution to those people; I was determined, and so was father – and I did my best for Lord and Lady Lansdowne.' Then came the question of rebuilding and returning to Derreen: 'Well – you can do so – for there was nothing personal and the people are sorry; and the country will be more settled now.'

'But we are getting old now, Father S. and if we re-build, we may not live to enjoy the new house.'

'Well I thought about this, and I said to myself; "Lady Lansdowne is so fresh – I remember her so young and fresh-looking – and she and Lord Lansdowne will return surely."'

My mother asked him if he could tell her the names of those chiefly to blame for the destruction and looting, but this was taxing his friendship too far, and though he promised to send a list by the hand of a trusted messenger before we left, I felt that he had no real intention of doing so; and the letter which came a few days later justified that suspicion.

Incidentally, it should be mentioned that while Father S. was an old friend of the family, and of moderate politics, the C.C. was a comparative newcomer, and a strong Republican; I think there was very little doubt that the Real Republican had nothing to do with the destruction of Derreen, which was the work of that far more dangerous Bolshevik party whose influence is world wide, and its aim the destruction of all private property.

The old Priest left us, and we wandered into the Hotel Grounds, and over the Golf Course, comparing the impressions we had gleaned from his talk. It was a delicious evening with a hint of rain in it, every breath of wind was a caress and we could barely to go indoors and waste any of the beauty of it.

Mr and Mrs M, who had met us at the Station on arrival, looked in after dinner; we heard the latest news, and made our plans for the morrow – a morrow which, though we scarcely owned it to ourselves, filled us with an unspeakable dread. My mother slept little that night, and was up early next morning; there was a drizzling rain, and a mist hung about the mountains, but it gradually lifted, and when we had travelled a mile or two on the Lauragh road we stopped to put the hood down that we might miss nothing of the delights of that drive.

The river on our right opened out; we passed Dinish Island with its rambling one-storied bungalow, and the little fleet of boats showed that the rich Midland Merchant who came there every Autumn with his numerous friends and guests had not yet been scared away from his play-ground; and left behind us the plot of reclaimed land in the midst of which, in an old houseboat, lived the man who had settled there many years before to avoid paying rent. Past the Priest's house and Ardea Castle, past Cloonee Lough, and over a rather crazy bridge where the old stone one had been destroyed; past the ruined

Constabulary Barracks, once so trim with its well-kept garden. We kept the coast road, and passed through Lehid Wood, which on the landward side bore some resemblance to the devastated areas in France and claimed kinship with many a new outhouse on neighbouring farms.

Knockatee on our left, and Loughaunacreen before us – those names of which the mere sound is an inspiration – and as we passed a double cottage by the road side, my Mother waved to a friend, and wondered how her sister-in-law – the woman whose melancholy left her 'no heart for to rise off the bed' had fared since a strong tonic and persuasive words had set her on her feet.

Round the point, past the rocks which used to be our happy hunting grounds for sea-urchins, and the little cove where the sea-sick ones had so often been landed when the fishing became too unbearable – past the ruins of the little old Church in the Cemetery, where we had visions of my Father and brother, with long streamers on their hats, driving in the funeral procession of Paddy Brien the boatman; and then Kilmakillogue Harbour opened out before us and we were really near home.

And as we passed each well-known cottage, we wondered: Was Sullivan in it? Did Shea join in the looting? Had Brien any hand in the burning? And our hearts ached to think of any of our old friends having had a share in such dastardly work. At Bunaw we stopped, and 'Nealy' Sullivan – Republican, trawler owner and carrier, made us welcome with a large hand grip, and sleepy eyes full of sympathy and understanding. He took us upstairs to the overcrowded parlour, and his nice little wife joined us, and we listened to their soft tones, telling us of those days of madness and destruction, and the hardships endured by old Mrs Searcy, the housekeeper, and by the gardener and his family, who managed to send away a cartload of their most cherished belongings, only to have them looted to the last hairpin by a gang in wait on the road we had just come over. The Nealys said little of what they had done in those dark days, but we knew well enough how staunch they had been, and how they had done all in their power to save anything from the wreckage, and to assist the homeless gardener and housekeeper.

As we left the house, a figure stepped forward, and there was the well-known face (though much altered with years) of Mick Guihan, my favourite among our boatmen, who taught us all to dance jigs, and himself knew more steps than any other man in the countryside. Yet this man was said to have been disloyal to us, and to have joined in the pillage; and I wondered how he had the face to come and meet us like that. He looked shamed, and said not a word when we silently shook hands with him; it was an embarrassing moment, till my Mother, with tears in her eyes, pointed to the long pole sticking out of the car, and 'I have brought a prawn net,' said she. 'That's good,' said he – and we drove on.

We heard afterwards that the stories about his joining in the bad work at Derreen were not true (though I fear he could hardly be exonerated from a share in the levelling of Lehid Wood) and I felt full of remorse for my coldness to him, for he was a very old friend. We passed him Tin Liz going at her fastest) on the road a few days later, and gave a backward wave in which I tried to show all the friendliness possible, and I was glad to see a smile beaming over the old face as it receded from view, and to feel that we might yet talk of the old days when we danced and fished together.

In a few minutes we were at the cottage which I will always think of as 'Holbrow's' – although several other employees have inhabited it since his time – and there at the little iron gate stood Seamus Sullivan the Keeper (nobody has ever been able to discover what he kept), the always melancholy expression in his face intensified by the large goggles he was now compelled to wear, and by the tragic circumstances of our return; and behind him stood Nora his wife, her serene countenance troubled with sympathy, and a warm welcome in her honest eyes.

'Oh – Lady Lansdowne I am glad to see you; welcome, welcome, Lady Waterford.' (I must always remain Lady Waterford there) and she threw her strong arms round us, and gave us a hearty hug. A wonderful woman this Nora, who as a slip of a girl had defied the custom of the country, and refused to let her Seamus marry the girl with seven cows whom his ambitious parents had affianced him to; and had – even at the eleventh hour – prevailed on his brother to get him away from the betrothal feast near Colorus. She, meanwhile, kept watch in the darkness on Bunaw point; and when a little beacon fire (the signal of success) blazed on the Colorus headland, she threw her shawl around her, and ran fleet-footed to the Priest at Lauragh, by whom she and Seamus were joined together in the dim dawn of Shrove Tuesday; leaving the lady with the cows disconsolate and furious!

We all loved this story, but we could hardly ever get her to talk about it; and when the babies arrived in quick succession, and her poor legs were so swollen that she could hardly get about her work in the little cottage, and would say with a laugh 'Faith – then if I'd known the way it would be I'd never have married him at all' – but the love-light never left her eyes, and is there to this day, reflected in the eyes of Maggie, Bridget, Julie, Florrie and all the other delightful young Seamuses!

'Well – indeed – Lady Lansdowne – I can tell you we were for sorry for what happened – and weren't you very good to come back at all,' murmured Mrs Seamus as she led my mother into the cottage.

'I want you to tell me all about it,' said my mother; and I drew Seamus to one side, and impressed on him that she wished to be told everything, and that he should keep nothing from her, and need have no fear that she would quote him or give him away. He looked at him solemnly, and said 'Lady Waterford, I will tell Lady Lansdowne the truth, and *all* the truth.' And so we passed into the cottage, and Seamus told again of the attack of September 1922 on the house; how lorries were brought up to the gate on the main road, and loaded with furniture and pictures, all the best things in the house, and then driven right away, so that no one knew where they had gone while other things were taken away in ass carts by local people who remained about the place all that evening until late at night.

Piecing together his rambling tale with help of notes in Arrowsmith's diary, I gained some idea of the happenings of those days, beginning on the previous Sunday when the old housekeeper had been awakened in the middle of the night by eight men, who, having gained admittance to the house proceeded to ransack it for clothes, rods, game bags, etc., and smashed two or three doors which barred their progress.

But the looting only started in real earnest on that Friday (September 1st 1922) when scores of men appeared with carts of all descriptions drawn by horses, mules, and donkeys, which they loaded up with the spoils. Some must have been transferred to the waiting lorries outside the gate; the rest found its way into farms and cottages within a radius of ten miles or so.

The next morning, Arrowsmith made his way on a borrowed bicycle to Kenmare, a weary 17 miles, to report to the Agent; and returned with a trap which took the housekeeper away the next day. In the evening when the place seemed to be deserted, he and Seamus went to collect a few things from the house, hiding them outside with a view to subsequent removal. While they were doing this, Seamus saw two men getting out of the dining room window on the yard side, and realizing that the looters had returned 'Mr Arrowsmith' said he 'this place is not safe for us, we'd best get out of it.'

The looting continued all that night; the remaining floors were bashed in, the cellar was broken into, and added zest to the plundering.

Then came Sunday morning, and these amazing people trooped off to Lauragh Chapel to Mass!

While they were away, Arrowsmith, Seamus, Sylvie Sullivan, the Stonemason's son (at one time yard man at Derreen) and a gardener named Jim Shea, took advantage of the short lull and rescued all they could lay hands on, but the looters soon returned, and that night was the worst of all. A madness had come over the people; they drank, and shouted, and looted; they quarrelled over the spoils, and tore things from each other – it was pandemonium.

Mr Maxwell came next morning on a sidecar; he took Arrowsmith's two children and the young housemaid (Lily Howick) back with him and piled the car with all the odds and ends it could hold. He had brought six carts from Kenmare on which to remove things from Derreen, but – except for the few saved during Mass, most of which he now took with him – there was nothing left to remove, so he told Arrowsmith to fill the carts with his own belongings and get away with his wife as soon as possible.

Nealy Sullivan took them to Kenmare on his sidecar, and they got away without being molested, but the six carts were attacked at Lehid and pillaged of all their contents, leaving the Arrowsmiths destitute of every possession. Their house was burnt that evening, and when Arrowsmith came out two days later to see if anything more could be saved he found it absolutely burnt out, and only the bare walls left. Derreen itself was not burnt then, but before Arrowsmith left the people had started hacking out all the woodwork: floors, doors, shutters, staircases etc. and when he returned on the Wednesday he found the house completely gutted, no woodwork left, all the outhouses removed, and nothing remaining except the walls and roof.

A few days later, the Arrowsmiths and Mrs Searcy, in company with a family who had been burnt out of a house on the opposite side of the river, left Kenmare in a little trading steamer for Cork, whence they could get a passenger boat to England. There was no cabin, and they were all huddled together under a tarpaulin; but their luggage gave them no trouble, for they possessed none.

'Seamus' said my Mother: 'I want you to tell me the names of the people who were at the bottom of this, and the people who were bad'; 'not,' she added, 'because I want to do them any harm, but so that I may know who were our friends.'

'Lady Lansdowne, I will tell you who were *clear*,' said Seamus, and then he gave the names of Sullivans, Sheas etc. – Dick, son of John, Pat with the foxy beard that was brother to Jer – and so on – house by house. Very often it was 'the young men were bad, and the old people could not stop them, though they were sorry.' When it came to Bunaw, he mentioned one or two bad ones, and then 'all the rest in Bunaw were *clear*.'

'But what about Mick Guihan?' we asked nervously.

'He was *clear* Lady Lansdowne – I give you my word he was *clear*.'

Afterwards, with lowered voice, he told of a meeting held several weeks before the attack, when the outrage has been planned by a few of the larger tenants, with the deliberate intention of getting rid of the Landlord, and dividing the land up amongst themselves and their friends. Among the names of these men, I was surprised to hear one he had already mentioned as being '*clear*'; and I protested.

'Lady Waterford,' said he, 'that man was *clear*; he took no part in the burning, and he was not at the house; but he was at the meeting and he was one of them that planned it.'

We talked of a widow woman to whom my Mother had always shewn special kindness, and who we knew had behaved abominably, not only to my Father's representative, but even to the Priest. My mother, always looking for extenuating circumstances, said that no doubt the woman was mad; we had always thought her queer.

'Mad, is it?' said Mrs Seamus. 'I tell you Lady Lansdowne – she is not mad at all, but a damned good lump of a rogue, that's what she is.'

In an untenanted part of the cottage we found piles of furniture, bedding, crockery etc. This was part of the restitution, of which Father S. had told us, and though there were a great many breakages, the things were by no means in such bad condition as we had been led to expect.

Before we left Curraghmore, my Mother had told me she wanted, if possible, to sleep one night in some house near Derreen: we had brought along a camp bed and some blankets, and Mr Maxwell has promised another outfit of the same kind.

Sitting in the Sullivans' clean little parlour that morning we both mentally chose it as our resting place, and before we left the cottage, we had, to their mingled consternation and delight, settled to sleep here the following night.

We went on now to face the real ordeal, Seamus going with us. At the gate to Derreen stood little 'Pats', most faithful of men, now the only gardener left in charge of the place. His dog-like eyes were full of tears, and as his firm grip closed on our hands he could utter no welcome or greeting of any kind, but the sorrow and sympathy in his eyes were more eloquent than any speech.

The front drive was blocked by a fallen tree, so we came on the house from the back, and oh! The desolation of it. 'Indeed' said Pats 'we are all gone grey looking at it.' It was worst from the back, because there were not many creepers there, and one saw right through the bare windows to the sky and grass beyond.

But I think we minded the porch most. I had always had such a friendly and welcoming air, with its grained oak seats and red cushions, and beyond, the little hall hung with maps and fishing paraphernalia, with a glimpse of the white staircase at the back. Now there was nothing but a heap of rubble and fallen masonry; and through the opening we saw one solitary beam, charred, black, and jagged, showing where the floor of my Father's little dressing room had rested.

The western side of the house looked less forlorn, and one gable and one gable over the room which was still called 'Charlie's bedroom' remained intact; while both here and on the front, the creepers seemed to have conspired together to hide the damage, and festooned the sightless windows with all the colour and brightness they could muster. Of the actual burning there was no sign, with the exception of the beam I have mentioned, and the walls seemed to be in perfectly sound condition. In the basement idle fellows had chalked their sentiments on the walls; but even these showed a diversity of opinions.

We spread our luncheon under the old larch tree (where we used to dance jigs on the board) and now that we had seen the worst, a certain peace descended on us, and the old house; even in its desolation, seemed to hold out its arms to us, and to whisper comfort for the future.

The tide had been flowing for nearly an hour when we got down to the ruined boathouse, and the sea had already covered half the length of the pier; but my Mother, nothing daunted, took Pats's arm (for the pier was slippery with wet seaweed) walked out to where the little waves were stealing in with gentle lappings, and after a few excursions with the prawn net, triumphantly produced two diminutive shrimps! With these and five periwinkles I had picked off the rocks, our predatory instincts were for the moment appeased, and after aadjuring Pats to bait the place well with mussels, on preparation for the morrow's prawning, we went off to look at shrubs. Pats led us to various pet spots where the best rhododendrons were planted; ever since the Head Gardener had left he had tended these with great care, and now beamed with pride when we admired their splendid condition. He had little or no horticultural knowledge, but a great love for all that his master cherished; 'This was one that Lord Lansdowne brought back the last time' – 'Some of these would need to be moved, and I could do it if I had the orders' etc. etc.

We had heard the bushes were badly damaged; and we were overjoyed to find that this was not the case, and that it needed but a few weeks tidying and trimming to put the grounds in good order. A few flowering shrubs had been dug up and removed; but since that happened the wily Pats had watched the others carefully, and as soon as a bud appeared, had snipped it off, and so robbed them of their fatal attraction.

Cattle had been deliberately driven into the grounds; they had smashed up a few bushes, eaten of the forbidden fruit, sickened , and died; 'those cattle belonged to the people who had caused the fire, and it was their cattle that died, and no others, and surely the hand of God was in it – didn't the Priest say so in the Chapel – without doubt it was the Hand of God.'

Later on, to pay off some spite, wild fellows had come in, and set fire to about twenty of the large clumps of bamboo. The weather was dry, and they blazed up with a great popping, which was so loud tht the Free Staters who were then in the neighbourhood made sure there was an ambush, and with immense caution surrounded the place. "And when they got in, there was nothing, only the bamboos." These same bamboos had since made a record growth, and now shewed splendid young shoots, some of which were as much as nine feet high.

The recent storms had made more havoc than the rebels, and many of the little paths were blocked with fallen trees and branches; but Pats led us by devious ways through "the King's Cozy" (where he shewed us how the tree ferns had seeded themselves) – and the "Lower Cozy" to "Knockatee Seat" where (the seat having gone west) we rested on camp stools, and let the calm beauty of the mountain sink into our souls.

My mother was anxious to see the Free Staters who were encamped at Joss's house near the Rath, (which had now been rechristened 'Fort Cottage'); and we had some papers to give them from Mr Maxwell. The officer was on the road when we motored past, and was obviously pleased at our wishing to see his little camp. 'Lieut. Jevons' was a dapper young man with a Dublin accent, who had served in the Great War; and he confided to us that he was fed up with the life in these lonely parts, and longed for a fight or any diversion to vary the monotony of existence. He had been over six months in Kerry, and was one of those who had been detailed to dislodge the rebels from the caves by the sea; and after his superior officer was killed was the first to effect an entrance. But nothing worth recording had happened since this incident, and he and his men had been reduced to fancy gardening, and had traced out little plots with whitewashed stones, embellishing the centre bed with flowers in a glass jar, precariously perched on forked poles.

Our next visit was to Mrs Keogh, whose house always reminded one of the visits paid there long ago, when Mrs Keogh was one of the slovenly Misses McSwiney, (careless as to fish-bones and fleas) whose parents we were taught to treat with a certain deference, Mr McSwiney's father having been the former occupant of Derreen House.

From thence we went on to see Mrs Pats Sullivan, the stout little woman whose smiled matched her figure in broadness, and who was just as staunch and true as her little husband. She always has a 'Wen' on her head, which she treated as a huge joke, till it became so large that she was persuaded to have it removed – 'But look at now,' said she with loud laughter, 'and haven't I two of them instead of the one!' She gave us the warmest of welcomes, – 'Glory be to God, and aren't you looking fine!' Here, as in every place, there were many enquiries after my Father; and when my Mother said he was not able to walk as well as he used to Mrs Sullivan said 'well of, we're all shoving along in years.' She asked after all my family, and 'have you any increase?' said she. On receiving a negative: 'Well, you are best so, you have enough.'

Coming down from this place, we passed the School, and went on to see Mrs Murphy at the Schoolmaster's house. She had buried her husband very recently, and was evidently feeling very lonely and forlorn; but she soon dismissed her own troubles to sympathize with ours; and when my Mother asked for a cup of tea, she responded with alacrity, and busied herself preparing home-made bread, butter, and honey; while she boiled the kettle in the adjoining kitchen. Her son 'Michael Edward' had saved a good many of my Father's books under pretence of taking them for himself – and we drank our tea in the company of many old friends on the bookshelves.

We were fairly tired out by the time we got back to Kenmare; but my Mother slept well that night, and looked ten years younger next day; she was full of plans for the future; a visit to Kenmare the following spring – my Father amongst his rhododendrons – building operation next Summer – granchildren's visits to Derreen. Mr Maxwell went with us on the second day, and when we reached Seamus's cottage, he and my Mother at once set about examining the restituted furniture in ther other part of the house. I meanwhile unpacked the things we had brought with us, set up the camp beds in the sitting room, and spread out our luncheon, which we presently shared with Mr Maxwell before proceeding on our rounds. Then, mindful of the flowing tide, we hurried with net and bucket to the shrimping ground, and caught a dishful of the prawns that were hovering over the delectable mussel bait laid by Pats. Mrs Seamus cooked them for our supper that night, and was persuaded to taste some herself, for the first time in her life; she said they were so lively, she was afraid to put them in the saucepan.

It was a grey afternoon, but the charm of Kilmackilogue drew one irresistibly; and I went for a few moments in the place of 'Father's seat' to drink it in alone, and to listen to the cry of the sea-birds which my so loved to imitate. Seamus, with the perfect tact and understanding inborn in these people, remained out of sight till I called him; and then we proceeded up by the outer walk in pursuit of the rest of the party, whom we presently found awaiting us in the motor. Dourus was our next point, as my Father was particularly anxious for a report on its condition; the middle path was too overgrown and wet for us, but we walked some way along the bohireen, and Mr Maxwell shewed us the worst of the unauthorized clearings. These open spaces, with their many stumps, and a desolate tree left standing here and there, had a melancholy air on this grey day: but one felt that some of them would ultimately prove a blessing, as parts of the peninsula were really overwooded; and a few open glades, with views of the sea and mountains beyond, would greatly improve it.

Rain had threatened all day, and now came down heavily; the motor had a perforated hood, and no wings; and the rain drove in upon us with great fury. We hedged ourselves around with umbrellas, and then put them down because they prevented us from seeing the beloved views; up they went again when the rain beat in too fiercely; but we could not bear to keep them open for long.

Past Dick Line's new house, with the shop attached to it; past the road to Coomingeera (it was said that some of the best of the Derreen linen was in a house up that way), along the little river and past Poul Koum – the scene of so many struggles with the wily salmon; along the shore of Glenmore Lake, beautiful even on this evening of driving rain; and here we were at Glenmore Schoolhouse.

Mrs Sullivan, daughter of the old schoolmaster, wife of the new one, and herself a teacher, fitly carried on the family tradition and name of Glenmore, besides rearing a family of delightful children of her own, one of whom – a little girl with curly hair and melting grey-blue eyes – was a most enchanting specimen of humanity. The Sullivans had been through some hard times in this lonely glen; it was infested with rebels, and they constantly had to feed these men, and go short themselves when provisions were hard to get. The husband of Mrs Sullivan's sister, who lived in Cork, had been murdered by rebels, and their little child was also being cared for in the Glenmore Schoolhouse by these excellent people.

On the journey back to our 'country residence' Mr Maxwell purchased a packet of candles for us at Line's shop for we thought Mrs Seamus would hardly have such luxuries in her store; then he dropped us at the cottage, and pursued his way to Kenmare.

Mrs Seamus produced the best teapot, and had a hot brew drawing under the quilted tea-cosy; fortified by this, and her excellent bread and currant loaf, we presently went out for a stroll, and ended by making a tour of the first part of the 'Ladies Mile'. The rain had ceased, the wind had dropped, and it was a heavenly evening. My Mother, despite the long day, was still 'young and fresh-looking', and was with difficulty dissuaded from making the longer tour. Some sheep browsing in the plantation, and a few trees cut down on the upper edge of it, were evidence of the prevailing lawlessness; otherwise all was calm and inexpressibly beautiful; and we longed for the presence of one whose initial was carved with my Mother's on the little stone seat, that he also might feel these healing influences.

At the cottage Mrs Dan Sullivan awaited us; and presently came also Mrs Mike Brian – and the little sitting room became a regular hall of audience. Mrs Dan's son Sylvie, had been one of the best; and shown both courage and intelligence at the time of the attack. Now his job had gone, so he had migrated to America, and his mother was very lonesome after him. She had another son at home, lately in the R.I.C. but he would be best out of the country too, as the young fellows would have no truck with him. When he left she would have only 'poor little Jimmy – the small lad' – 'What age was he?' we queried. 'Well I suppose he would be twenty-six.' She wept over the destruction of the laundry, which had been her pride, and her livelihood: 'Oh my God Lady Lansdowne, wasn't it very wicked to destroy such a beautiful place?' Then there were mutual enquiries after our respective families, and she waxed eloquent on the beauty of my children, and of their Father: 'A splendid man; and wasn't it a very funny thing, that everyone was so fond of him.' Mrs

Mike Brian's conversation was on softer tones, and concerned with more personal matters; my Mother is the most sympathetic listener in the world, and don't we all bring her our troubles?

At last we were alone, and could give some attention to Mrs Seamus, who was looking dubiously at the lively prawns and wondering how she should cook them.

We never ate a better supper than she gave us that night; new-laid eggs fried in butter, floury potatoes just bursting out of their skins, prawns of our own catching, delicious butter and bread made by our hostess; and was their ever a better waitress than dark-haired Maggie, flitting about on bare feet, her deep blue eyes – with wondrous long dark lashes – glowing mistily in the light from the candles.... Those same candles had nearly caused a coldness between us and Mrs Seamus; 'Why would you bring candles, hadn't we had enough of them in the house? Surely to goodness wouldn't we have them for the children doing their school work at night? There was no need to bring them at all.' She was really hurt with us over this, and it took all my Mother's tact to smooth her ruffled feelings.

After supper, we sat for some time in the Seamus's kitchen, surrounded by all the family; my mother questioned the children about their work in school, and looked at the tasks they had to prepare that night (one, I remember, was all about the care of the teeth), while I knitted by the light of one lamp hanging above the settle. The turf glowed redly on the hearth, and filled the little room with its fragrance; the talk grew softer and more intermittent; and though the five-year-old Florrie still sat up according to his impish custom, we felt it was time to go to bed. We strolled out into the garden, and feigning interest in the stars, we crept round to the back of the house to what Mrs Sullivan called 'the little place east'. Then we bid goodnight to all, and retired into our pyjamas and flea-bags, first surreptitiously stopping the pendulum of Seamus's clock, which had an echoing strike which would have awakened the soundest of sleepers. We had to wait until the same hour next morning to start it again, and devoutly hoped that the good people had noticed the liberties taken with their treasured timepiece.

Each time we turned in our bed, they creaked like the beams of a ship, so we were afraid to move for fear if waking each other; my Mother was also acutely conscious of a draughty hole in the canvas beneath her, but was too considerate to call me to pad it up for her; nut beyond these inconveniences, we had nothing to complain of.

She was afoot before anyone in the cottage next morning, to Mrs Seamus's evident surprise; and Maggie's dark lashes still drooped with sleep when she bought in the bucket of hot water which was to serve for our ablutions. While my mother was dressing in the attic above, I, still snog in my sleeping bad, wrote a letter to the one we had left behind us, and tried to tell him something of our experiences and impressions, then rolled up my little bed in its canvas bag, and took my turn at the bucket above.

After breakfast, while I was packing up, my Mother sorted out some of the restituted furniture and crockery. She gave the Seamuses a little picture, and several odds and ends, amongst which was a saucer inscribed with motto referring to the blessing of a good wife, which greatly pleased Mrs Seamus. She also had several more visitors: Mike Brien, Peter the Pump, Jeremiah Sullivan, and others. One of these young men was suspected of having looted, and when she saw him her intuition told her that he HAD done it, and was much ashamed. So she looked at him and said, 'Peter, I know you will bring back anything you took away', and he dropped his eyes, and said indeed he would. I believe she did far more good by taking the people in this way than if she had covered them with reproaches and abuse.

I photographed the house party, my Mother distributed largesse among the family, and with many blessings and hopes of a speedy return, we took leave of them, and went on our way.

We had promised to visit Lauragh Schools, so motored up there before returning to Kenmare. In the Girl's School we were welcomed by Mrs Ryan (née Murphy) who stood the children up as we came in; the attendance had fallen off considerably during the bad times, but was gradually improving now, and they were as nice a looking lot of girls as you could see anywhere. Little Julie Sullivan was struggling with arithmetic, and was presently reproved for doing the addition on her inky little fingers. Near her was Nealy Sullivan's small fair daughter, and beyond them one with sooty hair and eyes like deep pools of water.

In the other half of the School 'Michael Edward' was instructing the boys in Irish, and here also we were struck with the good countenance of the boys, with exception of one farouche little fellow, who glared darkly at us, and gave a most unpleasant impression.

One thing my Mother could not bring herself to do and that was to pass by Mrs McCarthy's house near Lauragh Chapel; so we returned the way we had come, and then on to Kenmare by the coast road, only stopping at Bunagh for a few moments to bid goodbye to the Nealy Sullivans.

It was a wonderful morning, still and clear, with such an atmosphere as is only found in Kerry, a slight mist veiling the mountain tops only enhanced their beauty, and every delicate shade of colour impressed itself on the senses which all blended softly together in perfect harmony. How could there be ill will or malice in the midst of such beauty? It seemed inexplicable.

We lunched sumptuously at the Maxwells – the capable Oona had cooked the repast in the absence of the maid – after which my Mother inspected two more furniture dumps, and came back quite amazed and delighted at the number of things which had been retuned.

We went next to meet the old Nuns at the Convent; the Lay sister who opened the door to us was wildly excited at our unexpected appearance, and leaving us in the parlour, ran off as fast as her old legs would carry her to summon the four sisters whom we knew. In they came, all chattering little magpies, and gathered in a circle around us. The Reverend Mother was very sick – poor thing – and could see no one, but they were so pleased that we had come, they hadn't seen any of the family for so long.... How was Lord Lansdowne, and would he come over soon...? And wasn't it a pity the way the country had gone. And it was dreadful when there was fighting in the Town, and firing all round them – though the Convent had always been respected.... And none of the young girls wanted to work now, and their beautiful lace industry had practically died out.... And so the dear old souls chattered on, taking the words out of each others' mouths like children, their eyes shining, and their fresh old faces flushed with excitement. In old days the Lay Sister sat rather apart, and took little share in the conversation; now the community had dwindled to such a small number (the young women of the present day find that particular order far too strict for their taste) that the old members seemed to cling together, without making any distinctions. They would have talked forever, but we had to tear ourselves away from their gentle hands; and soon were on the way to my brother's house on the other side of Kenmare.

Sheen Falls had been occupied by Republicans and Free Staters in turns, and at one time seventy of the latter had been billeted there; we expected to see a good deal of damage, and were much surprised to find absolutely none, beyond one broken-legged table. The commanding officer had been most careful and had even insisted that his men should pull their beds away from the wall for fear of scratching it. No doubt the housemaid had been obliged to use a considerable amount of soap and water after they left; but as we saw it the place was spotless and undamaged, and its owner could have stepped into it that very day, had he wished to.

On the way back, a visit to Lily Howick's Mother; then we were at the hotel again, entertaining the Hoods from Dromore, and hearing all their trials. They had not been away for two years (and had doubtless saved their place by this fidelity) they had been threatened more than once, and had suffered many hardships and losses, and some insults; but now things were gradually improving, and they hoped soon to get away for a much needed change and holiday.

After they had left us, we sauntered off to pay a visit to Mr John Brennan, elder brother to the faithful George – who had been for so many years my Father's right-hand man at Derreen. A tall and still fine-looking man, this one had the advantage of our old friend in height, and possessed the same musical voice, but yet he somehow lacked the gentle charm of George Brennan, and was never so handsome as he. He had a good deal to tell us of adventures with Republicans during their occupation of Kenmare, but appeared to have come through that time without any great loss beyond that of a few bullocks, and congratulated himself on the lucky chance which had on one occasion led the Rebels to seize his son-in-law's cattle instead of his own!

We left at 11.30 the following morning, motoring through the glorious mountains, over many a broken bridge, and past the Lakes to Killarney Station. The train started on the stroke of one o'clock, and we only just caught it; a couple of hours later we had packed our kit into our own car at Mallow, and were on our way home. We stopped for tea with Sir J. and Lady E. Keane at 'Tivoli' in Cappoquin, and afterwards walked up to see what was left of their old home. It had been a fine house, well proportioned, with decorations of the Adam period; now it was but a shell. One's heart ached for the owners – and I was thankful that Tyrone's age had debarred him from being appointed a Senator in the early days of the Free State.

Our trip was over; the fates had been wondrous kind, we had done all we planned and rather more. Two days later my Mother returned to England.

And already, though barely four weeks have passed since we left Derreen, an expert has been sent over to examine the walls, and report on the possibility of using them in the new structure.

And I hope that next Spring, when the Derreen Rhododendrons are in flower, the one who loves them most will be there to see the blossom.